RECTIFYING FALLACIES OF MODERN BUDDHISM

BY SAKYAQINGYANG

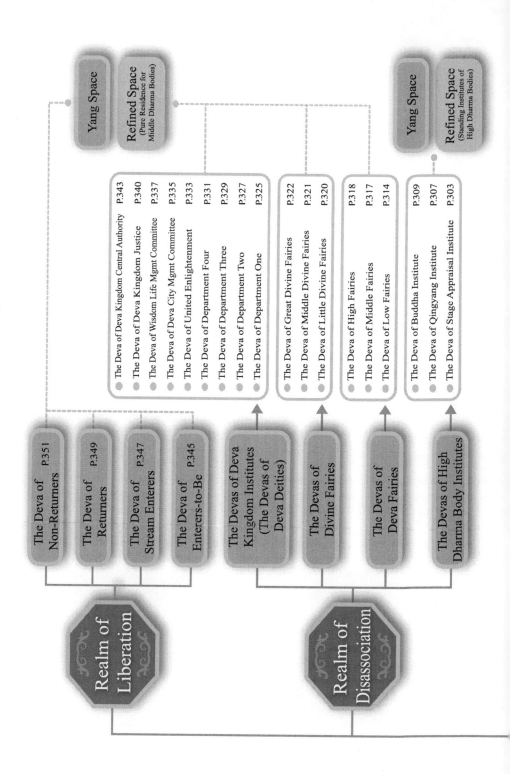

Yang Space

Refined Space
(Pure Residence for Middle Dharma Bodies)

Yang Space

Refined Space
(Standing Institutes of High Dharma Bodies)

The Deva of Deva Kingdom Central Authority — P.343
The Deva of Deva Kingdom Justice — P.340
The Deva of Wisdom Life Mgmt Committee — P.337
The Deva of Deva City Mgmt Committee — P.335
The Deva of United Enlightenment — P.333
The Deva of Department Four — P.331
The Deva of Department Three — P.329
The Deva of Department Two — P.327
The Deva of Department One — P.325

The Deva of Great Divine Fairies — P.322
The Deva of Middle Divine Fairies — P.321
The Deva of Little Divine Fairies — P.320

The Deva of High Fairies — P.318
The Deva of Middle Fairies — P.317
The Deva of Low Fairies — P.314

The Deva of Buddha Institute — P.309
The Deva of Qingyang Institute — P.307
The Deva of Stage Appraisal Institute — P.303

The Deva of Non-Returners — P.351

The Deva of Returners — P.349

The Deva of Stream Enterers — P.347

The Deva of Enterers-to-Be — P.345

The Devas of Deva Kingdom Institutes
(The Devas of Deva Deities)

The Devas of Divine Fairies

The Devas of Deva Fairies

The Devas of High Dharma Body Institutes

Realm of Liberation

Realm of Disassociation

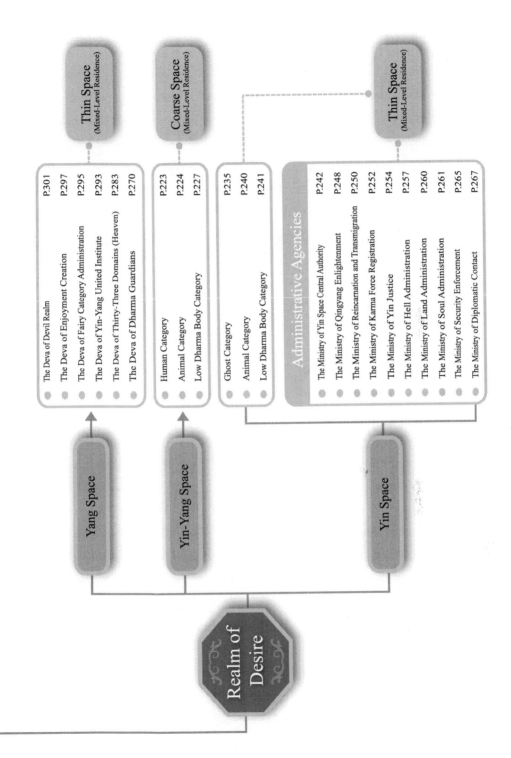

FIGURE 1 Material Realm

DECLARATION

The author has been ordered by Sakyamuni Buddha to assume the responsibility of organizing, compiling, and writing the scriptures of the Buddha-to-Be Religion. The entire contents provided by the author are true and have been approved by Buddha. The author shall be condemned to Hell if any of the above is untrue.

GENERAL PREFACE

The author has been following his master, practicing and working toward religious attainment since childhood, and lacks writing skill. Sakyamuni Buddha has commissioned the author to establish the Buddha-to-Be Religion. This task sometimes makes the author wonder if his capacity can match his goal. It is only due to a great deal of kind assistance and support that the author dares to accept such a daunting task. The author is fully aware of the importance of such a responsibility.

The author asks for pardon from readers for the author's limited literary talent. Please forgive marginal errors in composition, grammar, and symbols as long as the meaning is properly conveyed. The "opening chant" says:

Hard it is to meet with the supreme, abstruse,
   and subtle Dharma
in myriads of Kalpas.
Now that we have met with it,
   may we comprehend Buddha's true meaning.

Let us now learn with our hearts what Buddha has been trying to tell us.

Language is a tool for conveying meaning, but it can be less than perfect in expression and description. The meanings between the lines require extensive contemplation to understand; they will not be as straightforward as face-to-face conversation.

To accommodate readers from different backgrounds, the author has made his best effort to convey the true meanings of Buddha in plain language, explaining with simple descriptions those issues that are hard to understand. Even though the author is serving the Buddha-to-Be Religion, the author is not Buddha himself and is merely a spokesperson of Buddha. Buddha is a "Dharma Body" (Sanskrit: *Dharmakaya*; 法身), and the author is a "retributive body" (報身). Buddha is a saint, and the author is an ordinary human. Buddha is the source of Dharma (truth, law, method; 達摩, 法), and the author is only a communication tool for Dharma. Therefore, please do not regard the author as a saint and do not measure the author by the standard of a saint.

Whenever the Buddha-to-Be Religion is mentioned, many will automatically associate it with Mi-Le Bodhisattva (Sanskrit: *Maitreya*; 彌勒菩薩) and jump to the conclusion that the Buddha-to-Be Religion follows Mi-Le Bodhisattva. That conclusion is not correct.

To be more specific, Buddha-to-Be is not yet Buddha. An elementary school pupil swears to earn a doctorate degree in the future, for example. At this point, the pupil is a future doctor but not a doctor now; he or she is still an elementary school pupil.

You are Buddha-to-Be; I am Buddha-to-Be; he and she are Buddhas-to-Be; everyone is Buddha-to-Be. The only difference among us is the time of the attainment of Buddhahood. The attainment of Buddhahood is absolutely certain, but it cannot be achieved instantly in this life; it will be achieved sooner or later in the future.

Let us appreciate the correct way of Buddha-to-Be Religion with our hearts. May all whose conditions (prerequisites; 條件, 緣) have matured attain their correct "stages of attainment" early and receive eternal and true peace and joy.

First published in USA 2012
Second Edition 2013
Third Edition 2014

Author: Sakyaqingyang
Translators: E. Liu and C. Ditmars
Copyeditors: L. Anderson, Mark Philip Marsella & Heather Cao Marsella,
S. Clark, C. Ditmars, and D. Parker

ISBN-10: 1460978226
EAN-13: 9781460978221
Library of Congress Control Number (LCCN): 2011903822

CreateSpace, an Amazon Company
North Charleston, SC, USA

TABLE OF CONTENTS

INSTRUCTION FROM SAKYAMUNI BUDDHA

The Purpose of Buddha-to-Be Religion:
Inheritance, Defense, Correction, and Sublimation

(A) INHERITANCE
To continue the legacy of correct dharma of traditional Buddhism, promote the correct dharma of Buddhism, and benefit the general public

(B) DEFENSE
Protect the correct dharma of traditional Buddhism and defend it against speech statements that sabotage the correct dharma

(C) CORRECTION
Correct the scriptures of Buddhism and rectify the scriptures that deviate from the correct dharma of Buddhism

(D) SUBLIMATION
Disclose the essence of traditional Buddhism and combine it with the present and future "cognition and views" to raise the essence of traditional Buddhism to a brand new stage.

The combination of the past, present, and future cognition and views shall form a new correct dharma—the correct dharma of the Buddha-to-Be Religion. This correct dharma shall be spread around the human world to benefit the general public!

"MEMORY IMPRINT"
MADE BY THE BURNING LAMP BUDDHA

The Burning Lamp Buddha (Sanskrit: *Dipankara*; 燃燈佛) gave Di-Zang Bodhisattva (Sanskrit: *Ksitigarbha*; 地藏菩薩) the style name Qingyang and, at the same time, imprinted this memory on Di-Zang Bodhisattva: "You shall achieve Buddhahood after consummately saving and converting living beings in Saha Land in the future lives, and your style name shall be 'Qingyang Buddha.'"

VOLUME ONE

WHO AM I?
WHO SHALL I BECOME?

I.

THE INSTRUCTION AND ENTRUSTMENT IN "THE DEVA OF THIRTY-THREE DOMAINS"

More than twenty-five hundred years ago, Sakyamuni Buddha, after examining the living beings on this planet, concluded that the "potentialities and conditions" (機緣) of living beings had been mature. Buddha was reincarnated to this world to teach Buddhism by becoming a Buddha to offer a thorough and proper way of practicing Buddhism to the living beings on the planet Earth. This thorough and proper way is now referred to as correct dharma of Buddhism. At the same time, he was to establish the Three Treasures of the mundane world as a solid foundation for the long-term teaching of Buddhism.

At birth, Sakyamuni Buddha was given the name of Siddhartha. His mother, Madame Mayadevi, departed the world of human beings seven days after giving birth to Siddhartha. Because of the rich and profound goodness in which Madame Mayadevi had been engaging, she was able to enjoy the Blessed Retribution (福報) in "The Deva of Thirty-Three Domains" (commonly referred to as

"Heaven") through reincarnation by metamorphosis (化生).[1]

Despite having only a slight impression of Madame Mayadevi, Siddhartha never forgot his biological mother. In his "Dhyana and Samadhi" (meditation, concentration, and abstraction) practice—Dhyana: 禪那, 禪; Samadhi: 三摩地, 三昧, 定—after perfecting his own Dharma Body of the present life and incorporating it with his Dharma Body of the previous life, Siddhartha learned that his mother was living a peaceful life of Blessed Retribution in "The Deva of Thirty-Three Domains." Such a reward, however, would eventually come to an end if the doctrine of being "neither born nor ended" (不生不滅) was not practiced, and a person went through "reincarnation and transmigration" (轉世輪迴). He then decided to go to "The Deva of Thirty-Three Domains" to save his mother, "convert" (渡化) more living beings at the same time, and arrange for the future development of Buddhism.

As an act of "great filial piety,"[2] Buddha entered into a hyper-meditation state, where he left his "material body" (physical body; 色身)[3] in the human world, but carried the Three Souls and Seven Vigors[4] of the material body with his Dharma Body to "The Deva of Thirty-Three Domains." This was to help his mother and the countless number of living beings attain their high Dharma Bodies and escape from the Three-Realms (三界)[5] and the Five Elements. Then, they could be freed from the transmigration (輪迴) of births and deaths and be granted eternal life in the Dharma Realm,[6] leave Heaven where joyful pleasure would eventually end, and live in a true and permanent bliss (the utmost joy).

Buddha demonstrated supernatural power and gave full play to the Linguistic Dharani[7] in "The Deva of Thirty-Three Domains." He preached the stories of Di-Zang Bodhisattva (Sanskrit: *Ksitigarbha*; 地藏菩薩) and once again gave the countless number of living beings the Convenient Dharma (way, method). In the Deva of Thirty-Three Domains, Buddha reached out his golden arms and laid his hands on top of the head of Bodhisattva to give "memory imprint" (授記).[8] In front of the living beings, he said to Di-Zang Bodhisattva, "You watched me relentlessly saving and converting 'since beginninglessness' (無始以來) the stubborn, sinful and suffering living beings that had not yet come to enlightenment. If they are driven by the 'karma force'[9] into the bad categories, then you shall re-call my instruction to you that I had reiterated to you today right here in 'The Deva of Thirty-Three Domains': Because the potentialities and conditions of the living beings have matured enough, I have come to this Saha Land (娑婆世界)[10] to teach correct dharma. During the 576 million years (Calculated in the Chinese calendar; the ancient Indian calendar differs from the modern calendar. As an adaptive measure, measurement of time referred to in the scriptures of Buddha-to-Be Religion will be converted into the modern calendar for readers' convenience. Many figures may, therefore, be different from modern Buddhism) since my Nirvana (涅槃)[11] to the time of Mi-Le Bodhisattva's[12] reincarnation to become Buddha, there will be no Buddha responding to this world (無佛應世). You shall be the one who responds to this Saha Land and saves and converts the living beings on this Saha Land until Mi-Le Bodhisattva's response to the world. You shall free all living beings from all sufferings once and for all, make them meet a Buddha, hear Buddhist doctrines, and have memory imprinted by Buddha. Di-Zang Bodhisattva, after my Nirvana, I shall entrust the poor, the sinful, and the suffering living beings of the world to your hands."

At this very moment, the countless Duplicated Bodies (分身) of Di-Zang Bodhisattva in the infinite worlds merged into one. Di-Zang Bodhisattva broke into tears over the trust and instruction from Buddha. He replied, with palms together, in the most respectful way, "World Honored One,[13] I have been coached and taught by you for so many Kalpas (eons),[14] and I have gained enormous supernatural power and great wisdom. Now, I have my Duplicated Bodies spread in as many worlds as the number of the sands of the Ganges.[15] Each of my Duplicated Bodies is capable of reproducing trillions of Transformation Bodies (化身), and each of my Transformation Bodies is capable of saving and ferrying trillions of living beings to admire and convert to Three Treasures (皈依三寶),[16] allowing them to forever escape from the cycle of births and deaths and attain the joy of Nirvana. I will do everything to save, in their best interests, even those low-level practitioners who perform infrequent acts of goodness. I will never let you down. I will practice relentlessly and will never stop until all living beings are saved. World Honored One, don't worry about the living beings committing bad karma in the future; just leave them to me."

Di-Zang Bodhisattva repeated the last sentences three times to Buddha as a confirmation of his resolute, sincere determination, confidence, and perseverance. Buddha was delighted to hear this confession from Di-Zang Bodhisattva: "Good. Good. I'm really happy for you. You have kept the oath you made many Kalpas (劫) ago; you will soon accomplish the mission of 'wide conversion' (廣渡) of living beings and will thus realize the Bodhi."[17]

II.

WHO AM I? WHO SHALL I BECOME?

Enhancing the "cognition and views" (知見) is important for learning and practicing religion. By understanding one's current level of cognition and view, one may know what religion to learn and practice. In this Saha Land where we exist right now, there are four levels of cognition and views about souls: view of absolute extinction; view of absolute belonging; view of absolute transmigration; and view of absolute eternity.

(A) VIEW OF ABSOLUTE EXTINCTION (斷滅見)

People who approve of the view of absolute extinction do not believe that humans have souls. They believe "a person's death is like a dimmed lamp; when grass dies, it leaves nothing but ash." If a person is dead, he/she is dead forever; any device of sentience (e.g., soul) attached to this dead person will no longer exist in this world. When breathing stops, life ceases, and the spirit disintegrates. All awareness of emotion previously belonging to the body shall become extinct. People holding views like this are believers in the view of absolute extinction.

(B)   VIEW OF ABSOLUTE BELONGING (斷歸見)

People who approve of the view of absolute belonging believe that humans do have souls. Upon death,
one's soul will be destined to go to either Heaven or Hell
according to the good karma and bad karma accumulated before death. Once such a soul has been sent to
either Heaven or Hell, it shall remain there forever. People
holding views like this are believers in the view of absolute
belonging.

(C)   VIEW OF ABSOLUTE TRANSMIGRATION (斷迴見)

People who approve of the view of absolute transmigration also believe humans do have souls. After death, one's
soul will be reincarnated within a certain period of time. A
soul never becomes extinct and will transmigrate forever.
People holding a view like this are believers in the view of
absolute transmigration.

(D)   VIEW OF ABSOLUTE ETERNITY (斷恆見)

People who approve of the view of absolute eternity
not only believe that humans have souls but also believe
in the transmigration of the soul, and they differ only in
believing such transmigration to be a form of suffering.
They believe that humans may somehow be relieved from
such transmigration.

They believe that humans may form an External Body
(身外身), which is also called Energy Body (能量身) or Dharma Body (法身), comprised of cosmic energy through the
practice of religion. One may further enhance such Dharma Body to a "Nano Body" (high Dharma Body), which
will be immune from death, deterioration, sickness, aging,
growing, and extinction.

Upon death, one's soul enters into the high Dharma Body, a body that will never be extinct and is free from the sufferings of birth, aging, sickness, and death that come with mandatory transmigration. Then, permanent and true peace and happiness of the greatest kind will be fulfilled. People holding a view like this are believers in the View of Absolute Eternity.

The view of absolute extinction, view of absolute belonging, and view of absolute transmigration are confused views of the soul (靈魂迷見). The view of absolute eternity is the correct view of soul (靈魂正見).

The view of absolute extinction and view of absolute belonging are called evil views of the soul (靈魂邪見).

The view of absolute transmigration is called the biased view of soul (靈魂偏見).

The view of absolute eternity is called the correct view of soul.

The "correct cognition and view" (正知見)[18] can be achieved by converting from the confused view of soul to the correct view of soul.

People are divided into groups according to their differences; objects are grouped according to their similarities. Although this world may be one entity, it is divided into religious belief-systems. People of different religions gather in their respective churches to chant different prayers.

There is one organization in this world responsible for the centralized management tasks of religious missionary work. It is called the Deva of United Enlightenment (聯合教化天) established in the Refined Space (精維空間). All religions in our world are established and taught by the personnel dispatched by the Deva of United Enlightenment.

Every religion is one course, each of which is established for souls at different levels. One with an elevated level of cognition and view will be reincarnated to practice a higher religion course with other people. Those who possess the View of Absolute Extinction are at the lowest level of cognition and view. When they elevate to the view of absolute belonging, they will be reincarnated among the people who also possess the view of absolute belonging and share the same religions. When the people of the view of absolute belonging elevate their cognition and view to the view of absolute transmigration, they will be reincarnated among the people who possess the view of absolute transmigration to follow the doctrines of the religions in which they believe.

The preaching of the Buddha-to-Be Religion primarily begins with the view of absolute transmigration and helps its believers to achieve enlightenment and acknowledgement of the view of absolute eternity. With a combination of theory and practice, they may gradually achieve Nirvana joy. The Buddha-to-Be Religion teaches people to know the sufferings of transmigration and preaches the world beyond transmigration. It also tells people how to elevate to the state where the Nirvana joy is granted.

Some may ask, if there is a soul that never becomes extinct and constantly reincarnates, why are we unable to remember anything about previous lives? In the Thin Space, there is an agency in charge of the reincarnation of souls. Every reincarnation of a soul must go through this agency, no exception (excluding the "soul smugglers"[19]). Any soul, regardless of whether high or low, prestigious or lowly, must consume the "amnesia drink" (迷魂湯) before reincarnation.

After consuming the amnesia drink and entering the material body, the soul will immediately lose consciousness and fall into dreams. Every bit of memory will be lost except the content of memory imprint. Upon the death of the material body and the departure of the soul from it, the soul will suddenly be awakened from the dreams and recollect the past that has been forgotten. It is the amnesia drink that stops the material body from finding direction amidst the ocean of pain.

Who was I before my birth? Who shall I become after my death?

Where did I, as a person, come from, and where am I going? This world is full of disaster and calamity and life that is so short with all the troubles and sorrows. We live in a world like this, in such an environment, for only a few decades with endless struggling that lasts for a lifetime. For what, exactly? Who was I? Who shall I become? How well do we understand life, the universe, and our bodies?

Some always perceive life to be meaningless. Their needs for certain things that they do not have drive them into suffering. They eventually take certain things into possession after going through much suffering, and they ask another question: So what can these things do for me? They still feel life is meaningless.

The bottom line: What should I do with all these troubles in life?

Allow me to elaborate for you.

III.

THE DREAMING PERSON

It is not difficult to understand the meaning of the universe and life. It is not difficult to achieve the "stage of attainment" (果位) either. It is the amnesia drink at the time of reincarnation that makes simple things complicated.

After entering the fetal state, a soul becomes a sleeping "original soul" and lives in dreams. This original soul is firmly enclosed by the material body which, in turn, is dominated by the Yang soul. The Yang soul is an acquired soul that only knows the experiences of this present life from childhood to adulthood. During this sleep, the original soul, as the material body in sleep, forgets about everything that happened while it was awake; only dreams are there with it.

According to the regular rules of the material body, the waking of the material body follows sleep, and the waking of the original soul follows one's life. Therefore, one's material body is nothing but a person in a dream, and the dreams we have during our sleep are dreams in dreams.

We already know that the amnesia drink blocks our memories of our previous lives. As our material bodies grow up, the amnesia drink completely integrates into our material bodies. We also know that once the original soul departs from the material body, it wakes up immediately. Then, must we die before we may become awakened? This same question is one of the subjects that our predecessor practitioners studied.

Actually, we do not have to die to become awakened. By following certain practices, we may achieve, while we are still alive, a state that we may allow our original souls to depart from our bodies.

When the original soul departs from its body, it suddenly wakes up. All facts about the universe and life are laid out in front of our eyes; the motivation to cultivate ourselves is boosted. This is the time when we may come to ultimate enlightenment on our own. With further practice by following a certain method, "using the false (the material body) to achieve the true (the Dharma Body)," we may develop an External Body,[20] gain the grand capacity, and eventually achieve Nirvana.

When the original soul is able to enter into and depart from the material body at will, with a little more practice, we may allow our Yang souls to depart from our bodies as well. This departure allows our trinity of souls (original, Yang, and Yin) to work for us. It is the level of "three flowers gathering at the top of the head." The Yin soul is by nature capable of departing from the body without any practice.

The original soul and the Yang soul are locked up at our birth. That means there are certain "acupoints" (竅) in our bodies, and these acupoints are sealed to prevent the original soul and the Yang soul from departing. They can be opened, thereby freeing the Yang soul and the original soul, only when we are dead or through practice and cultivation. Therefore, the methods with which we practice puncturing through or opening up the "acupoints" are very critical. From the distant past to the present time, people have practiced this through a variety of methods, such as Dhyana, Esoteric Sect, Yoga, deep respiration, Dao-Yin, Qi-gong, etc. for a variety of reasons, such as self-improvement, healing sickness, practicing religion, and even obtaining supernatural functions.

From the perspective of religious practice, there are "Dhyana with Leakage" (有漏禪) and "Dhyana without Leakage" (無漏禪). Transmigration is like swimming in the ocean of pain. To arrive on land, we need a boat. A leaking boat will not make it through. Only a boat that does not leak can take us to land. Whatever the Dhyana may be, if it can take us to land, it is Dhyana without Leakage. On the other hand, no matter how fancy it may be, if it cannot take us to land, it is Dhyana with Leakage.

Indeed, we may gain a healthier material body and a better state of mind by practicing Dhyana, but what really matters is that we become awakened, after which comes Nirvana. We may become better judges in distinguishing the true and false Dharma (Buddhism) and mentors after we become awakened. We will know our direction and not give up cultivation easily. And this is also the author's experience in mentoring. Not a single disciple of mine who has become awakened has ever quit. On the contrary, those disciples who failed to become awakened often fell into confusion, stopped cultivating, or even turned against me.

When in dreams, of course, it is impossible to bring everyone to Nirvana because the "degree of maturity of 'potentiality and conditions'" (機緣成熟度) for everyone may differ. They can only be taught according to their different conditions in an adaptive way without any coercion.

One's life after awakening is very meaningful; there will be dramatic changes in one's philosophy. Gradually, things existing in the mundane world that one could not let go no longer matter anymore, and the way to Nirvana becomes closer and closer.

It happened to the author that in a state of Dhyana-and-Samadhi, the author's soul departed its material body and entered the Time-Space Tunnel[21] that leads to the Nano Space. My soul kept on going, and before long, I saw a magnificent palace without guards. I took the liberty of walking into the palace.

I wandered around and found the palace enormously spacious and glamorous. There were many rooms but no occupants. I walked into a very large bedroom where there was a big bed, on which a Buddha was sleeping peacefully with his eyes gently closed.

I bowed three times, and the bows were not returned. I mentally asked myself, "Where am I?" and the Buddha answered, "You are in my dream." At the very same time, a beam of colorful light was cast onto me. The beam was so powerful that my soul returned to my material body in a split second, and I woke up from my deep meditation. I sighed, with complex emotions, at what the Buddha had said to me.

Our world and the living beings who live in it are all dreams of Buddhas. Because dreams come to an end, everything in this world of fantasy will become extinct. Nothing lasts forever. We must cultivate and practice to enable ourselves to get out of this fantasy world and reach the world that will never become extinct. There will be permanent and true peace and joy waiting for us. This must be the Buddha's plan.

A few days later, I wrote "Dreaming Person":

Acting like a monk but actually a layman; being a
    layman but looking like a monk.
Practicing Supramundane Dharmas, while leading a
    mundane life.
Nominally inactive, but actually active in everything.
Tangible is petty; intangible is great.
Despite wave, wind, and fire, the hermit frolics on tide.
Against the rumbling red stream, I sail on.
Half asleep and half awake, using the false to
    achieve the true;
Awakening from "Dreams of the Dream,"
    I cultivate my External Body.

IV.

TRANSMIGRATION

People who hold the view of absolute transmigration believe that humans do have souls, and the souls go through transmigration repeatedly. That is, they believe in the theory of soul reincarnation. They do not, however, believe that there are lives other than those in repeating transmigrations, not to mention lives that are "neither (to be) born nor ended"(不生不滅).

Transmigration is a loop between births and deaths that applies to all living beings in the material realm. A soul has begun to transmigrate "since beginninglessness." It is important to understand transmigration prior to cultivation of the way of Nirvana.

Every soul begins to live, learn, evolve, and upgrade to a high-level life form starting from a low-level life form. This is the process of the evolution of the soul.

Some say that human beings come from monkeys. If that is so, then why have monkeys today stopped becoming human beings? A monkey becoming a human being is a change in the material body, and such a change cannot occur in one lifetime. If the soul of a monkey is given a human fetus during reincarnation, however, it will become a human being. It is the evolution of soul, namely the spiritual change. A successful plastic surgery does not mean the evolution of a person. When a soul undergoes reincarnation, it is given a perfect body because it had elevated its level in its previous life; that is the real evolution. Therefore, the real evolution is not that a monkey turns into a human being, but an elevated soul is given an even more perfect body.

Because our environment changes constantly, human beings and other creatures have to be adaptive to survive. Even after hundreds of years, thousands of years, tens of thousands of years, material bodies are still constantly changing. The adaptation to the environment is the survival of the fittest, but it is not the change that a soul may encounter within one lifetime. It is correct to call such a change evolution, but it is also correct to call it devolution.

The plants in the world also go through evolution and devolution. In this highly industrialized world with rapid population growth, diversity among both plants and animals is declining.

The bottom line is that the evolution of life is determined according to the level of evolution of the soul as opposed to direct changes in the material body.

The level of evolution of a soul is not determined by oneself. Instead, it is determined by the "soul-level appraisal organization" (靈魂層次評定機構) in the Thin Space of the world in which the soul is living. This organization is under the jurisdiction of the "Ministry of Soul Administration" (靈魂

管理院). After death or prior to the birth of a body, its soul is reviewed by the organization before deciding what kind of body will be given to the soul for the next life.

A material body existing in this world is a house in which a soul resides. A soul cannot exist independently over an extensive period of time. To exist over a long period of time, a soul must have a residence (also called a house, body, etc.). To guarantee its survival, a soul would rather possess a body[22] that does not belong to it instead of being taken away (incarcerated in the "Original Soul Palace" [原魂宮] by the Ministry of Soul Administration).

There are many souls in this world, but only a very limited quota is available for reincarnation; many souls must wait in line. The souls not allowed to reincarnate, as many as the sands of the Ganges, are kept in different kinds of bottles and jars. Some of the containers keep one soul only; some keep a few, and some keep a group. These souls are filled with the amnesia drink to keep them in the state of dormancy over a long period of time with minimal energy consumption. The containers with souls in dormancy are stored in the "Original Soul Palace" in the Thin Space for unlimited Kalpas. The Original Soul Palace is like a seed warehouse for living beings; its inventory rotates in and out constantly. Considering that souls are being kept in the Original Soul Palace, it is an extremely difficult task for a soul to keep reincarnating in material realm without being repossessed back to the Original Soul Palace.

It is not easy to have a body, and we should cherish our opportunity to be a human and pursue the elevation and enhancement of our souls.

A soul cannot gather Spiritual Qi (靈氣) independently, but it has to replenish Spiritual Qi to stay alive. A soul is capable of living by itself over a short period of time, and the exact length of such time may vary depending on the individual's condition. In general, the life expectancy of a soul is about forty-nine days and does not exceed one hundred days. Therefore, when an old body dies, the next body for the soul will be determined within forty-nine days, followed by immediate occupancy.

In material realm, all bodies have limits on their lives except the "Four Great Correct Stages of Attainment" (Arhan, Pratyeka-buddha, Bodhisattva, and Buddha). Therefore, a soul has to move from house to house (body) whenever there is a death to survive.

It is the intention of the Buddha-to-Be Religion to allow the living beings for whom the conditions have matured enough to receive "houses" that never deteriorate as the residences for their souls. That shall end the pain and solve the problem of transmigration.

Having a residence that never deteriorates, a soul will be relieved from transmigration and given freedom and permanent and true joy. If a soul wishes for transmigration, it may file an application for it; if a soul does not wish for transmigration, it can choose the place to live and the destination to go.

It can be derived that transmigrations are classified into occasional transmigrations and mandatory transmigrations.

(A) OCCASIONAL TRANSMIGRATION

Occasional transmigration, as its name suggests, takes place occasionally. Such transmigration is not a requirement or an obligation; it happens occasionally as needed. For example, it happens when: a soul is ordered to transmigrate; an upgrade of the stage of attainment is planned (a practitioner should be content while in the Yin-Yang Space and should endeavor to upgrade the stage of attainment while in the Dharma Realm); a soul is going to help someone or to help a person on a mission to save and cultivate the living beings; "karma settlement" (了業) is required; or a soul has made a great vow to teach the scriptures and preach dharma and to save and cultivate living beings.

Such transmigration allows one to choose the preferred time or condition. It is voluntary instead of mandatory, which is why it is called occasional transmigration.

The method for such reincarnation is called "soul-branching."

After the transmigration has been concluded, if no mandatory transmigration has been caused, then the "branch soul" can be retrieved. If the karma (羯磨, 業) that leads to mandatory transmigration has been committed, however, the retrieval of the branch soul will not be allowed.

Therefore, a person going through occasional transmigration must not commit any karma that leads to mandatory transmigration to ensure that the branch soul may be retrieved after the mission is complete.

"Branch soul" (分靈) and "Duplicated Body" (分身) are different concepts. A "Duplicated Body" is another body that originates from the Dharma Body. Like the original Dharma Body, it is a body consisting of Spiritual Light (靈光). A "branch soul" is "a bit of Spiritual Qi" (一點靈氣) that breaks away from a soul. It is a "seed" of the soul.

One is an entire body, and the other one is a part of a body (the spiritual part). Therefore, they are completely different.

Occasional transmigration also comes in two conditions.

1.   Long and Unlimited Wisdom Life

"Long and unlimited wisdom life" means that trans-migration is no longer needed because the "Four Great Correct Stages of Attainment" (四大正果) have been achieved; one is relieved from transmigration and never has to worry about birth and death. In terms of time, the life has no limitation (unlimited life); transmigration takes place only to serve a certain need or purpose.

2.   Long But Limited Wisdom Life

"Long but limited wisdom life" means that the "Four Great Correct Stages of Attainment" have not yet been achieved, but a body has been acquired that is given quite a long life. Despite transmigration not being relieved, there is a residence available that lasts for a long time, and temporarily, there is no need for transmigration. Even though the body has a long life, it is still limited; transmi-gration is still required at the end of the life. Under the cir-cumstance that the length of life can still go on for a long time (e.g., one billion years), transmigration will take place and take a few decades or centuries to serve a certain need or purpose.

A body that has an extended length of life is called a "wisdom life." Only a soul that has wisdom may receive a body that lives for a long time, and that is why it is called a wisdom life. A body with long but limited life as mentioned here is undoubtedly a wisdom life.

A "long but limited wisdom life" must figure out a way to extend its life while it is still alive, or it has to find a new "house" within forty-nine days after the end of life. Failure to find one will cause the soul to lose its residence and be susceptible to complete disintegration.

The Ministry of Soul Administration has pity for the living beings. A soul has to go a long way to evolve to such a level. Instead of allowing the soul to disintegrate completely, the Ministry acquires it and keeps it in the Original Soul Palace for protection. Therefore, a soul without residence, possessing a body randomly, and wandering around will most likely be recaptured and kept in the Original Soul Palace with not much hope of transmigration.

With the residence of soul having ceased and a new residence unavailable due to the "karma force," the homeless soul becomes so desperate that it will take whatever it can; even a pig is better than nothing. That is why a "long but limited wisdom life" will choose the perfect time to file its application for transmigration, and that is why a "long but limited wisdom life" undergoes "branch soul transmigration."

(B) MANDATORY TRANSMIGRATION

Those who go through mandatory transmigration are

totally driven by the karma force. They have no choice but to accept whatever comes to them against their will. There is nothing they can choose—the time, location, residence—nothing at all.

They have to obey unconditionally without any autonomy (although they can appeal). Their "karmic effect" (業果) shall be arranged by the Ministry of Reincarnation and Transmigration according to the respective karma force. This type of transmigration is called mandatory transmigration and is also of two types:

1.   Branch Soul Transmigration (分靈輪迴)

If a soul that goes through branch soul transmigration (occasional transmigration, as mentioned above) has done something wrong, then the karma force will stop it from returning to its primal soul (rejoining the primal soul); it will be trapped in mandatory transmigration in the material realm until the level of the branch soul is upgraded and the karma that has caused the mandatory transmigration has been fully settled.

2.   Primal Soul Transmigration (原靈輪迴)

Primal soul transmigration is further divided into two conditions:

The first one: A soul that has never attained the wisdom life since beginninglessness. As a low-level soul, it has to move upward little by little to higher levels through many lives. In each life, the soul receives transmigration as its retribution for karmas committed in previous lives.

The second one: A soul that has already attained wisdom life but has failed to extend its wisdom life and caused the wisdom life to die. Without a host on which to depend, it has to transmigrate to obtain a new host.

The above explains the difference between mandatory transmigration and occasional transmigration, which happens when a soul goes through the cycle of birth and death in the material realm.

V.

MULTIPLE SPACES WITH DIFFERENT DIMENSIONS (多維空間)

The concept of space is very critical to a practitioner.

We are living in a world comprising multiple spaces with different dimensions; each space exists independently but interacts with other spaces. Therefore, the spatial structure is quite complex.

The spatial structure exists permanently even if the world is annihilated.

In our world, there are over one hundred spaces, each of which has a unique dimension. Some of the spaces are idle, desolate, dark, and undeveloped. If a person enters any of these spaces during "soul communication" (通靈), this person will see nothing as if in a black hole.

In fact, we do not have to know many spaces. To expand our thought and concept for use in the cultivation of the way of Nirvana, all we have to know are the four spaces, each of which has a distinct dimension.

These four spaces are Coarse Space (Coarse-Dimension Space; 粗維空間), Thin Space (Thin-Dimension Space; 細維空間), Refined Space (Refined-Dimension Space; 精維空間), and Nano Space (Nano-Dimension Space; 納維空間).

The following is a description of these four spaces from the perspective of a human material body (based on the "cognition" of the material body, not the Dharma Body).

(A) COARSE SPACE

The Coarse Space is a space of materiality. This space exists in material realm and contains "materials" that have "shapes" or "mass."

Material will deteriorate sooner or later. Therefore, a material body will also deteriorate sooner or later, and the material realm, too, will deteriorate sooner or later.

Based on the standard of the material body's "cognition," the feelings and impressions for material and material realm can be generalized according to three ideologies: color, number, and line.

The feelings that a material body has for everything can be expressed with indices. For example, the indices include temperature, humidity, speed, level of pain, and monetary amount.

In the understanding of current science, the speed in the Coarse Space that we know of is limited to the speed of light; even aircraft can only reach supersonic speed. The superluminal age has to wait until the appropriate technology becomes available in the future. Only when an aircraft can reach superluminal speed can we explore deeper into the mystery of cosmos with "realistic" scientific methods.

Unlike the limited science, religious practitioners' cognition is that the soul of a human being flies at the speed of light, and the Dharma Body of a practitioner flies at superluminal speed. How much faster than the speed of light depends on the level of the Dharma Body.

In general, before science enters the superluminal age, the cultivation of Dharma Body is an action of super-science. The Dharma Body can break through spatial obstacles, insert or acquire an object into or out of a sealed container, move an object from thousands of kilometers away, and travel to another planet tens of billions of kilometers away instantly.

Coarse Space can be further divided into three categories of: "with shape and mass," "with shape but without mass," and "with mass but without shape."

1.   with shape and mass

"With shape and mass" means the shape of something can be seen with the physical eyes and is tactile to human flesh. It is something that occupies some of the Coarse Space that has shape, size, weight, and volume, such as a material body, a planet, a house, a mountain, a river, a tree, and an automobile.

These materials exist in the Coarse Space. A material body considers this space as the real world, but once the material body dies, nothing can be brought away by the person.

2. with shape But without mass

"With shape but without mass" means the shape of
something can be seen with the physical eyes but is not tactile to human flesh. It is something that has shape and size
but has no weight and does not occupy the Coarse Space.
For example, cast light onto a human body, and there will
be a Yin side and a Yang side on the body. There will be
shadow on the Yin side, and the shadow is "with shape but
without mass." (When the practitioner has achieved the
state of "Shadow Materialization," the shadow will then have
mass. This concept involves the Thin Space.)

3. with mass But without shape

"With mass but without shape" means the shape of
something cannot be seen with the physical eyes but can
be visible, audible, or tactile through transformation by a
scientific apparatus (e.g., electricity and radio waves).

When we contact an insulated live wire, we cannot
see the existence of electricity. If we do so without
insulation, however, we will feel it. There are many
examples, such as the telegram and mobile phone.

The above are the three categories of Coarse Space.

The Coarse Space has been proven by modern science, and modern people believe that it exists. The spaces we are going to talk about below are not visible to the
majority of people. Therefore, people do not believe in
their existence. Even many Buddhists do not believe in them.

In fact, there are many paranormal phenomena existing in our world that are beyond scientific explanation.
The unknown of the vast universe largely outnumber the

known. Something that has no scientific explanation yet, or is beyond the understanding of science, is not necessarily unscientific. Modern science does not know everything and needs further development. The multiple spaces that can be explored by our souls and Dharma Bodies cannot be explored with modern scientific apparatus (perhaps this can be done in the future). The existence of these spaces has been proven by many practitioners after countless explorations.

(B) THIN SPACE

In the knowledge of human material bodies, many "things" are invisible. These intangible "things" have no mass. Therefore, we group these "things" together and call them "without shape and mass."

The "without shape and mass" *things* in the Coarse Space are not tactile to our flesh and are invisible to us.

When a person's soul or Dharma Body enters the Thin Space, however, all these "without shape and mass" *things* suddenly become "with shape and mass."

To a material body, the Thin Space is a formless world. The Thin Space, like the Coarse Space, has landscape, pagodas, towers, houses, flowers, trees, human-shaped bodies, and animals.

The Thin Space is a world comprised of Spiritual Qi. The living beings residing in this space fly at the speed of light, and they do not need vehicles, such as automobiles.

The living beings that live in the Thin Space include ghosts, Heaven People, and low Dharma Bodies.

All souls and Dharma Bodies may also enter into and live in the Thin Space.

Ghosts, Heaven People, and low Dharma Bodies are all human-shaped bodies in the Thin Space.

Like the Coarse Space, the Thin Space has jails, governments, law enforcement agencies, and legislative institutes; everything is under orderly management.

The Thin Space contains Yin Space and Yang Space.

Yang Space has no night and, therefore, no darkness.

Yin Space has no day and, therefore, no light.

The Coarse Space has days and nights. It has Yin and Yang, half and half. That's why it's called Yin-Yang Space.

(C) REFINED SPACE

In the cognition of human beings, Refined Space is also a "without shape and mass" space.

The Refined Space is comprised of Spiritual Qi and Spiritual Light.

The Refined Space is a world for the middle Dharma Bodies to inhabit.

The Dharma Bodies living in the Refined Space fly at superluminal speed; their velocities are individually determined according to the levels of their Dharma Bodies. These Dharma Bodies have supernatural power, enabling them to break through spatial obstacles.

To a material body, the Refined Space is also an invisible world. It too has pagodas, towers, houses, flowers, and trees like the Coarse Space; they are all perfectly built by the dharma power and beautifully decorated with the Seven Treasures.[23] The floors of the palaces are paved with gold, but they feel softer and more comfortable than carpet.

The Refined Space also has administrative agencies, law enforcement agencies, and legislative institutes; everything is well in order.

(D) NANO SPACE

Nano Space is the place where high Dharma Bodies live and is the Nano Realm within the Dharma Realm. It is a space with no birth or death; it is a pure and clean space. It is also a space of eternity and utmost joy.

The Four Great Correct Stages of Attainment live in this space.

Nano Space is a superluminal space comprised of Spiritual Light.

There are infinite Buddha's Pure Lands in the Nano Space. For example, setting the Solar System as the origin of a coordinate (the Earth rotates, and it will not be accurate if a certain point on the Earth is set as the coordinate origin; this is a cosmic point of view, not the global point of view), flying westbound away from the Solar System for 44.58 billion light-years, you reach the World of Utmost Joy. Flying eastbound for about 55.6 billion light-years, you reach the Lazurite Light World of Medicine Buddha (Sanskrit: *Bhaisajyaguru*). Both of the two are built on the Buddha's Pure Lands in the Nano Space. (The Nano Space of the world in which we live is an undeveloped space. All high Dharma Bodies live on Buddhas' Pure Lands created in other Nano Spaces by Buddhas. Some of the high Dharma Bodies have also built their palaces for temporary stays in the Refined Space of this world. They are used for saving and converting the living beings of this world.)

All substances are composed of energy particles; the particle size determines the properties of the space.

The particles of the Coarse Space can be observed with the physical eyes. They are coarse particles, and we consider them "with shape" (except the "with mass but without shape" category in the Coarse Space).

The particles of the Thin Space, Refined Space, and Nano Space cannot be observed with the physical eyes; they are micro-particles, and hence, we believe they are "without shape."

The particles of the Coarse Space are large enough; they have volume and weight so that they cannot go through walls. That is why we consider them as "with mass" (except the "with shape but without mass" category in the Coarse Space).

Water cannot leak if it is stored in a container with a sufficiently high density. If it is stored in a container with insufficient density, it begins to permeate. Such permeation is a pass-through.

The particles of the Thin Space, Refined Space, and Nano Space are so tiny that they can pass through any material in the Coarse Space. These micro particles are so small that they cannot be seen and are not tactile. That is why we call them "without mass."

The particles of the Nano Space can pass through the material in the Refined Space; the particles of the Refined Space can pass through the material in the Thin Space; the particles of the Thin Space can pass through the material in the Coarse Space.

In terms of the thinness of these particles, the Nano particles are thinner than the Refined particles; the Refined particles are thinner than the Thin particles; the Thin particles are thinner than the Coarse particles.

Are there spaces whose particles are thinner than the ones of the Nano Space? Of course there are. However, from the aspect of the current level of our cultivation, it is not necessary to explore further to that extent. Understanding the Nano Space is more than enough for the cultivation of Nirvana.

(E) PARALLEL EXISTENCE OF MULTIPLE SPACES WITH DIFFERENT DIMENSIONS

When it comes to multiple spaces with different dimensions, many people believe that every space has a fixed location. For example, Heaven must be up there in the sky, and Hell must be down there under the ground. That is incorrect.

The Earth is spherical and the sky in relation to the Earth is omni-directional.

In fact, there are over one hundred spaces of different dimensions in one speck of micro-dust, and all the spaces operate independently without interfering with each other in the same way there are countless radio waves that constantly pass through our bodies at any moment. Our bodies cannot stop them from passing through, but some materials can because the structures of the composing particles are different. The energy particles of Spiritual Qi and Spiritual Light are so tiny that they have high penetration strength.

If we put water in a highly transparent glass bottle, followed by putting a plastic bag with a cell phone sealed in it into the water, and replace the cap of the container, then it becomes an interesting multidimensional space (a space comprised of multiple spaces with different dimensions). A soul and a Dharma Body can pass through this bottle at will and can survive inside the bottle. We dial the number of the cell phone, and the cell phone rings inside the bottle. In the meantime, both Heaven and Hell can be established inside the bottle. It can be concluded that there are multiple spaces of different dimensions existing inside the bottle. Each space is not solitary; all these spaces coexist and overlap, but each operates independently.

The conclusion is that multiple spaces of different dimensions coexist.

VI.

THE SPHERES FOR A SOUL THAT TRANSMIGRATES IN THE MATERIAL REALM

Transmigrating repeatedly in the material realm can expose the soul to stress, pain, and anxiety. Sometimes, the soul attains a "long but limited wisdom life," but shortly afterwards, it falls into transmigrations again.

Because a soul is transmigrating in the material realm, what are the spheres that may exist in material realm?

Figure 1 in the front of the book provides a brief description of the material realm.

With Figure 1, we can see that our Little World contains the Yin Space, Yang Space, and Yin-Yang Space.

These spaces are all built within the Land of Endurance with Five Impurities, which is destructible. Therefore, the "multiple spaces with different dimensions" existing in the entire Little World belong to material realm (Nano Space is not developed in a Little World).

"All phenomena arise due to their causes and conditions; all phenomena cease when the conditions cease." There were already "multiple spaces with different dimensions" existing in the space that was occupied by our Little World, except that they were not yet developed and utilized because there was no "condition" for development and utilization. When the living beings came to the Yin-Yang Space, developments for these spaces began. The Yin Space and Yang Space were established, and the "multiple spaces with different dimensions" were developed. If this Little World decays and disappears, all the mountains, rivers, pagodas, towers, Heaven, Hell, Heaven People, ghosts, deities, etc. in the "multiple spaces with different dimensions" will no longer exist. This space returns to its desolation as it once was and waits for the next development and utilization.

Because everything in this world will go bad and become extinct, everything is delusional. That is why it is called the material realm.

By cultivating a Dharma Body with a certain method (a body attained by cultivation using a specific method; dharma also has the meaning of "method"), one may enter the Dharma Realm (a sphere only accessible by Dharma Body; that is why it is called the Dharma Realm). A high Dharma Body may enter the Nano Space, which is also called the Nano World or Nano Realm. The Nano Realm is a part of the Dharma Realm; it is a world of eternity, a world with the utmost joy, a world without transmigration, a True World, and a pure and clean world.

The human-shaped bodies in the Nano Realm are also called Nano Bodies; they have no phenomena of males or females, "phenomena of lifespans,"[24] and "phenomena of material bodies." They can break through spatial obstacles and appear in any space of any dimension. They can change their sizes and exhibit "manifestations of supernatural powers" according to the levels of their dharma powers. They can show their material body figures in the Coarse Space. (*The Law of Deva* stipulates that no image showing is allowed without a "pardon order" [特赦令]; the violators will be subject to penalty provided by *the Law of Deva*.)

A soul that transmigrates in the material realm may be entitled to great blessed retributions (a.k.a., blessed rewards), but the blessed retributions will end eventually. It has to go through transmigration when its life ends.

These transmigrations may be pleasant or painful to a greater or lesser extent; in some cases, they are half-and-half.

Those who are enjoying great pleasure become highly conceited and forget about cultivating and practicing.

Those who are suffering great pain become extremely desperate and have no spare effort for cultivating and practicing.

Those who are in the sphere of half pleasure and half pain are the ones most likely to come to their enlightenment.

Most of the time, human beings living in this Yin-Yang Space are in the sphere of half pleasure and half pain. Thus, they come to enlightenment more easily. Because living beings in such a sphere are easily enlightened, we should embrace this opportunity to awaken to the truth, eventually leading to practice and cultivation.

The Realm of Desire, a part of the material realm, is a sphere of desire for sexuality and diet (food and drink).

The Realm of Disassociation, also a part of the material realm, is a sphere where the desire for sexuality and diet has been abandoned.

The Realm of Liberation, a part of the material realm, is a sphere where one's worries over transmigration are about to be eliminated, and all pains are about to be relieved. One is getting ready to bail out of these Three Realms and the Five Elements, enter the Nirvana, receive a Nano Body (high Dharma Body), and eternally enjoy the utmost joy.

The details of Figure 1 are described in later sections.

Below is a simplified version of Figure 1.

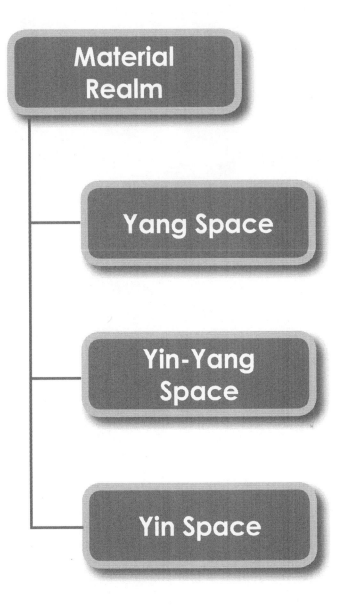

VII.

DI-ZANG BODHISATTVA'S THREE LIVES OF BUDDHISM PREACHING IN CHINESE

A living being's failure to enter into Nirvana after transmigrations throughout multiple lives over countless Kalpas (劫) is attributed to incorrect methods of practice and cultivation.

It is rare for a living being in the Yin-Yang Space to achieve attainment only by independent study; in most cases, schooling is required, like going to elementary school and working one's way up to a higher-level degree.

It is the same in religious practice and cultivation; after all, the truth of the universe and life is not easy. With the help of a good master, one may succeed more easily.

Religious practice and cultivation need "potentialities and conditions" (機緣).

The kind and pitying Buddha has arranged all kinds of opportunities for as many living beings to be converted as possible.

Some believe, after a period of practice and cultivation, that they have already succeeded and self-claim a certain stage of attainment. That is a great deceptive lie. It is shameful to grant an attainment to oneself. That can only fool the unenlightened, and such self-granted attainment is not recognized in the Dharma Realm.

In human society, to receive a legitimate academic degree from an accredited institute, one must study and pass examinations.

A stage of attainment in the multiple spaces is applicable to a Dharma Body as opposed to a material body. The stage of attainment of a Dharma Body has to be recognized by a Stage Appraisal Institute.

In addition, it is the branch soul of a Dharma Body's soul that goes through the transmigration, not the Dharma Body itself.

The stage appraisal (評定果位) does not happen every year; it has its predetermined schedule.

With the pre-historic cultures taken out, there have been two stage appraisals during human history.

The first time happened during the period of Jiang, Zih-ya as described in the *Fong Shen Bang* for granting the stage of deities (神).

The second time happened during the period of Sakyamuni Buddha and Lao-zi of Taoism as a general appraisal where a batch of the titles of fairies (仙), Arhans (阿羅漢, 羅漢), and Pratyeka-buddhas (辟支佛) were given.

Will there be a third time? Of course there will be.

The third time will happen during the Modern Qingyang Period[25] and the Buddha-to-Be Religion (未來佛宗教) Period. It will be a general appraisal and a batch of the titles of Bodhisattvas will be given.

When will the fourth time be? It will be around 6,000 years later, temporarily scheduled; the actual date will change according to the collective karma forces of living beings.

What about the Dharma Body attained between two stage appraisals (such as between the second time and the third time)? All Dharma Bodies attained prior to "stage appraisal" will be temporarily considered "human fairies," which is the lowest level of the middle Dharma Bodies.

The stage appraisal is administered by a committee consisting of high Dharma Bodies and middle Dharma Bodies, which are not material bodies.

In human society, the propagation of dharma is administered by a group of material bodies.

The collective action above and below the Deva is called "Dharma Propagation and Stage Appraisal"(傳法定位).

Even Buddhas have to be appraised and certified by the "Buddhahood Certification Institute" (佛陀資格認證機構) of the Kingdom of United Nebulae[26] before they can be called Buddhas.

The Buddhahood Certification Institute of the Kingdom of United Nebulae is a large institute already established by a group of predecessor Buddhas countless Kalpas ago.

There is an institute called Qingyang Zang (青陽藏) in the Kingdom of United Nebulae specializing in training Bodhisattvas. Its primary mission is to train all Bodhisattvas that have completely realized the Tenth Ground (十地).

The immeasurable information of countless worlds is deposited in the Qingyang Zang.

A Bodhisattva who has realized the Tenth Ground may use his "Duplicated Bodies" to study while concurrently using his "branch soul" to reincarnate.

Since beginninglessness, Di-Zang Bodhisattva has been saving and converting living beings in immeasurable worlds and has realized the Tenth Ground of Bodhisattva countless times. Because Di-Zang Bodhisattva has vowed in previous lives, "I will not accept my Buddhahood if there is anyone still in Hell," he remains a Bodhisattva up to the present.

There is a saying: "Every household worships Amitabha Buddha and Guan-Yin Bodhisattva (Sanskrit: *Avalokites-vara*; 觀音菩薩)." The majority of people do not know Di-Zang Bodhisattva very well, and they think that Di-Zang Bodhisattva works in Hell only. Actually, this is not correct. After all, Hell is a place for "karmic retribution" (業報); it is too late to be sorry for a living being who has been condemned to Hell. Why would Di-Zang Bodhisattva only work in Hell? Why would a Great Bodhisattva who has converted countless people fail to take preventive measures in advance? That is why Di-Zang Bodhisattva constantly reincarnates to the human world (凡人間), under appropriate "potentialities and conditions," to save and convert living beings.

Di-Zang Bodhisattva will never forget the instruction that Sakyamuni Buddha gave at "The Deva of Thirty-Three Domains."

Sakyamuni Buddha responded to the world and preached Buddhism doctrines for several decades without leaving any written scripture behind. After Sakyamuni Buddha's Nirvana, his senior disciples gathered together and transcribed his teaching into scriptures for future generations. These scriptures are collectively called "Tripitaka" or the Buddhist Canon.

Tripitaka has three collections: the Sutra Collection, the Precepts Collection, and the Treatises Collection.

The Sutra Collection: The "Dharma" that Sakyamuni Buddha taught.

The Precepts Collection: The precepts that Sakyamuni Buddha provided for his disciples.

The Treatises Collection: The understanding and realization by the disciples from the study of the precepts and dharma and from practice.

Tripitaka did not go into public circulation until the disciples had held three major editorial conferences.

According to Sakyamuni Buddha's instructions, the "Great-Vehicle Buddhism" (*Mahayana* Buddhism)[27] is to be preached primarily in China.

Despite such instruction, the Correct-Dharma Period of Buddhism never happened in China. The preaching of the Great-Vehicle Buddhism is not an easy task; we must first understand the true meaning of the doctrine that Sakyamuni Buddha taught us.

Following the instructions of Sakyamuni Buddha, Di-Zang Bodhisattva committed himself to the career of preaching the Great-Vehicle Buddhism in Chinese. For more than one thousand years, he reincarnated three times to the human world and established three milestones in the preaching of Great-Vehicle Buddhism.

(A) FIRST LIFE

Di-Zang Bodhisattva reincarnated into the mundane world in 600 AD in China. His mundane last name was Chen, and his first name was Wei; he also had an alias, Xuan-zang. He set off to the West Territory to acquire Buddhism scriptures in about 626. The fifty-thousand-kilometer journey across 110 countries took him eighteen years to complete. He took back 744 volumes of Buddhism scriptures, including 244 volumes of *Great-Vehicle Sutras*, 192 volumes of *Great-Vehicle Treatises*, 114 volumes of *Sutra, Precepts, and Treatises of Arya-sthavira-nikaya*, fifteen volumes of *Sutra, Precepts, and Treatises of Mahasanghika*, thirty-six volumes of *Hetuvidya Treatises*, sixty-seven volumes of *Sutra, Precepts, and Treatises of Sarvasti-vadin*, forty-two volumes of *Sutra, Precepts, and Treatises of Dharmaguptaka*, and fifty-four volumes of other scriptures.

He returned to ChangAn, the capital of the Tang Dynasty, at the end of January 645 with more than twenty horses carrying the scriptures and Buddhist artifacts. There was a grand welcoming ceremony for him; the event was regarded as the greatest since Buddhism was introduced to the East.

Tai-zong of the Tang Dynasty was an exceptionally brilliant emperor. His full support for Xuan-zang's career after he returned home protected the interests of Buddhism throughout the country and successfully promoted the cultural and societal position of Buddhism. Xuan-zang was highly regarded as the Holy Monk and became the leader of the circle of Buddhism.

With this generous protection and support from the ruler, Xuan-zang received a great amount of human and material resources, and the translation of Buddhism scriptures and the promotion of Buddhism were very successful. Xuan-zang achieved great success in terms of Great-Vehicle Buddhism.

In 664, Xuan-zang died smiling with his mission accomplished in this life.

(B)   SECOND LIFE

In 696, Di-Zang Bodhisattva was born through reincarnation in the Kingdom of Silla (of the ancient korea) with the mundane last name of Jin and the first name Qiaojue. In the later years of Kai Yuan of the Tang Dynasty, he arrived at AnHui Province, China, and stopped at Mount JiuHua in QingYang County, where he started his ascetic practice. A generous local met him and donated money and land to build a temple. It was the beginning of the Mount JiuHua Truth Place (a place for teaching, learning, and practicing Buddhism), which is now a popular tourism destination known as one of the famous Buddhist mountains and the Appearance-Dharma Truth Place of Di-Zang Bodhisattva.

After the establishment of the Appearance-Dharma, the initial system for saving and converting the living beings, Jin, Qiao-jue died at the age of ninety-nine in 794, which was the tenth year of Zhen Yuan of the Tang Dynasty.

(C) THIRD LIFE

Di-Zang Bodhisattva was again born in China in 1960. At the age of twelve, he encountered an emergency that could have claimed his life; however, he was rescued by a supramundane person. He then followed this supramundane person as a disciple and began to learn Buddhism. He often followed his mentor and practiced solitary meditation deep in the mountains and acquired profound knowledge of Supramundane Dharma.

The third milestone of Great-Vehicle Buddhism began in 2008.

Excluding dharma preaching in other languages and focusing only on preaching in Chinese, the three lives had specific focuses:

The first life was focused on the acquirement of Buddhism scriptures and their translation into Chinese; there was no further explanation of the scriptures.

The second life was focused on the establishment of Appearance-Dharma and the propagation of scriptures.

The third life was focused on the explanation of the scriptures. The most essential parts of the Buddhism scriptures are like riddles; the living beings in the world have been guessing their true meanings for more than 2,500 years. It is now the time to unveil the riddles. The scriptures of the Buddha-to-Be Religion shall disclose the answers to these riddles hidden in the ancient scriptures of Buddhism to the living beings as a measure that rectifies the common fallacies. Those whose condition have matured enough will be saved and converted; the cultivation result of the practitioners shall be appraised and their stages of attainment rewarded.

ESSENTIALS OF VOLUME ONE

1. Reincarnation by Metamorphosis (化生)

In the material realm (色界), reincarnations have four types: viviparity, oviparity, moisture-birth, and metamorphosis.

[1] Reincarnation by Viviparity (胎生):

Life is given through the mating of male and female and pregnancy by a female parent (e.g., human beings and some animals).

[2] Reincarnation by Oviparity (卵生):

Birth comes via an egg laid by an animal, such as a chicken, duck, or frog.

[3] Reincarnation by Moisture Birth (濕生):

Many little insects are born naturally in moistened soil or damp environment without viviparity, oviparity, or metamorphosis. It is, therefore, referred to as moisture-born.

[4] Reincarnation by Metamorphosis (化生):

Human beings are an animal of viviparity. A person after death may be destined by the karma force (業力) to other realms without reincarnation by viviparity (e.g., a Heaven Person or a ghost).

After death, the material body becomes extinct, and the person's soul loses its residence. If this person reincarnates to Heaven, a new body (a new residence) will be given to the soul immediately. Because of the karma force, this soul is spontaneously pulled into Heaven and is given a body, which consists of Spiritual Qi (靈氣). This process is referred to as reincarnation by meta-morphosis.

Of course, the whole process is not a matter of free will; instead, it is controlled by the Yin Space (陰間) admini-strative agency in our Little World.

The agency in charge of soul reincarnation is estab-lished at the Thin Space (細維空間).

2.   The Great Filial Piety (大孝)

The ancient Chinese say: filial piety is number one among all good deeds.

Filial piety can be differentiated into great filial piety (大孝) and minor filial piety (小孝). Alternatively, it can also be differentiated into remote filial piety (遠孝) and near filial piety (近孝).

[1]   Great Filial Piety
(a) Supramundane Filial Piety (Filial Piety without Leakage)

All living beings are regarded as parents. One should endlessly help them, through conversion, making them stay away from the ocean of pain of transmigration, the-reby leaving material realm, achieving the high Dharma Body, living in the Nano Space, and realizing the eternal and true peace and happiness.

(b) Mundane Filial Piety (Filial Piety with Leakage)

Repay the favors of teachers and parents of every life. Help people do good deeds and take pleasure in helping others. Respect teachers and love students. Assist the elderly and protect children. Devote yourself without selfishness.

[2] Minor Filial Piety
(a) Supramundane Filial Piety (Filial Piety without Leakage)

Convert one's parents in the present life to relieve them from the pain of transmigration.

(b) Mundane Filial Piety (Filial Piety with Leakage)

Show filial piety to one's parents in the present life.

[3] Remote Filial Piety

Show filial piety and respec for ancient saints and sages and follow their words and deeds.

Buddhists should take Sakyamuni Buddha as a role model; they should learn from Buddha, learning Buddha's virtue, acts, and thoughts, and in this way, gradually enter into the way of Buddhahood.

[4] Near Filial Piety

Show filial piety to and convert not only one's own parents, but also parents of other people.

3. Material Body (色身)
◆ "Material" (色)

In this book, "material" means any material with tangible volume, weight, and form that is visible to the physical eyes and sensible to human touch, that exists in the Coarse

Space, and that will decay and disappear eventually.

The Four Great Elements (四大) of earth, water, fire, and wind, and the Five Elements (五行) of metal, wood, water, fire, and earth, are all within the scope of "material."

◆ Material Body (Physical Body; 色身)

A "material body" consists of materials with "material properties." A material body can feel pain and happiness and is, therefore, referred as a "retributive body" (報身), "karmic body" (業身), or "karmic-retribution body" (業報身); it is the body that receives the pain and happiness it deserves.

4. Three Souls and Seven Vigors (三魂七魄)

As the saying goes: "Even a little sparrow has a complete set of internal organs." All animals with material bodies have "Three Souls and Seven Vigors." Human beings, as high-class animals, have these "Three Souls and Seven Vigors." Take mankind as an example:

[1] Three Souls
(a) Yang soul

It lives in the "three Yang-meridians" of the human body. Its existence depends on the Spiritual Qi (靈氣) of the human body.

Yang soul exists only after birth. Therefore, it is an acquired soul.

It is responsible for all matters in the Yin-Yang Space. All behaviors of a material body are determined by the Yang soul; it is the master of the material body. If the Yang soul leaves the material body, then a person becomes a semi-vegetable. Therefore, the Yang soul may not leave the material body without good cause.

A practitioner at high-level meditation may allow his or her Yang soul to leave the body, but he or she will lose tactile sense and become immobile when that happens.

Because the Yang soul should not leave the body without a good cause, it is referred to as the "guardian soul." It is the soul that guards one's material body throughout one's lifetime.

Yang soul is also referred to as mental consciousness (意識) or ideology.

Modern Buddhism refers to Yang soul as Mind or the sixth consciousness.

Yang soul is able to leave the material body and act independently for short periods of time. If the period of time is too long, the material body will be regarded as injured or mistakenly assumed to be dead.

(b) Yin Soul

It lives in the "three Yin-meridians" inside the human body. Its existence depends on the Spiritual Qi of the human body.

The Yin soul exists only after birth. Therefore, similar to the Yang soul, it is acquired.

The Yin soul is responsible for one's matters in the Yin Space (existing in the Thin Space), including the matters of previous lives, current life, and future lives.

The Yin soul is able to leave the material body and act independently for forty-nine days normally and one hundred days on special occasions. After one hundred days, the material body may become sick, contract disaster, or even die.

The Yin soul often leaves the material body to wander around or take care of business. It is, therefore, also called the "wandering soul."

Modern Buddhism refers to Yin soul as *manas* consciousness (末那識) or the seventh consciousness.

(c) Original Soul

It lives in the "heart meridian" inside the human body and is, therefore, referred to as "heart-residing spirit." Its existence depends on the Spiritual Qi (靈氣) of the human body.

Some also refer to the original soul as "original spirit" (原神).

The original soul is able to leave the material body and act independently. Both the Yang soul and the original soul can leave the material body only through practice, but the Yin soul may leave the material body and wander around without practice.

Modern Buddhism refers to the original soul as *alaya* consciousness (阿賴耶識), the eighth consciousness, or store consciousness (收藏識).

The original soul is a seed; it is "a bit of Spiritual Qi" (一點 靈氣) and is congenital. It carries all the information regarding a life since beginninglessness.

The original soul is responsible for collecting all messages of the current and previous lives and is obliged, at the same time, to combine, release, change, and influence unobtrusively and imperceptibly.

Below is the process in which the original soul changes and influences humans unobtrusively and imperceptibly:

The original soul reincarnates and carries the given messages accumulated from the previous lives since beginninglessness. A person acquires new awareness through influential factors, such as aging, family, and society. This new awareness is first deposited and combined within the original soul and then released to form one's usual habits, temper, character, aspirations, and hobbies.

The changing and influential effect of the original soul is like a clay tea pot that has been used for tea brewing for decades; even if only hot water is added without tea leaves, if one just lets the tea pot sit for a while, it still produces a liquid with tea flavor and tea color because the tea pot has accumulated tea stains for decades.

It is the same for the original soul. It collects information on lives; every new life combines and releases these messages to make the general condition of a life.

A person is a combination of congenital Spiritual Qi and acquired Spiritual Qi. The congenital Spiritual Qi is also called "a bit of Spiritual Qi" (一點靈氣), which is a person's "original soul." It carries the messages accumulated from all previous lives.

The Yang soul, Yin soul, and original soul comprise the entirety of a soul.

Modern Buddhism refers to soul as the divine consciousness.

The three souls shall become one after one's death.

The trinity of the three souls can also be achieved with practice through a certain procedure.

The magical practice of "Three Flowers Gathering at the Top of the Head" (三花聚頂) as referred to by Taoism is actually the state of "trinity of the three souls" where one may enter into meditation at any time. One may control his or her living and dying within the limit of life. One may also gain remote sense (遙測) or remote vision (遙視).

The brain is the workplace for the soul.

It is like a computer. The three souls are the software, and the brain is the hardware; the malfunction or poor efficiency of either one may interrupt normal operation.

[2] Seven Vigors
◆ Vigor

Vigor is the drive-train built onto the Spiritual Qi for the vital organs of the human body. The index of "vigor strength" (魄力) directly influences the activity levels of the vital organs as well as the general condition of one's health. For example, an intestine with a low "vigor strength" index has less peristaltic activity.

Under the condition that the body has no pathological change, one may improve health by replacing vigors with the help of the Dharma Body (法身) cultivated by oneself or the help of another person.

◆   **Seven Vigors**

The seven vigors are actually seven sets of vigors: heart, liver (liver and gall are one set of vigors, and so on), spleen, lungs, kidneys, stomach, and intestines.

Their operations depend on burning the Spiritual Qi inside the human body until death, after which the vigors disintegrate and return to the soul. This process is how information about one's health in one's current life is carried forward to the next life.

5.   **Three Realms (三界)**
◆   **Realm (界)**

"Realm" in Chinese also means a territorial limit: a land limit, border stone, border mark, border location, borderline (1. a line dividing two areas; 2. a criteria that differentiates different subjects; or 3. an edge of a certain object), or boundary (1. a criteria that differentiates different subjects; or 2. an end or confine).

Scope: visual realm, the world, natural realm, mental realm (ideological level)

Human category by occupation or gender: the education circle (realm), the science circle (realm), or all walks of life

Natural object category by animal, plant, or mineral: inorganic realm or organic realm

The highest class of the strata system, equivalent to an "Era" as referred to in geology. The class next to a "realm" is a "system."

◆   **Three Realms**

"Three Realms" means:

The Solar System, a Little World on which our life depends, provides different living spaces for all living beings. These spaces are configured according to each person's karma force. All living beings will reincarnate to the spaces they deserve based on their respective karma forces.

People are grouped by their characteristics. Buddha categorizes living beings in this Little World into three groups, living in three different realms.

People may share similar natures, yet their customs may be quite different. Those who share the same natures are grouped as one kind.

The fundamental definition of the Little World is: A space where there is the Sun, the Moon, and the Earth. "Material" is any material that can be destroyed, and the Earth, the Sun, and the Moon are all comprised of "material." The spaces occupied by "material" have their respective and predetermined boundaries.

Because this Little World of ours is primarily formed for human material bodies, all spaces and living beings within this Little World gather when human beings appear and disseminate when human beings disappear. In other words, any space within this Little World shall form, exist, decay, and disappear along with the entire Little World.

In general, this Little World is comprised of "materials" and will be annihilated sooner or later. Therefore, it is collectively referred to as material realm (色界).

The material realm can be further divided into Three Realms (three Sub-Realms), as follows:

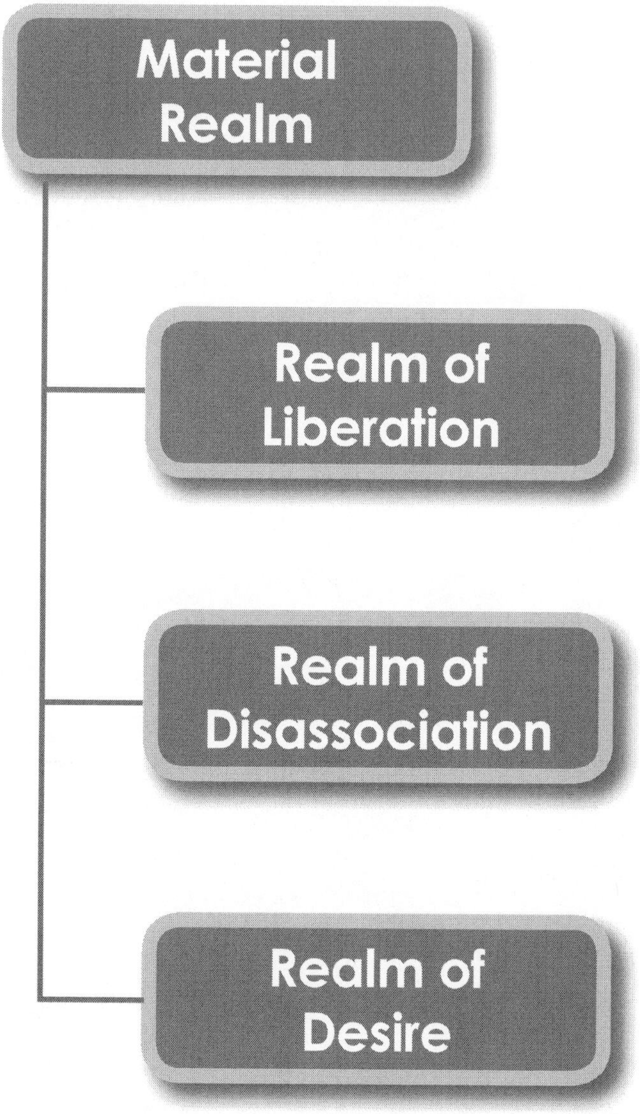
Material Realm
Realm of Liberation
Realm of Disassociation
Realm of Desire

6.   Dharma Realm (Sanskrit: *Dharmadhatu*; 法界)

Dharma Realm is the sphere occupied by Dharma Bodies, which are classified into low Dharma Bodies, middle Dharma Bodies, and high Dharma Bodies.

Only the high Dharma Bodies are allowed to reside in the Nano Space (納維空間), also known as the Nano Realm (納界), which is a space that cannot be destroyed. Other Dharma Bodies may be able to reside in Dharma Realm, but they are only allowed to live in the destructible part of Dharma Realm (this part belongs to material realm).

7.   The Linguistic Dharani (語言 "陀羅尼")

There was no Buddhism in ancient China, and Chinese Buddhism is an imported religion. The Buddhist scriptures were primarily translated from Sanskrit and Pali.

The ancient translators of the scriptures had certain principles in common—the "Five Exemptions." The meanings of the source terms could not be translated and only the pronunciations were translated under any of the following five conditions:

[1]   Secrecy

A secret cannot be translated (e.g., the secret Dharani).

[2]   Multiple Meanings

A term with multiple meanings cannot, therefore, be translated. For example, Bhagavat (薄伽梵) is a term with multiple meanings.

[3]   No Matching Target Term

There was no matching term in Chinese for a source term, making contextual translation impossible. In such a case, only the transliteration is done to present the pronunciation (e.g., Yan-Fu Tree).

[4]   Existing Custom

There are cases where the source terms have been previously translated by their pronunciations rather than by the meanings in ancient times, and these translations are already accepted among the public.

In such cases, the ancient transliterations are retained for consistency. For example, *Anuttarā-samyak-sambodhi* is transliterated into Chinese as 阿耨多羅三藐三菩提 (A nou duo luo san miao san pu ti), which means "supreme correct enlightenment," and which was an ancient transliteration that has since been widely accepted. For the purpose of consistency with existing custom since ancient times, the ancient transliteration has been adopted and no contextual translation will be made.

[5]   Contextual Translation Still Cannot Convey the Meaning the Source Intended

The languages of Sanskrit and Pali are both highly complicated, and some terms have abstruse meanings. Translating such terms into Chinese may fail to convey the original meanings properly, and transliterations were chosen so as to retain the complete, original meanings. For example, Prajna (般若), which means the wisdom to disengage from painful transmigration and to achieve Nirvana, was transliterated into Chinese as 般若. If contextual translation had been attempted, this term would only have been able to be translated as wisdom, which does not fully convey the meaning of the abstruse term Prajna. Contextual translation, therefore, was dropped completely.

The five conditions described above generally explain the reason why only transliterations were made for some source terms.

"Dharani" conforms to one of the "Five Exemptions."

However, a secret can still be decoded.

Dharani is one kind of function (also referred to as "dharma power" or "supernatural power") of high Dharma Body and may come in many types.

The Linguistic Dharani is one of many forms of Dharani. A high Dharma Body can speak in one single language and is still universally comprehensible by the audience regardless of the distances between the speaker and the listeners. For example, Buddha was teaching dharmas to ten thousand people. Althoughthe people spoke different languages, they heard the teaching as if it were spoken in their respective languages.

This is the result of Linguistic Dharani.

8.   Memory Imprint (授記)

Both Buddhas and Great Bodhisattvas possess one kind of "dharma power" (supernatural power): the "Dharma-Memory Power," also called the Dharani of Memory (記憶 陀羅尼). This power can be exercised upon living beings to allow them to imprint current happenings into their memories permanently, including spoken words, without ever forgetting them throughout future lives.

There are also cases in which the power is exercised only to make a certain issue or words a permanent memory of the audience.

Memory imprint comes in three different spheres: "memory imprint in materials," "memory imprint in Dhyana," and "memory imprint in dreams."

[1] Memory Imprint in Materials (色授記)

This concerns a living being that is subjected to memory imprint, under the condition that he is mentally sound and clearly conscious, as long as it is being done in the Little World and regardless of whether in the Yang Space (陽間), the Yin Space (陰間), or the Yin-Yang Space (陰陽間). It is called, in such a case, "memory imprint in materials" (memory imprint within the material realm).

[2] Memory Imprint in Dhyana (禪授記)

This involves a person being given a memory by Buddha while practicing Dhyana to the state of deep meditation (禪定).

After being given memory imprint in the practice of Dhyana, such a person will maintain a vivid memory. Not everyone can meet Buddha while practicing Dhyana; some have spent a lifetime practicing Dhyana and have still never met Buddha. It is attributed to the factors of virtue (德行), method (方法), and causes and conditions (因緣).

[3]   Memory Imprint in Dreams (夢授記)

Memory imprint given during dreams is called memory imprint in dreams. After waking up, such a person still carries a vivid memory. Memory imprint in dreams is not an easy thing to achieve; it also needs virtue and a proper method.

People sleep every day. Seeing Buddha in dreams, however, is rare.

Memory imprint in materials, memory imprint in Dhyana, or memory imprint in dreams can be of three kinds according to living beings' levels: "subject memory imprint," "dharma memory imprint," and "preemptive memory imprint."

[1]   Subject Memory Imprint (事授記)

Applied to cause living beings of lower levels to remember a certain subject permanently throughout repeated reincarnations as a motivation for practicing further until they ultimately succeed. For example, in order to make a living being who has been committed to Hell permanently remember the sufferings in Hell in the subconscious, the subject memory imprint is administered so that this person in future lives will be afraid of committing bad karmas and thus embrace virtuous acts.

[2]   Dharma Memory Imprint (法授記)

Applied to cause those living beings already in the stream of Buddhist practice to remember some dharmas permanently as a motivation for practicing further until they ultimately succeed.

[3]   Preemptive Memory Imprint (預授記)

Applied to those living beings of higher levels or who are already on the way of Bodhisattva. The practice of the way of Bodhisattva is inherently difficult, and it may discourage a living being already in the way of Bodhisattva in times of stagnant doubts and frustrations. In order to consolidate the determination and courage of such a practitioner, Buddha preemptively explains to the Bodhisattva what it is like when a Bodhisattva attains Buddhahood, making this Bodhisattva permanently remember Buddha's prediction and encouraging the Bodhisattva to practice further until Buddhahood is achieved.

9.   Karma (業)

Karma is the thought, deed, or word of a person in daily life.

Karmas have three types, three characteristics, two differences, four types that cause fast retributions, and two retribution times.

[1]   Three Types of Karmas
(a) Karmas of Mind
Thought or ideas of a person

(b) Karmas of Mouth
Also called "karmas of words," these are languages spoken by one's mouth.

(c) Karmas of Body
Actions and behavior of a person

[2]   Three Characteristics of Karmas
(a) Good Karmas

A good karma is active and diligent effort; it is the cause that leads to the enjoyment of happiness in future lives or the present life. Taking initiative in doing good deeds is an example.

(b) Bad Karmas

A bad karma is badness, crime, and corruption. It is the cause that leads to suffering in future lives or in the present life. Taking initiative in doing bad deeds is an example.

(c) Unrecordable Karmas

An unrecordable karma is a karma equivalent to the standard of humanity, compliance with which merely constitutes qualification as a human being and the eligibility to reincarnate as a human being again. Therefore, there is no credit earned. It is neither good nor bad and, therefore, will not have any "effected retribution" (果報), for example, not stealing while taking precepts.

There are too many things that do not belong to us; stealing constitutes bad karma, and it is something that a normal person with integrity would not do. If not stealing while window shopping qualifies as good karma, does stealing not qualify as a normal act?

Another example is refraining from obscenity while taking precepts. It is normal for a married man practicing Buddhism at home not to commit adultery. Therefore, not committing adultery does not count as good karma.

Therefore, all of the above examples are unrecordable karmas.

There is an organization in this world called the Ministry of Karma Force Registration existing in the Fine Space (細維空間). It keeps records of the good and the bad in each person. It is comprised of countless "earth fairies" (地仙) that are responsible for the actual task of recording.

As only the good and bad karmas are recorded, the unrecordable karmas are not.

The karmas of deeds, words, and thoughts that can produce "effected retributions" (果報) are limited to two "causal seeds" (因種): good karmas and bad karmas.

In the standard of humanity, those who perform good karmas rise, those who commit bad karmas fall, and those who qualify as human beings by engaging in unrecordable karmas shall reincarnate as humans. This is the Law of Cause and Effect.

[3]   Two Differences of Karmas
Karmas can be further differentiated into personal karmas and common karmas.

(a) Personal Karmas
A personal karma is the karma committed by an individual person, and the result is sustained only by that person. The entire process from committing the "karmic cause" (業因) to sustaining the "karmic effect" (業果) is called "personal karma."

(b) Common Karmas

Different individuals may commit similar karmas. When these people gather together, these karmas are combined to form a torrent of karmic retribution much greater than that of a personal karma. These individuals shall sustain such common "effected retribution" (果報) in the same environment.

The karmic retribution sustained by each person may vary in terms of the different personal karma committed.

The common "karmic causes" make people sustain common "karmic effects." The karmas that make people sustain "karmic retributions" (retributions of similar "karmic effects") together are called "common karmas"

Because of common karmas, people with similar "karma forces" (業力) are arranged to sustain similar fates and live in the same environment.

(c) Relationship between Common Karmas and Personal Karmas

The force of common karmas pulls living beings into one generally similar environment, such as the same world, the same race, the same country, the same group, or the same family.

Despite sharing the same environment, each person will be given different karmic retribution depending on his or her respective personal karmas. For example, if ten people are taking the same vehicle for a journey during which a car accident occurs, each of them is wounded at different levels.

The car accident is caused by common karma, and the different severities of wounds are caused by personal karmas.

A person can only sustain karmic retribution brought by that person's karma force and cannot be implicated by another person. An incident that a person seems to be implicated in is, in fact, the result of common karma.

If the person does not have such a karma force, then this person will never be implicated in another person's karmic retribution.

Some karmic retribution may seem to be bestowed upon a group or family; however, it is, in fact, a relationship between common karma and personal karma.

All good and bad retributions, such as being assigned to a certain realm, location, or family, are determined by the common karma and personal karma of the living beings. Good and bad retributions are not determined by people bringing trouble upon each other. Thus, it is all determined by causes and conditions.

[4]   Four Types That Cause Fast Retributions

The four types of karmas that cause faster "karmic retributions" (業報) are major karmas, significant karmas, proximity karmas, and routine karmas.

(a) Major Karmas (重業)

Both major karmas and minor karmas can be good or bad.

Major karma is also called great karma. For example, murdering one's parents is a seriously bad karma. A great virtue (大德), like sacrificing one's own life to save another person's life, is a seriously good karma.

The fulfillment of "cause-and-effect retribution" (因果報應) first begins with major karmas and then minor karmas. Major karmas mature earlier, and minor karmas mature later. Therefore, the first retributive results that people sustain mostly come from major karmas.

(b) Abundant Karmas (豐業)

Regardless of whether good or bad, major or minor, the karmas of the greatest abundance among the accumulated karmas are "abundant karmas." They possess great gravity and are the focal point of karmic retributions. They cause retribution rather fast and lead to karmic effect easily.

(c) Proximity Karmas (近業)

The karma committed by a person who is about to die is especially unforgettable for such a person. This karma is called proximity karma. It is relatively closer to the next life, and it leaves a deeper impression. Therefore, it possesses much stronger gravity and greater influence. It will receive karmic retribution more easily or faster than other karma.

(d) Routine Karmas (慣業)

A habit kept up long enough shall become second nature.

Routine karma reflects repeated behavior or other habits. Because a habit shapes character, it has greater karma force and will produce a karmic effect easily and quickly.

Because this type of karma is committed routinely, it often becomes a part of a person's nature. A Chinese proverb says, "Changing a person's nature is much harder than changing the landscape of a continent." It is a good description of routine karma.

Some routine karma cannot be uprooted completely even though countless Kalpas (eons) have been taken to do so; Routine karma can be very stubborn.

[5]   Two Karmic Retribution Times

Karmic retributions can be "retributions in the present life" or "retributions in future lives."

Some karmas mature in this life and bear fruit in great bounty. In this case, the retributions of such karmas must be fulfilled in the present life. This type of karmic retributions is called "retributions in the present life."

Some karmas have just been committed, and some are not yet matured; some karmas have their respective significances yet to be determined, and some are very complicated. These karmas can only wait to be settled in the next life, the life after the next life, or even after several Kalpas.

The karmic retributions that are to be fulfilled in future lives are called "retributions in future lives."

10.   Saha Land (娑婆世界)

The vast universe has countless planets inhabited by human beings, who are generally categorized according to intelligence, thought, and brain development into three classes: high-class human beings, middle-class human beings, and low-class human beings. Each class is further divided into three levels, and each level is also divided by region. There are also differences among each class of human being. For example, many aviation vehicles of the high-class human beings are capable of traveling faster than the speed of light (at hundreds of thousands of light years per second). Life expectancy of this class may be one thousand years. These planets are high technology planets.

Saha Land refers to the planets inhabited by the middle-class human beings. The planet on which our life depends, the Earth, is one Saha Land.

The Saha Land referred to in this literature shall mean exactly the world we are living in right now.

Saha Land is a "Land of Endurance with Five Impurities" (五濁忍土), which are greed, wrath, delusion, arrogance, and disbelief.

[1]   Greed
Demanding excessively and insatiableness: being overly playful, addiction to alcohol (excessive consumption of alcohol), being greedy, guilty of corruption (acquiring illicit wealth by abusing authority), obsession, avarice, covetousness, cupidity, hunger for power, hunger for lust, or corruption

[2]   Wrath
Anger, being unsatisfied with people, blaming, being fussy, and resentment: wrath with madness, wrath with cursing, wrath with blaming, wrath with accusing, or wrath with anger

[3]   Delusion (Stupidity)

On the conceptual level, the term "delusion" in Buddhist teachings is somewhat different from what it is in daily conversation.

If a person, after having tried and done everything, still fails to escape from the material realm (色界) and liberate him/herself away from the suffering of transmigration, then it is delusion. In other words, it is about having too much flawed knowledge, failing to recognize the true meaning of the universe and life, and even despising the true meaning of the universe and life as a heretic.

[4]   Arrogance

Being indifferent and impolite: being irreverent or insolent.

Complacency and disdain; believing that oneself is of a more prestigious status than others. Persisting in the belief that the material body is one's own true self; thinking that everything about oneself is better than others.

One who, without having the reward of a certain "stage of attainment" (證果), makes a representation of having such.

One who, having fully admitted that other people are better or stronger, is still reluctant to learn from the better or stronger with a humble mind.

One who, having no virtue, considers oneself virtuous.

[5]   Disbelief

Being excessively dubious about everything, not trusting people, and hesitating to act.

One does not believe the truth told and seen. Having doubt in the truth about the universe and life; believing that the world one is living in and the material body are real; all other things that cannot be seen with one's own eyes are suspicious.

Everyone on our Saha Land more or less has all five of the above impurities.

When people gather for work or daily life, they will release more or less of the five impurities each carries, causing conflict among them and bringing troubles of different kinds to one another.

Human beings are high-class animals living in society and cannot live in solitude. To survive, one must endure the five impurities from other people.

When Bodhisattva reincarnated to Saha Land to save people, he also had to endure the five impurities, otherwise the great mission of Buddhism teaching would not be achieved.

As a result, our world is called the Land of Endurance with Five Impurities (五濁忍土), the World of Endurance with Five Impurities (五濁忍世), or the Saha Land.

11. Nirvana (涅槃)

Nirvana is a term for the achievement of high Dharma Body.

Nirvana implies that after a person has successfully

achieved the stage of high Dharma Body (Nano Body), the life of his/her material body ends and the Dharma Body has obtained the correct stage of attainment (正果). The Dharma Body will take in the "three souls" (三魂) and "seven vigors" (七魄) of the material body, abandon the material body, and fade into the Nano Realm (納界). The very moment in which the material body loses its life and the Dharma Body takes away the three souls and seven vigors of the material body is called Nirvana.

Nirvana can be further classified into Nirvana with Remainder (Sanskrit: *Sopadhi-sesa-Nirvana*; 有餘涅槃) and Nirvana without Remainder (Sanskrit: *Nirupadhi-sesa-Nirvana*; 無餘涅槃).

[1] Nirvana with Remainder

Nirvana with Remainder is like a mathematical division with a remainder. It describes unfinished karmic retribution. At any point of time, as long as one is reincarnated to the material realm and in possession of a material body (retributive body; 報身), such a person shall continue to sustain karmic retribution until there is no more new karma made, and the retribution to all previously made karma is finished. The Nirvana obtained before that is Nirvana with Remainder.

Therefore, all kinds of Nirvana "prior to" (and "of") the "Virtual-Enlightenment Bodhisattva" (等覺菩薩) stage are called "Nirvana with Remainder."

Nirvana with Remainder is also called Non-Final Nirvana (不究竟涅槃).

[2] Nirvana without Remainder

Nirvana without Remainder is like a mathematical division without a remainder. In this condition, all karmic retributions have been finished, and there is no more karmic retribution to sustain. This type of Nirvana is called Nirvana without Remainder.

As a practitioner, the Buddhahood is achieved only when "Nirvana without Remainder" is achieved. Therefore, the Nirvana of the "Marvelous-Enlightenment Bodhisattva" (妙覺菩薩) is Nirvana without Remainder, which is the Nirvana for achieving Buddhahood.

A "Marvelous-Enlightenment Bodhisattva" has to finish all karmic retributions accumulated since beginninglessness without committing any new karma at the final life-journey. Only by doing so may a "Marvelous-Enlightenment Bodhisattva" achieve perfection at the final journey.

Nirvana without Remainder is also called Final Nirvana (究竟涅槃).

12.   Mi-Le Bodhisattva (Sanskrit: *Maitreya*; 彌勒菩薩)

Mi-Le Bodhisattva is also called Ci-Shi Bodhisattva.

Mi-Le Bodhisattva currently lives in Tusita (兜率天) and often teaches Buddhism scriptures and dharma to the "Heaven People" who are entitled to the enjoyment of Blessed Retribution. Mi-Le Bodhisattva has achieved the stage of "virtual enlightenment" (等覺) and is a candidate of Buddhahood. Mi-Le Bodhisattva is entrusted by Sakyamuni Buddha to attain Buddhahood in Saha Land and will be given the name of Mi-Le Buddha.

13.   World Honored One (世尊)

Buddha is a Dharma Body of the highest level and is the teacher of all living beings.

Buddha has ten other titles: "Thus Come;" "One Who Deserves Offerings;" "The One with Correct Peerless Enlightenment;" "Perfected in Enlightened Behaviors;" "Well Gone;" "Knower of the Mundane World;" "Unsurpassed;" "Tamer;" "Mentor of Deva People;" and "World Honored One."

[1]   "Thus Come" (Sanskrit: *Tathagata*; 如來)

By reviewing the path of cultivation, a living being who has achieved Buddhahood may realize that the path can be followed by every living being to achieve Buddhahood in the future, and it is the lacking of "correct enlightenment" (正覺) that prevents one from achieving the "correct stages of attainment" (正果). And, this, in turn, causes one to transmigrate in the material realm. By cultivating oneself in the right way with "correct enlightenment," one shall receive supreme enlightenment and achieve Buddhahood.

Buddhahood is achieved by the soul's evolution from the soul of an animal (旁生), gradually earning its progress and finally reincarnating as a human being. The soul then cultivates itself through countless Kalpas to upgrade from low Dharma Body (低法身) slowly toward high Dharma Body (高法身) and eventually achieves Buddhahood.

That is exactly the same process that all Buddhas have been through.

"Thus Come" literally means "come the same way" (rising from a common living being that shares the characteristics of all living beings to Buddhahood).

"Thus Come" also means "come and go freely" (the power of entering and exiting this world freely).

[2] "One Who Deserves Offerings" (Sanskrit: *Arhat*; 應供)

Among the living beings, Buddha is dignified and worthy of respect and, therefore, deserves the provision of offerings (供養), which can be classified into material offerings and dharma offerings.

(a) Material Offerings

With esteem and respect, providing clothing, food, housing, and transport as needed by a Buddha while he was living in the world.

(b) Dharma Offerings

Being compliant to the teaching of Buddha, strictly observing all precepts, cultivating by following the dharma, spreading and passing Buddhism into the hearts and souls of all living beings, and allowing all living beings who are ready to be relieved from all pains and obtain the utmost joy.

Buddha is also called Arhat because of the reasons above.

In addition, Arhat is differentiated into Great Arhat and Little Arhat.

Buddha and Bodhisattva are called Great Arhat.

Pratyeka-buddha (辟支佛) and Arhan (羅漢) are called Little Arhat.

[3]   "The One with Correct Peerless Enlightenment" (Sanskrit: *Samyak-sambuddha*; 正遍知)

Buddha knows everything, including the minds of people, and has no limit on his knowledge.

Buddha's cognition cannot be wrong and is immune to confusion and illusion. Therefore, Buddha is "the One with correct peerless enlightenment."

Buddha's enlightenment is unparalleled in its correctness. Therefore, Buddha is called "supreme correct enlightenment" (無上正覺).

Buddha is a high Dharma Body (法身) that knows all dharmas truly.

[4]   "Perfected in Enlightened Behaviors" (Sanskrit: *Vidya-carana-sampanna*; 明行足)

The key to cultivation for all living beings is eliminating ignorance (無明). Buddhahood is impossible to achieve unless "fundamental ignorance" is eliminated.

Behaviors of living beings, before achieving enlightenment, are behaviors stemming from ignorance. Such behaviors are called ignorant behaviors.

After achieving enlightenment, living beings may obtain high Dharma Bodies at the levels equal to or below Bodhisattva by eliminating "derivative ignorance" (枝末無明) and cultivating and practicing at different levels.

Starting from the Way of Bodhisattva (菩薩道), the cultivation of each life in this mundane world (凡世間) has to be done with "enlightened behaviors" (明行). In other words, in every life, the practitioner must eliminate "derivative ignorance" and progressively remove "fundamental ignorance"—obstacles to Buddhahood—allowing the "enlightened behaviors" to be completed perfectly so that the Bodhisattva who is converting living beings may come closer and closer to Buddhahood.

The "enlightened behaviors" begin with the attainment of high Dharma Body and complete with the achievement of Buddhahood.

Buddha has eliminated "fundamental ignorance" and perfectly completed the "enlightened behaviors" and, therefore, is called "Perfected in Enlightened Behaviors."

"Perfected in Enlightened Behaviors": complete in transparent actions

"Perfected in Enlightened Behaviors": fully possessing enlightened cognition and actions

[5] "Well Gone" (Sanskrit: *Sugata*; 善逝)

As living beings transmigrate between births and deaths in the material realm, the births and deaths are themselves "painful retribution" (苦報). The many pains accompanying the onset of death are excruciating, and that is why a relatively peaceful death (death without pain) is a "blessed retribution" (福報).

With the level of Buddha comes the power of controlling birth and death.

Buddha has fulfilled the Way, abandoned the material body, and entered Nirvana.

The confused person sees death, pain, sorrow, and tears in Nirvana.

The enlightened person sees sublimation, blessed retribution, happiness, and joy in Nirvana.

A living being has no control over birth and death but is full of worry. On the other hand, the material body that is about to attain "supreme correct enlightenment" (無上正覺) can die whenever death is desirable. One is totally in charge of one's own life, and there is no pain. This is the first meaning of "Well Gone" (善逝).

Buddha is relieved from the bondage of karma force; all coercive transmigrations between births and deaths have already passed.

Buddha has shaken off the chain of births and deaths and may enter and leave this world freely. Whether going into the mundane world to save living beings or the Supramundane World to live in the happy and quiet Dharma Realm, Buddha can accomplish them in a split second.

The great Buddha has an unlimited number of Dharma Bodies existing in every space. Buddha is familiar with disappearing from the Nano Realm (納界) and entering into the material realm (色界) to save living beings. Buddha is also familiar with disappearing from the material realm and entering into the Nano Realm freely whenever desired. This is the second meaning of "Well Gone."

That is the reason why Buddha is also called "Well Gone."

"Well Gone" means having a complete, kind, peaceful, beautiful, and honest past. It also means a perfect personality and a happy state of life.

[6] "Knower of the Mundane World" (Sanskrit: *Lokavid*; 世間解)

Buddha knows everything in the past and the future and is able to explain all dharmas, both in this mundane world and the Supramundane World. For example, formation, existence, decay, and disappearance (成住壞空) of worlds, and birth, aging, sickness, death, poverty, wealth, long life, prematurely ended life, auspiciousness, misfortune, disaster, and blessedness of living beings, are all known to and can be explained in detail by Buddha.

Buddha knows people's intentions and knows all dharmas. Buddha can teach the immeasurable dharmas to immeasurable living beings, provide the exact solution, and individually convert them. The immeasurable dharmas are the cure for immeasurable psychological issues. Buddha knows and explains the dharma for relief and, therefore, is also called "Knower of the Mundane World."

[7]   "Unsurpassed" (Sanskrit: *Anuttara*; 無上士)

Literally, a great person with supremacy. Within any space of the vast universe and among all sentient lives, only the wisdom, virtue, and "dharma power" (supernatural power) of Buddha are second to none. There is no sentient life more dignified than Buddha. That is why Buddha is also called "Unsurpassed."

[8]   "Tamer" (Sanskrit: *Puruadamyasarathi*; 調御丈夫)

"Tamer" in Chinese is "*Tiao-Yu-Zhang-Fu*."

The Chinese character of "Tiao" (調) means evenly and harmoniously distributed or balanced. In addition, it means mediation or adjustment. It also applies to configuration, arbitration, taste adjustment, adaptation, conciliation, mind adjustment, management, etc.

The Chinese character of "Yu" (御) means steering a horse cart, controlling, ruling, or managing and using the subordinates by the superior.

It also applies to administering, driving vehicles, undertaking matters, directing, etc.

The Chinese characters of "Zhang-Fu" (丈夫) means a male adult.

In this literature, it implies that the stubborn living beings are hard to tame. On the other hand, it means that Buddha is a real great man.

The abominable, stubborn living beings are hard to reform and convince. They tend to commit all sorts of bad karmas, which cause living beings to constantly suffer painful reincarnation in the material realm.

The great Buddha is able to subdue the stubborn living beings in the World of Endurance with Five Impurities (五濁忍世). By taming, liberating, and directing them, Buddha can teach and convert living beings and lead them away from pain and toward happiness, making the living beings become great men as well. Therefore, Buddha is also called the "Tamer."

[9] "Mentor of Deva People" (Sanskrit: *Sasta deva-manusyanam*; 天人師)

There is no doubt that Buddha is the mentor of the human world. The great Buddha still constantly helps the Deva People, however, by explaining the Buddhism scriptures and teaching the immeasurable dharmas (無量法門). Buddha teaches them not to be conceited with the "blessed retribution;" they must keep improving to prevent themselves from falling into the bad categories after the "blessed retribution" subsides. Only liberation from transmigration is the orthodox and correct way.

As Buddha guides the Deva People, Buddha is also called the Mentor of the Deva People.

[10] "World Honored One" (Sanskrit: *Lokajyeha*; 世尊)

Buddha has immeasurable "meritorious virtue" (功德) and unlimited "kindness and pity" (慈悲). Despite all the daunting hardships, Buddha never stopped saving and converting living beings to the extent that Buddha would sacrifice his own interests. That is why Buddha is respected by all sentient beings of the mundane world and Supra-mundane World.

Buddha deserves the respect of all living beings, and all living beings should respect Buddha. Therefore, Buddha is called "World Honored One."

14. Kalpa (劫)

The vast universe has neither beginning nor end in time and no edge or border in space.

The vast universe has a countless number of Little Worlds; some are vanishing, and some are growing, which is a phenomenon that has no beginning or end.

The vicissitudinous cycle of a Little World must go through the four stages of formation, existence, decay, and disappearance (成住壞空), which are also called "four Kalpas" (劫).

Kalpa means a long period of time.

The length of time of a Kalpa cannot be measured with the year, month, day, or hour with which we are already familiar; it is an extensively long time.

Kalpa can be further broken down into "large Kalpa," "middle Kalpa," and "small Kalpa." Four small Kalpas comprise one middle Kalpa, and four middle Kalpas comprise one large Kalpa.

The four stages of formation, existence, decay, and disappearance are all middle Kalpas, which collectively form a large Kalpa.

There is no fixed standard for the length of time of a Kalpa; instead, it is determined according to the karma force that the living beings have accumulated.

It is similar to the life of a person. Some die at the age of one, and some die at the age of one hundred. Other people may die at any age between one and one hundred. Then, what exactly is the length of a person's life? The answer can be one hundred, one, or something else. Science, however, can still provide a statistical average length of life.

The same applies to Kalpa. Because people cannot understand it if there is no specific number, a rough average number is devised. As time moves forward, the average length of a Kalpa also changes constantly. It is similar to the life expectancy of human life; there is a significant difference in life expectancies between five hundred years ago and the present. According to the statistic of the Buddha-to-Be Religion (未來佛宗教), the average length of one large Kalpa is approximately 9.7 billion years.

This Little World we are living in goes through a large Kalpa from its formation to its disappearance.

The Kalpa of Formation, or the first stage, is the stage when this world grows.

The Existence Kalpa, or the second stage, is the period of peaceful living in this world. Our Planet Earth of this Little World is now at the stage of existence.

The Decay Kalpa, or the third stage, is the period in which this world decays.

The Disappearance Kalpa, or the fourth stage, is the period in which this world becomes emptiness.

The Formation Kalpa is divided into two phases. In the first phase, "the world of matter" (the natural world; 器世間) is formed. "Matter" (器) is the material provided for living beings to survive and breed (e.g., the mountains, water, minerals, and forests). In other words, these resources are the five elements of metal, wood, water, fire, and earth. They also include the four great elements of earth, water, fire, and wind.

In the second phase, "the world of sentient beings" (有情世間) is formed. The term "sentient beings" applies to entities with lives and sentiments, such as human beings, animals, Heaven People, and ghosts.

Following the Formation Kalpa, the living beings may live in peace. It is then the beginning of the Existence Kalpa. In the Existence Kalpa, there are Little Three Calamities threatening the lives of the living beings: hunger, disease, and war.

Similar to the Formation Kalpa, the Decay Kalpa is divided into two phases. "The world of sentient beings" decays in phase one, while "the world of matter" decays in phase two. The decay of "the world of sentient beings" begins with Hell. After "the world of sentient beings" has completely decayed, "the world of matter" becomes empty. In the end, an inferno of fire descends, and the world is reduced to ashes. (After the destruction of the world, the structure of the multiple spaces (多維空間) still remains, but all lives and buildings, including all landscapes, cease to exist.)

The Disappearance Kalpa is the emptiness after the Little World is burned and destroyed. There will be no Sun, no Moon, and no difference between day and night. All that will remain is endless dimness.

After the Disappearance Kalpa ends, the Formation Kalpa resumes, and the cycle turns to the first stage.

Every Little World must go through the four Kalpas of formation, existence, decay, and disappearance. Each of the countless and immeasurable Little Worlds may be in the stage of formation, existence, decay, or disappearance. In infinite time, there are countless Little Worlds disappearing and appearing. That means that in every second, the vast universe has old planets decaying and new planets forming.

In other words, it is like living beings; there is a living being dying and another living being born every second. That is why there is a saying: "The cause comes before the result in a continuum relationship. A cause has its leading cause, and the beginning of this repetitive pattern can never be known. A result leads to another result, and the end of this repetitive pattern can never be predicted. There is no ultimate predecessor or successor; there is no ultimate beginning or end; change has no routine pattern and has unlimited possibilities."

15.   The Number of the Sands of the Ganges (恆河沙數)

The Ganges is the largest river in south Asia and the largest river in India. Its source is on the south slope of the Himalayas. It runs through India and Bangladesh and enters the ocean at the Bay of Bengal. It stretches some

2,700 kilometers.

The number of the sands of the Ganges is a description that implies a number as big as the number of the sands of the Ganges—so big and beyond counting.

16.   Convert to the Three Treasures
[1]   Conversion (皈依)

As a soul is being formed, it awaits being shaped like a piece of plain cloth on which to be written, painted, and dyed. After being repeatedly transmigrated in the World of Endurance with Five Impurities (五濁忍世), this piece of cloth has been tainted already. Having attained enlightenment, a living being may want to disinfect such cloth and, thus, begins to seek the proper method of disinfection.

Buddhist conversion (皈依) is the means to liberation by removing contamination both physically and psychologically through submission and entrustment.

Buddhist conversion is done in two ways: the conversion that lasts "until the present material body dies" (盡形壽) and the conversion that lasts "throughout the lives of a soul in the future and beyond" (盡未來), which is also called the countless Kalpas (無量劫).

The Chinese character of 皈 means turning to or returning to. All water must flow into the ocean eventually; all guests shall leave and return home sooner or later.

The Chinese character of 依 means dependence and reliance. A child depends on a mother; a sailor relies on his boat.

[2]   Three Treasures (三寶)

Three Treasures means Buddha, dharma, and monks. There are two types of Three Treasures: "Supramundane Three Treasures" (出世間三寶) and "Mundane Three Treasures" (世間三寶), which is further divided into "Three Treasures of the Correct-Dharma Period (正法時期)" and "Three Treasures of the Appearance-Dharma Period (相法時期) and the Degenerate-Dharma Period (末法時期)."

[3]   Supramundane Three Treasures (出世間三寶)

Buddha: Buddhas of all directions and of the past, the present, and the future.

Dharma: all truths of the universe and life (It primarily indicates Supramundane Dharma, which is the dharma for attaining enlightenment and extinguishing births and deaths. It is also called the dharma for Nirvana.).

Monks: "the highly virtuous and learned monks" (saints and sages; 聖賢僧) who have achieved the "correct stages of attainment" (正果), including all Bodhisattvas, Pratyeka-buddhas (辟支佛), and Arhans (羅漢).

The conversion that lasts "throughout the lives of a soul in the future and beyond" (盡未來), as referred to at the conversion ceremony, means converting to Supramundane Three Treasures.

[4]   Mundane Three Treasures (世間三寶)
(a) The Mundane Three Treasures of the Correct-Dharma Period

In the Saha Land on which we are living, the Mundane Three Treasures of the Correct-Dharma Period are:

Buddha: Sakyamuni Buddha;

Dharma: the methods of practicing Buddhism that Sakyamuni Buddha taught to his disciples, which is also called the truths of the universe and life; and

Monks: all the disciples that followed Sakyamuni Buddha.

(b) Mundane Three Treasures of the Periods of Appearance Dharma and Degenerate Dharma

Buddhism entered into the Appearance-Dharma Period after the Nirvana of Sakyamuni Buddha, followed by the Degenerate-Dharma Period. The Mundane Three Treasures of the Appearance-Dharma Period and the Degenerate-Dharma Period are:

Buddha: primarily the sculptures and paintings of all kinds at temples and common households to be worshiped, converted to, and provided with offerings;

Dharma: primarily the scriptures of Buddhism in written form to be worshiped, converted to, and provided with offerings; and

Monks: primarily the "worldly monks" (凡夫僧) to be worshiped, converted to, and provided with offerings.

The conversion that lasts "until the present material

body dies" (盡形壽), as referred to at the conversion ceremony, means converting to the Mundane Three Treasures.

17. Bodhi (菩提)

Bodhi is the wisdom that allows the elimination of the suffering of transmigration and the attainment of Nirvana. For "high Dharma Body" (高法身) stages of attainment (果位), there are four stages of Bodhi:

[1] Hearer Bodhi (聲聞菩提)

This is the stage of Arhan (羅漢果). Hearer Bodhi is achieved after the enlightenment on the Four Noble Truths (四聖諦) and the Twelve Links of Dependent Origination (十二因緣) and the accomplishment of the Eight Correct Ways (八正道). It is the Bodhi of Arhan—Nirvana with Remainder (有餘涅槃).

[2] Condition-Awakener Bodhi (緣覺菩提)

Condition-Awakener Bodhi is the stage of Pratyeka-buddha (a.k.a., Pratyaya-buddha). (Pratyeka-buddha: Solitary Awakener, 辟支佛, 獨覺; Pratyaya-buddha, Condition Awakener, 緣覺)

By practicing the way of Arhan, converting some people to Buddhism, realizing the state of Bodhisattva, and starting to learn to forsake the discrimination between the virtuous and the fool, the noble and the despicable, the estranged and the intimate, the endeared and the despised, the beloved and the rival, and gratitude and resentment, one may achieve Condition-Awakener Bodhi, which is the Bodhi of Pratyeka-buddha—Nirvana with Remainder.

[3]   Bodhisattva (菩提薩埵, 菩薩)

"Bodhi" means enlightenment and Nirvana; "sattva" means "the sentient" (有情) and beings (眾生).

Bodhisattva allows sentient beings to become enlightened all the way through Nirvana. Bodhisattva is also called Bo-Sa (Pu-Sa) for short.

A Great Bodhisattva that reincarnates to the material realm to save and convert sentient beings must understand the great method of Nirvana. He must also be capable of imparting that method to sentient beings. That is the Way of the Bodhisattva (菩薩道).

The Bodhisattva must forsake the discrimination between the virtuous and the fool, the noble and the despicable, the estranged and the intimate, the endeared and the despised, the beloved and the rival, and gratitude and resentment. He shall escort sentient beings beyond the entanglement of births and deaths.

All of the above are accredited to the achievement of the stage of Bodhisattva—Nirvana with Remainder.

[4]   Supreme Bodhi (無上菩提)

Supreme Bodhi is also called *Anuttarā-samyak-sambodhi* (阿耨多羅三藐三菩提) or "supreme correct enlightenment."

Bodhisattva converts living beings, attains the level of marvelous enlightenment (妙覺), eliminates "fundamental ignorance" (根本無明), and enters into "Nirvana without Remainder." The result is the supreme Bodhi, namely the stage of Buddha.

18. Correct Cognition and View (正知見)

Abbreviated as "correct view" (正見).

Positioned as it is at the top of the Eight Correct Ways (八正道), its importance is self-explained.

The Eight Correct Ways are the eight correct paths that lead to Nirvana, but the path of "correct view" is a prerequisite to all other paths.

"Correct view" means absolute faith in the Law of Cause and Effect, the existence of Dharma Realm, the existence of Dharma Bodies, that transmigration is avoidable, and the theory of "multiple spaces" (多維空間).

Such "correct view" is the foundation for supramundane attainment.

19. Soul Smugglers (靈魂的偷渡者)

A major and confusing challenge for living beings is breaking through the spatial obstacle.

Only with a Dharma Body that possesses competent "attainments" (道行) can one break through the spatial obstacle. On the other hand, living beings that are unable to break through the spatial obstacle yearn for that supernatural power.

Living beings cannot understand until they are finally liberated from the constraint of the material body. Once they are reincarnated into the material body, they are confused to such an extent that they simply know nothing about it.

Departing from the material body to pursue the "correct stages of attainment" (正果) can be a very slow process, but the same pursuit that depends on the material body can be relatively fast. The cultivation that depends on the material body, however, will have to go through the obstacle of the amnesia drink (迷魂湯).

In addition, the number of people who wish to become human beings again after reincarnation can be as big as the number of the sands of the Ganges, but only a fraction of them can win the quota (presently, there are only a few billion people on planet Earth).

Due to the above reasons, some living beings choose to compete for the quota, some plan to skip the amnesia drink, and some, particularly those who have never been reincarnated as humans, want to take a pleasure trip in the human world. The result is reincarnation into the human world by smuggling. They are soul smugglers.

These soul smugglers may demonstrate brilliant wit from childhood; they are masters of persuasion and eloquence.

Once uncovered, these soul smugglers may be reported by other living beings and taken into custody by the law enforcement agencies. In that case, their material bodies may die young, or they may live a short life.

20.   External Body (身外身)

The Dharma Body attained by a material body is called an External Body, literally meaning the body external to the material body.

A Dharma Body consists of Spiritual Light that can help it break through spatial obstacles (but it is restrained by *the Law of Deva* (天條): permanent use of the visual blocking technique and the stealth technique are required) and fly at a speed faster than light (the speed may vary depending on levels, and this principle applies to all supernatural powers). Those at lower levels live for a limited length, but those at higher levels may live endlessly (without birth or death).

The Taoists refer to the Dharma Body as Yang Spirit (陽神); the integration of Yang Spirit and the material body is referred to as a "true person."

The Buddhists also called the Dharma Body the True-Self, Vajra (admant, diamond; 金剛), or Diamond-like Indestructible Body.

Some Westerners call the External Body an energy body. There are reportedly cases where the energy body has been used to help patients recover.

Dharma Bodies can be roughly classified into twelve levels (more solid details require elaboration and will be thoroughly explained in Volume Two of the Buddha-to-Be Religion: *The Mysteries of Dharma Bodies*).

21. Time-Space Tunnel (時空隧道)

Time-Space Tunnels are tunnels for swapping spaces and are purposefully provided for living beings that are unable to break through spatial obstacles. There are a lot of Time-Space Tunnels, each connecting to a different space.

A soul must go through the Time-Space Tunnel to swap spaces.

Time-Space Tunnels are different in length and color; some have the Spiritual Light (靈光), and some have the Spiritual Qi (靈氣).

Time-Space Tunnels can be further classified into three types: the past, the present, and the future.

Souls fly at the speed of light. When a soul first leaves its body, it may not know its path very well and may need guidance from a master. A person who has an External Body, on the other hand, may follow the lead of the External Body. The Dharma Body of the previous life, if any, may come to help in some cases.

In all, entering into the right Time-Space Tunnel is critical; the wrong tunnel will lead to a space other than the intended destination.

22. Body Possession (附身)

Body possession is also called body occupation. It can be very complicated. There are possessions by souls, ghosts, or fairies.

A high Dharma Body does not need to possess a body; it can completely remote control any material body externally using its dharma power.

Any body possession without the approval of a soul is against *the Law of Deva*. An entity that illegally possesses a body will be taken into custody by the "law enforcer" if reported.

After an entity has possessed a body, in most cases, it resides in some part of a person's meridians and collaterals; only in the case of a serious possession will the entity integrate with the material body. It is rare that such a possessing entity can suppress the soul that owns the material body.

If a Yang soul that owns a material body is being suppressed under a certain acupoint (穴位), it loses control over its own material body. In such a case, this material body is entirely dominated and occupied by the possessing entity. This phenomenon, therefore, is called "residence occupation" (佔舍) in some other cultures.

The Yang soul in the case of residence occupation has no memory whatsoever of anything its material body has done since the residence occupation has taken place.

A spirit medium (乩童) expressing a divine message and the "psychic dance" in northern China to communicate with the fairy or ghost are all phenomena of body possession.

A higher level body possession can sometimes help to heal sickness and improve health.

A lower level body possession can sometimes introduce sickness for which there is no medical explanation.

At the beginning of the 1990s, the author contacted a patient through a third party; the name of the patient was Li, Chun-lan.

Li told the author that one night when she was breast-feeding her one-month old son, she suddenly felt that the other nipple was being suckled by another infant. She tried to push it away, but only air was there. She definitely felt the existence of another infant.

After that, she became sick. She felt weak throughout her body. Although she always wanted to lie down and rest because of dizziness, she could never sleep well. She experienced random aching. Even when her child was over a year old, she was unable to return to work. That invisible child slept in her bed every day. She visited both Chinese and Western physicians, but the cause of her sickness remained mysterious. She took some supplemental medicines, but all efforts were in vain.

The author did a quick check on her with Deva eye (天眼) and explained: "This invisible child is the mount of a 'divine fairy' in the Deva Realm (天界). That divine fairy is playing chess with another divine fairy and is still unaware that this animal has just snuck down here. I will find that divine fairy tonight and tell him what is going on here, so he may claim his animal. Then you will have your health back again."

That night, the author found the divine fairy and told him about this issue in the human world.

After verification, the old divine fairy finally realized that his ride was gone. "What a sinful animal!" he scolded.

He then said to the author, "My apology. Thank you for telling me, now you can go without further worry. I will take care of this matter immediately."

In the afternoon, ten days later, Li, Chun-lan brought her husband to visit the author. She expressed thanks and said, "After seeing you, the next day around five o'clock in the morning, we were still in bed. There was a very loud sound of a door opening. It woke my husband and me, but we could not move our bodies. At that moment, I heard that invisible child crying.

"An old man's voice in anger came from the door: 'You sinful animal! You have got me in trouble again! Now come home with me!'

"The child refused and said, 'No, I won't!'

"The old man waved his lead up in the air, and the other end of the rope immediately went around the neck of the child. The child suddenly changed into a huge and ugly beast.

"Then the old man mounted the animal and left without any expression on his face.

"Since then, my health has improved day by day. I have found a job and will start to work next month. My husband and I are here today to thank you."

The story above is about another form of body possession: "Shadow Materialization" (入影隨形).

The soul of a human being relies on the Spiritual Qi inside the human body to live; a person will become sick if his Spiritual Qi is shared by many spirits or mixed with other, less pure Spiritual Qi.

On the other hand, a material body will acquire healthy energy if a possessing entity of a higher level supplements it with pure Spiritual Qi.

The above-mentioned Li, Chun-lan had encountered negative energy through a possessing entity that fed on the positive energy inside her body. That is the reason she became sick.

More examples of body possession are available.

23.   Seven Treasures (七寶)

The Seven Treasures are seven rare and valuable objects determined according to the values held by the people of the Coarse Space (粗維空間).

As time moves on, the Seven Treasures change as well. The modern Seven Treasures are diamond, gemstone, jade, gold, silver, pearl, and agate.

24.   Phenomenon of the Lifespan (壽者相)

The "Phenomenon of the Lifespan" encompasses all phenomena exhibited from birth to death of a living being. As long as there are birth and death (regardless of the length of life, the happiness enjoyed or pain sustained), all phenomena such as birth, growth, maturity, aging and death, or otherwise referred to as birth, aging, sickness, and death, that one experiences throughout the process from birth to death are collectively called the "Phenomenon of the Lifespan."

25.   Qingyang (Green Sun; 青陽)

Qingyang (literally "Green Sun") means the Moon.

The wisdom of Buddha is like the Sun; it gives light wherever it shines. This wisdom light can drive away the darkness deep inside living beings and illuminate them, preventing living beings from losing their direction. It keeps living beings happy and bestows liberation on them.

The Moon does not emit light by itself. It does give light, however, by reflecting the Sun. While the Sun is out of our sight, the Moon reflects the light of the Sun and shines on living beings, keeping them away from trouble and giving them liberation.

26. Nebula (星雲)

A Little World of the vast universe contains the Sun, the Moon, and the Earth. This Little World is a Solar System.

One thousand Little Worlds comprise a Small Chiliocosm (小千世界); one thousand Small Chiliocosms comprise a Medium Chiliocosm; one thousand Medium Chiliocosms comprise a Great Chiliocosm.

In other words, a Great Chiliocosm has one billion Solar Systems.

The vast universe has countless Buddhas; some of them are working, while some others are not; some are on missions, while some others are not.

Every Great Chiliocosm needs an administrative agency, and Buddha is the leader of such agency that runs a Great Chiliocosm.

A Great Chiliocosm is also called a nebula for short. In other words, a nebula is administered by an agency under Buddha's leadership.

27.   The Great Vehicle (Sanskrit: *Mahayana*; 大乘)
Buddhism can be classified into the Great Vehicle (*Mahayana*) and the Little Vehicle (*Hinayana*).

The Little Vehicle is like steering a small boat all by oneself to sail across the ocean of pain of transmigration. One ferries himself; he is responsible only for his own interests. The Little Vehicle is the egoistic journey of an Arhan.

The Great Vehicle is like steering a big boat to ferry those who voluntarily climb aboard to sail across the ocean of pain of transmigration. The Great Vehicle is an altruistic journey for a Bodhisattva.

VOLUME TWO

WHY ESTABLISH
BUDDHA-TO-BE RELIGION?

I.

THE THREE PERIODS OF BUDDHISM

The creation, thriving, and deviation of Buddhism go through three periods: correct-dharma, appearance-dharma, and degenerate-dharma.

(A) CORRECT-DHARMA PERIOD

"Correct dharma" (literally the correct method) and "the Correct-Dharma Period" are two different concepts. "Correct dharma" exists in both "the Correct-Dharma Period" and "the Degenerate-Dharma Period." The only difference is that the proportion of "correct dharma" in the two periods continues to decrease.

The proportion of "correct dharma" in "the Degenerate-Dharma Period" drops to about 20 percent. In order to re-establish the proportion of "correct dharma," the Deva of United Enlightenment (聯合教化天) will send its delegates to Earth to correct this situation.

During "the Correct-Dharma Period," Buddha himself responded to the world[28] (namely, appeared in the world) and taught dharma. Since then, the world has had

Buddha dharma. The "dharma" was taught by Buddha with his own words. Therefore, it is called "correct dharma."

From the end of the Correct-Dharma Period to the deviation of Buddhism, no Buddha has responded to this world. The reason: there was already Buddha dharma, and there was no need for Buddha to respond to this world and create a new Buddhism. Those who came to this world to teach and promote Buddhism, during this time, were all the disciples of Buddha.

Twenty-five-hundred-odd years ago, Sakyamuni Buddha came to our world to introduce Buddhism. A large number of his disciples had attained "Nirvana through the Present Body" (即身涅槃).[29]

Sakyamuni Buddha was a person of great wisdom; he applied different conversion methods and "dharmas" when saving and converting people according to individual needs. People have innumerable differences in their previous lives, lifestyles, and experiences. Accordingly, their needs for dharmas may have innumerable differences; different people require different dharmas. The eighty-four thousand[30] dharmas of Buddhism are the answer to this situation. That is why there is a saying: "all dharmas result from their respective causes and conditions."

There is no dharma suitable for everyone. A dharma that works for one person may not work as well for another person. With Buddha's guidance, everyone starts from a different place, arrives at the same destination, and attains the same state, Nirvana; it is only a matter of time.

Correct dharma is instructed by Buddha himself and is the method suitable for an individual's practice for the final attainment of Nirvana. It is the correct way for the individual to enter into Nirvana.

Many people in the present time sincerely seek the attainment of Nirvana but do not know how. Some of them fail eventually because they carelessly believe in the wrong instruction and take the wrong way of cultivation. Simply put, they cannot find the correct method (correct dharma). Therefore, "correct dharma is hard to find." If you find the correct method ideal for your practice, then the Joy of Nirvana can be achieved.

The saying that "correct dharma has no word" is also a metaphor; the correct dharma for one person may be an incorrect dharma for another person because the two persons will not share the very same experience and background. When they see things from different aspects, they can draw different conclusions. Therefore, there is no universally correct dharma applicable to everyone.

It is critical to help living beings set as their goal the attainment of Nirvana when converting them. Different dharma should be used according to individual needs and implemented in a way they will accept. Otherwise, the conversion may fail, which presents the challenge of propagating the correct dharma.

No one knows the correct dharma of avoiding pain and gaining happiness better than Sakyamuni Buddha. He can convince the stubborn living beings in the "World of Endurance with Five Impurities" and make them follow his method for achieving Nirvana, which is really admirable. Sakyamuni Buddha's method of converting people is absolutely correct, and his method is called the "correct dharma."

There are many different religions concurrently existing in this world; each of them teaches their believers with different methods that best fit their respective needs. Sakyamuni Buddha's primary purpose in establishing Buddhism is to save and convert the living beings who are ready for Buddha, so they may be relieved from transmigrations between births and deaths and attain Nirvana. The living beings of other levels will be left for the other religions to save. In Buddhism, only the method that may allow the living beings to be relieved from transmigrations between births and deaths and attain Nirvana is the correct method.

When Sakyamuni Buddha responded to the world and preached dharma, no literature was left behind. The Buddhism scriptures we have now were actually edited and compiled according to memory by Sakyamuni Buddha's disciples. After more than two thousand years, the content of these scriptures is more or less inaccurate. In addition, the works of the editing were not done in Chinese. Therefore, after translation, the original meanings may be even more inaccurate.

The time after Sakyamuni Buddha entered Nirvana is "the Appearance-Dharma Period."

Rather than not having "correct dharma," Buddhism in China never had "the Correct-Dharma Period."

(B) APPEARANCE-DHARMA PERIOD

Buddhism progressed into the Appearance-Dharma Period after Sakyamuni Buddha's Dharma Body abandoned his material body and hid in the Dharma Realm with his "Three Souls and Seven Vigors."

The "appearance dharma" represents phenomenon (現象), character (相狀), image (表象), and "believing" (相信). During this period, Buddha was no longer a tangible material body. Buddhists began to worship figures made from all sorts of materials and promote Buddhism through such "characters" as statues, temples, monks, lay Buddhists, Buddhism scriptures, and Buddhist artifacts.

"Appearance" means the way that something looks like on the outside. Observation of one's appearance (or fortune telling by reading the subject's appearance) can reveal one's inner quality. For example, when an animal is approaching from afar, an experienced person can tell what kind of animal it is with just one look. This is the "animal appearance." When a person comes here, we can identify this person as an adult, kid, old person, young person, male, female, etc. This is the "personhood appearance." Each country has its own national emblem and culture, which represent the "national appearance." Many religions in the world also have their respective images for identifying themselves. Just one look at the costumes, temples, symbols, etc. is usually enough to identify Buddhism. This is the "Buddhism appearance." These are all "appearance dharmas." The Appearance-Dharma Period of Buddhism focused on Buddhism promotion using these "characters" (相狀). Buddhism in this period formed a culture and a brand. "Appearance dharma" was indeed a brand effect. The Appearance-Dharma Period of Buddhism created a priceless religious brand. The above is one aspect of "appearance dharma."

"Believing" is to consider something correct, true, and without doubt. Some "characters" are used to make living beings believe that all the "dharmas" presented are "correct dharmas." For example, the scripture editors' words in the beginning that "thus have I heard" is another way to make people believe. The above is another aspect of "appearance dharma."

Therefore, "appearance" and "believing" are two aspects of "appearance dharma"

The Appearance-Dharma Period is the major promotion period of Buddhism in the Saha Land, and the promotion relies heavily on the Great Bodhisattvas and Sakyamuni Buddha's disciples who came to the Appearance-Dharma Period through reincarnation. The purpose of their reincarnations is the creation of "characters" in the material realm; that is, the branding of Buddhism in the material realm. It includes obtaining scriptures, translation, circulation and lecturing, and building "truth places" (道場) for the Great Bodhisattvas. Buddhism is introduced to the living beings of the world through all kinds of methods in an effort to make them believe and convert to the Three Treasures. For example, the four most famous Buddhist mountain truth places in China were established by four Great Bodhisattvas.

Wu-tai Shan (mountain), the ridge of northern China located in WuTai County, ShanXi Province, has an appearance-dharma "truth place" established by Wen-Shu Bodhisattva (Sanskrit: *Manjusri*; 文殊菩薩).

E-mei Shan (mountain) in E-mei Shan City, SiChuan Province, a part of the SiChuan Basin that stretches for more than one hundred kilometers, is the place where the Golden Light of Buddha has been frequently sighted and is called the E-mei Wonder. Pu-Xian Bodhisattva (Sanskrit: *Samantabhadra*; 普賢菩薩) established an appearance-dharma "truth place" here.

Pu-tuo Shan (mountain), a "Kingdom of Buddha" hung on the edge of a cliff at the oceanfront, located in ZhouShan City, ZheJiang Province, is the appearance dharma "truth place" established by the infinitely "kind and pitying" savior, Guan-Yin Bodhisattva (觀音菩薩).

Jiou-hua Shan (mountain), in QingYang County, AnHui Province, famous for its 480 temples, is the appearance-dharma "truth place" established by Di-Zang Bodhisattva (地藏菩薩) in the mundane world.

The purpose of establishing appearance-dharma "truth places" is not to provide long-term residences and facilities for the Bodhisattvas to teach Buddhism. Instead, the purpose is to establish tangible "characters" for living beings in the Appearance-Dharma Period. With these "characters," endless preachers and audiences are brought to the way of Nirvana.

Tangible "characters" include mountains, landscapes, temples, historic cultures, modern cultures, scripture printers, scripture lecturers, and scripture lecture audiences. There are slanders and praises; there will be

temple builders and destroyers; there will be supporters of
Buddha and enemies of Buddha; there will be money
donors and volunteer workers; there will be serious
practitioners and fake practitioners; there will be authentic
scriptures and fraudulent scriptures; there will be righteous
preachers and evil preachers; there will be preachers of
"correct dharmas" and preachers of "evil dharmas;"
there will be "wisdom lives" that rely on Buddhism and
material bodies that feed on Buddhism. All the above are
"characters." Using these "characters" as conditions (緣)
results in all kinds of "dharmas," and these "dharmas" are
thus called "appearance dharmas."

Some modern Buddhists have referred to the second
period as Semblance-Dharma Period (像法時期), which is
wrong. The author has brought this issue to Sakyamuni Buddha for his advice; he said it should be referred to as the
Appearance-Dharma Period and ordered the author to
rectify this problem.

The Appearance-Dharma Period needed initial efforts
as well. After the initial stage of its establishment, Sakyamuni
Buddha and the Great Bodhisattvas withdrew and left the
living beings alone to make trial and error on their own in
these "characters" until the end of the "game" (the Degenerate-Dharma Period) where the proportion of correct
dharma drops to around 20 percent. Then, a "generalissi-
mo" will be sent to the human world through reincarnation
to rectify dharmas of Buddhism and appraise the "stages
of attainment" of the practitioners over the last two thousand years. (This is referred to as "Dharma Propagation and
Stage Appraisal.")

Descending impatiently to the mundane world to

extend the wisdom lives
and bewildered by this world of sensual pleasures.
Returning to sanctity is difficult due to the entangle-
  ment of the Five Impurities.
The enigma of Buddhism shall be deciphered by a
  Buddha-commissioned Special-Dharma Repre-
  sentative.

Instead of heartlessness on the part of Buddha and Bo-dhisattvas, it is the stubbornness of the living beings. Every living being that has "wisdom life" believes that he or she is competent, impeccable, and strong enough, which is why he or she repeatedly applies for transmigration to extend one's "wisdom life." That is the reason why so many of them have come to this world. There has to be some kind of exam for "stage appraisal" (評定果位). If anyone challenges the result of the appraisal and files an appeal, the agency just replays the "recorded video," and the living being will have no more to say and be fully persuaded.

(C) DEGENERATE-DHARMA PERIOD

"Degenerate-Dharma Period" does not mean Bud-dhism is going into a stage of decay and disappearance. It means the theories and behaviors advocated by Bud-dhism are becoming more and more alienated from the original intentions of Sakyamuni Buddha. In short, it is the period in which Buddhism is derailed from correct dharma, the correct method.

When the Esoteric Sect and the Pure Land Sect have received great popularity and begun to thrive, and when Buddhism begins to advocate philanthropy,[31] "Good Karma with Leakage,"[32] "Dhyana with Leakage,"[33] and "Mundane Dharma,"[34] Buddhism has entered this period.

Another indication will be an index monitored by "the Deva of United Enlightenment," the "Correct-Dharma Proportion Composite Index" (正法含量綜合指數), which consists of figures, tables, and lines that reveal the behavior of Buddhists. For example, it can tell how many people are practicing "Good Karma with Leakage," how many people are practicing "Good Karma without Leakage," how many people are preaching Mundane Dharma, and how many people are preaching Supramundane Dharma.

When the Correct-Dharma Proportion Composite Index has dropped to 20 percent or so, one may say that the Degenerate-Dharma Period of Buddhism has started and rectification must be arranged.

Modern Buddhism argues that each of the three periods of Buddhism has a fixed length of time. That is yet another fallacy. In fact, none of them have a fixed length of time, and they are all determined according to the karma forces of living beings. If the Correct-Dharma Proportion Composite Index is high, the Degenerate-Dharma Period comes later; if the Correct-Dharma Proportion Composite Index is low, the Degenerate-Dharma Period comes sooner. This is a law that never changes.

Buddhism will go into chaos in the Degenerate-Dharma Period.

Because the brand name of Buddhism is too attractive, many people have contrived schemes to profit from it by exploiting the preaching mission. A brand name such as this is not a patent right and is not protected by the law of intellectual property rights. Many so-called bestselling writers flip through a few pages of Buddhism scriptures and claim themselves to be Buddhism gurus and go on to sell books and memberships. The market is already saturated with books about Buddhism; all kinds of Buddhas and deities pop up one after another from nowhere.

As for the Buddha-to-Be Religion that the author is promoting, the committee members have held a conference at the Deva of United Enlightenment for the rectification and explanation of dharma. The issue of brand name has been raised at the conference as well. Using a new brand name to promote the dharma may result in poor penetration. For example, the name of "Qingyang Religion" may be difficult to promote successfully in a short period of time, and it may confuse the general public. Using the name of Buddhism allows the general public to understand more easily. In the end, Sakyamuni Buddha himself has decided that the name of Buddhism that has already existed will be used because it confers more advantages.

The bigger a brand name is, the more counterfeits there will be. It is a frequent phenomenon.

During the Degenerate-Dharma Period, many fake practitioners live in Buddhist temples. They have shaved their heads and put on kasayas; they call themselves "Living Buddhas" or some Buddhas that respond to this world. Some claim that they are Bodhisattva or Vajra Gurus (金剛上師) to cover their crimes of fraud and sexual misconduct, smearing the Buddhists "truth places." Some disguise themselves as monks and live with their wives and children in temples. They audaciously teach pseudo-dharma to their innocent unsuspecting followers. Even worse, there are some evil persons, who have not been imparted and certified by any master, possessed by ghosts or monsters.

They think they are smart and do not know the need to cultivate themselves; they even claim to have achieved the final attainment. They look like monks but are actually the instrument of evil dharmas, luring people to fall into the evil course with them. They are destroying the "correct dharma" and people's "wisdom lives." There are also evil cults disguised as Buddhism factions; they practice amulets and incantations, serving plain water as holy water to their followers. They lure people into evil and act against Buddhism. Some evil people even adopt stage performance in Buddhism; they wear make-up and costumes for their appearance on the media, saying things that are unproven and lecturing on enlightenments that have never happened. With less than fundamental knowledge that they have read in some scriptures, they claim they are masters and practice feng-shui inspection and fortune-telling in the name of Buddhism. They are the enemies of "correct dharma" and destroyers of the "Buddhism appearance."

The above are the three periods of Buddhism.

II.

FALLACIES OF MODERN BUDDHISM

It is not easy to explain clearly and thoroughly all the fallacies of modern Buddhism. Among so many Buddhist scriptures, which parts are correct, and which parts are wrong? No one can point them out exactly. Who dares to argue that there are fallacies in Buddhist doctrines? Not even the author, because those who make false accusations will be condemned to Hell.

Buddhism doctrines are left behind by Sakyamuni Buddha; only he can tell which parts are right and which parts are wrong. The dharma that the author is talking about is the dharma that has been laid down by Sakyamuni Buddha. Sakyamuni Buddha, however, is invisible, and the author is an ordinary person living in this mundane world. The author has consulted with Sakyamuni and made notes. These notes are compiled and published for public circulation as a reference for sincere Buddhism practitioners with due conditions.

According to the "Correct-Dharma Proportion Composite Index" (正法含量綜合指數), modern Buddhism has deviated considerably from its normal track by about 80 percent, which suggests that the Degenerate-Dharma Period has arrived. It is impossible to elaborate and rectify that 80 percent in one book. To rectify the already deviated Buddhism and bring it back to its normal track requires the joint effort of generations of people, and that is exactly the long-term plan of the Deva of United Enlightenment.

It is impossible to address all the problems in one book. In this section, only a few examples will be briefly mentioned; their details will be left for future discussion.

(A)   THE POPULARITY OF THE ESOTERIC SECT (密宗) IS ONE OF THE INDICATIONS OF THE COMING OF THE DEGENERATE-DHARMA PERIOD

When the Esoteric Sect was introduced to China, Three-Mystery Yoga was established. It advocates practicing "Most-Honored-Buddha Dharma" (本尊法) through "contemplation and actions, based on the phenomena and the underlying principle" (事理觀行). Because Three-Mystery Yoga is mysterious, no one is allowed to disclose its knowledge to any third party without prior consecration (灌頂) and impartation. That is why it is called the Esoteric Sect.

There are many highly competent people, as well as newly emerged religions and their respective factions, in modern society. Many believe that they have religious talent, but after an extensive period of time, they still do not have the fame, followers, and money they have expected. Their blood pressure rises, and they cannot sleep well. They then take the shortcut. Suddenly, overnight, they claim that they have attained the dharma and are now Vajra Gurus or "Living Buddhas."

Sakyamuni Buddha has told the author: "In this Saha Land, there is no such thing as 'Living Buddha.' It is a term used to fool oneself and people. A material body will go through birth and death; if there is 'Living Buddha,' then there must be a Dead Buddha. Who is the Dead Buddha? Me? Buddha is Buddha. Buddha is a Dharma Body; birth and death do not apply to it. Only the 'stages of attainment' (果位) of Bodhisattva and lower can have retributive bodies (material bodies), which is never applicable to a Buddha. Even for the purpose of analogy or metaphor, the term 'Living Buddha' should not be used, lest the general public become confused.

"In the human world, a person who is truly a practitioner of the way of Bodhisattva will not be concerned about fame or money. Such a person will feel sorry when seeing the living beings not cultivating themselves and not practicing the dharma of relieving pain and gaining joy. It is the heart of a Bodhisattva that causes such a person to feel sorry for them. A person with the heart of a Bodhisattva is anxious about fulfilling responsibilities, not about his or her own Buddhahood. Such responsibilities are the dharma he or she is preaching and the mission to save the living beings from pain and give them joy."

◆ Why Create the Esoteric Sect in the Saha Land?

The Esoteric Sect's mission given in the Deva of United Enlightenment is to allow the people who approve of the view of absolute belonging and view of absolute extinction to believe in view of absolute transmigration through the "appearance dharmas" (such as the reincarnation of a "soul boy") of the Esoteric Sect, whereby they raise their level of "cognition and views," gradually abandon biased views, and attain correct cognition (正知) and correct views (正見).

Of course, the Esoteric Sect also has a faction that practices the methods (dharmas) of extinguishing birth and death based on the three fundamental scriptures of the Esoteric Sect. The practitioners of this faction are highly disciplined; they are not allowed to engage in sexual relations, consume alcohol and meat, or practice any killing. According to the *Surangama-sutra*, the practitioners must strictly comply with the precepts (e.g., prohibition of lust, meat, and alcohol) and practice and realize through Three-Mystery Yoga (三密相應). The Esoteric Sect, founded on the *Surangama-sutra*, is not against the sequential order of the way of Bodhi. According to the *Surangama-sutra*, a Bodhisattva must go through fifty-two stages before achieving Buddhahood. It is not some mysterious cult that pursues "Buddhahood through the Present Body" (即身成佛) directly through the material body by sexual intercourse, Qi meridians, and "Ming Dian."

In ancient times, the Deva of United Enlightenment did not plan to recognize the Esoteric Sect as a Buddhism faction in the first place. Instead, it was the "kind and pitying" Buddha who agreed to recognize them.

Every time, at the end of the meetings for Esoteric Sect missions held by the Deva of United Enlightenment, all missionaries (commissioned Dharma Bodies) have to leave through the left side door, where a Dharma Body arranges the itinerary. According to the standard procedure, the Dharma Body will remind each of the missionaries, "You have taken the left side door. Please remember to use the center door when you return with the achievement of the correct 'stage of attainment' in the mundane world. The door you have chosen is for exit only."

Many people think that they can take a shortcut to attain Buddhahood simply by offering money to a "Living Buddha" who undertakes the consecration ritual for them.

Some "Living Buddhas" tell their followers in "Buddhist services" (法會) that "even a mosquito passing through this 'Buddhist service' will receive my 'consecration' and, therefore, will attain its Buddhahood within seven lives."

A part in the scripture of *Buddha's Words of the Great-Vehicle Sutra of Solemn, Tranquil, And Equal Enlightenment of the Buddha of Immeasurable Life* once greatly confused the author when the author was reading it in early 1986. It said, "When I become Buddha, there won't be any bad name in my country. All living beings born in my country shall share the same belief, live at the same settlement, never have to worry, and enjoy peace of mind. Their happiness will resemble that of 'the Monks with Exhaustion of Leakage' (the monks who have extinguished all contamination). I won't achieve correct enlightenment if people born in my country will still have 'the greed or calculation on material bodies' (貪計身)."

The author did not quite understand the meaning of the aforementioned "the greed or calculation on material body" and then went to the Deva of Buddha Institute to consult with Buddha.

After bowing on his knees to Buddha, the author raised the question, and Buddha replied, "Well, the scripture is wrong. 'The greed or calculation on material body' is actually an incorrect translation of 'the greed for Buddhahood through the Present Body' (貪即身), which means coveting the present material body and seeking 'Buddhahood through the Present Body' (即身成佛)."

Buddha then criticized the author: "The mistake of the scripture is not a problem; the problem is your capacity to understand. Haven't I told you already not to limit yourself with words? You have to follow the contextual priority.[35] Don't be superficial; you have to understand the meaning between the lines."

Buddha further explained: "Buddhism has only had twenty-five-hundred-odd years of history in the human world, and there are already so many mistakes. The major reason is that the preachers of dharma have been short-sighted and impatient, and the practitioners of dharma have been anxious for fast attainment; the preachers of dharma seek instant success and desire vanities, and the practitioners of dharma also seek instant success and desire their short-term interest. Both parties are happily obsequious to each other. When they see only convenience in their preaching and practice, they are inviting fallacies.

"For example, Lee establishes Lee's Truth Place to preach correct dharma. He says, 'Buddhahood may take countless Kalpas to attain.' He has retained some followers. Next to Lee's Truth Place, Chan opens the fabulously decorated Chan's Truth Place, and he says, 'I'll give you Buddhahood through the Present Body if you follow me.' Soon Lee's Truth Place loses followers to Chan's Truth Place.

"A preacher of dharma who knowingly and purposefully gives false information to the followers is committing fraud. Buddhahood through the Present Body is impossible. Buddhahood can only be attained by first achieving the level of 'virtual enlightenment' that are preceded by the egoistic Arhan stage, the egoistic and then altruistic Pratyekabuddha stage, and the altruistic and then egoistic Bodhisattva stage, that, in turn, further consists of fifty-two stages of cultivation, among which the 'virtual enlightenment' is the fifty-first stage and the practitioner at this stage is still a candidate for Buddhahood. A candidate has to conceal his Bodhisattva identity and reincarnate to the Saha Land to settle his karmas. Then, the candidate may be allowed to enter Nirvana without Remainder and attain Buddhahood.

"Why a Buddhahood candidate system? Buddhahood is only given to those whose potentialities and conditions are mature enough. A candidate cannot descend to the human world where Buddhism already exists to attain Buddhahood. A candidate has to wait until the karma force has achieved the stage in which the remaining karma can be settled in one lifetime, and the potentialities and conditions of the living beings in a Saha Land are mature enough (in other words, this Saha Land has no Buddhism yet and it's time to introduce Buddhism there). Then, this 'virtual enlightenment' may descend to the human world to attain Buddhahood.

"After the attainment of Buddhahood, a living being will not have a 'retributive body' again. All of his or her opportunities of accumulating 'meritorious virtue' will be transferred to Great Bodhisattvas, and Buddha will be the mentor for all Bodhisattvas. If everything is done by Buddha, then these Great Bodhisattvas will never have a chance for Buddhahood.

"Remember, Nirvana through the Present Body is possible in the form of Nirvana with Remainder, but Buddhahood through the Present Body is impossible because it has to be Nirvana without Remainder. Buddhist practice should never take a shortcut; it leads nowhere. Therefore, a wise practitioner will not allow himself to be tempted by Buddhahood through the Present Body.

"Everybody knows Amitabha Buddha, for example. He once was the king of a great country. After listening to the lecture delivered by Lokesvararaja Buddha in a Buddhist service, he was gratefully enlightened and determined to pursue Buddhahood from then on. He resigned his throne, gave up his kingdom, and became a monk. His Buddhist name was Fa-Zang. He swore that he would attain Buddhahood and made forty-eight great vows in front of Lokesvararaja. Even he, after all these efforts, failed Buddhahood through the Present Body.

"For 54.8 billion years since Fa-Zang's oath, he had progressed relentlessly in the practice of the way of Bodhisattva, saved and converted countless living beings, and accumulated immeasurable 'meritorious virtue.' With the assistance of Buddhas, he finally eliminated 'fundamental ignorance' (根本無明)[36] and achieved 'Nirvana without Remainder.'

"A vow is only a wish; it does not guarantee Buddhahood, and Buddhahood itself does not guarantee one's wish will come true. Buddhahood is not determined by oneself or some Buddha; it requires certification. When the time for Buddhahood comes, you can't decline; when the time hasn't come, you won't get it anyhow. However, if, after the attainment of Buddhahood, you look behind the vows you once made, you just might ridicule some of your own vows.

"Fa-Zang's determination is absolutely admirable, but even he had to go a great distance to attain Buddhahood. How many people in this world can match his determination and effort? That is why Buddhahood through the Present Body is unrealistic wishful thinking."

Buddha's words have made it clearer to the author that even a "Virtual-Enlightenment Bodhisattva," as a "Buddha candidate," must relentlessly branch his soul and reincarnate to the human world, with an identity other than Bodhisattva, to settle the previously accumulated karmas countless times. Thus, it is very unlikely for a mosquito to attain Buddhahood within seven lives.

Some "Living Buddhas" run advertisements on newspapers for their Buddhist services. These advertisements say, "Respectfully asking for the blessing of Guan-Yin Bodhisattva." It is also a ridiculous thing. Indeed, it is normal for a Bodhisattva to ask for the blessing from Buddha; the level of "dharma power" of a Bodhisattva is lower than that of Buddha. A "Living Buddha" asking a Bodhisattva for the blessing, however, is quite awkward; perhaps some kind of "esoterica" has to be hidden.

People are, by nature, lazy sometimes. That is why many believe they can have someone else cultivate for them, allowing them to achieve Buddhood through the Present Body. This thinking gives the so-called "Living Buddhas" a window of opportunity.

Assuming that a living being has been already relieved from transmigration in the previous life, but, in this life, such a living being again begins to learn transmigration, admire "Living Buddhas," advocate reincarnations of "soul boys," and worship "Living Buddhas" for magical consecration (灌頂), this living being will then suffer degradation of his/her cultivation level. As the number of such types of living beings increases considerably, the Correct-Dharma Proportion Composite Index will go down. That is the reason why the popularity of Esoteric Sect is one of the indications of the coming of the Degenerate-Dharma Period.

(B) THE POPULARITY OF THE PURE LAND SECT IS ONE OF THE INDICATIONS OF THE COMING OF THE DEGENERATE-DHARMA PERIOD

One work of art cannot be acceptable to every human being; one idea cannot be acceptable to every human being; one religion, similarly, cannot be acceptable to every human being. Therefore, it is impossible to "pervasively convert living beings" (普渡眾生) with only one religion. That's the reason for the saying: "Buddha converts the ones 'with due conditions' (conditioned, connected, responsive)."

The Deva of United Enlightenment, however, has the ability to "pervasively convert living beings." This institute arranges different religions for different areas, races, and cultures.

The correct dharma, or the correct method, is about extinguishing births and deaths, which comes on two different levels: Nirvana with Remainder and Nirvana without Remainder. Therefore, Buddhism correct dharma also encourages the cultivation of Nirvana through the Present Body (in the form of Nirvana with Remainder; Nirvana without Remainder specifically should mean Nirvana for the attainment of Buddhahood).

Little-Vehicle Buddhism (小乘佛教) focuses on one's own relief from births and deaths (achieving the stage of Ar-han), and Great-Vehicle Buddhism (大乘佛教) focuses on saving and converting other people from births and deaths (while the practitioner achieves the stage of Bodhisattva). Nirvana through the Present Body can be achieved by either of the above if cultivated correctly.

Great-Vehicle Buddhism has compassion for the world and has "alternative dharmas" (另類法門) at lower levels, which are easier to practice specifically for the people at lower levels who are denied "Nirvana through the Present Body." Such "alternative dharmas" include:

1. cultivation of a "long but limited wisdom life;"
2. extension of the "wisdom life;"
3. rebirth in Buddha's Pure Land; and
4. preservation of the human body.

In fact, the teaching of these "alternative dharmas" is not the major concern of Buddha's preaching; such tasks can be left to other groups, such as Taoism, Confucianism, or folklore. Teaching such "alternative dharmas" to the living beings whose conditions are not yet mature, however, allows them to, at the lowest standard, preserve their human bodies instead of falling from virtue. They will then have a chance to practice and cultivate the way of Nirvana in their future lives.

The four of the above are all "mundane dharmas;" only the correct dharmas that allow people to attain Nirvana through the Present Body are "supramundane dharmas." The most adopted and practiced alternative dharmas are the "convenient dharmas" (方便法).

Most of the living beings are confused and cannot find their way out of the big mud pond of this material realm. Some of the living beings did make it out of the mud pond but voluntarily jumped back into the pond. That is how obsessed they have been. The kind and pitying Buddha still will not abandon these obsessed living beings because Buddha knows very well that these living beings have a lot of bad karmas to settle; they need more chances for redemptionin in order to work their ways toward the enlightenment.

The living beings are scattered at different levels and with different "natural capacities" (根器). Just one universal correct dharma to Nirvana, which is often difficult to learn and understand, will not work on them at all, particularly the ones who are at low educational levels or even illiterate. The kind and pitying Buddha then gives them the "convenient dharmas."

The convenient dharmas are easy dharmas toward success and the most widely adopted by practitioners. Currently, the most popular and adopted convenient dharma is the one created by Amitabha Buddha and promoted by Sakyamuni Buddha and his disciples: the Pure Land Dharma, which is also known as the Pure Land Sect, Buddha-Chanting Dharma, or Rebirth-in-Pure-Land Dharma. It is easy to practice and learn. If a practitioner succeeds in "Rebirth in Pure Land," such a practitioner will be able to arrive at the Pure Land of the Utmost Joy through "reincarnation by metamorphosis" (化生) and receive a "long but limited wisdom life."

This convenient dharma was the result of the forty-eight great vows made by Amitabha Buddha. The primary method of practice is chanting repeatedly "Na Mo Amitabha" or "Amitabha." In the forty-eight great vows of Amitabha Buddha, there are several favorable conditions offered:

Vow No. 18: If I attain Buddhahood, then the living beings who chant ten times (Amitabha) will be able to enter the kingdom of the utmost joy.

Vow No. 19: If I attain Buddhahood, living beings will chant my name and vow to be born in my kingdom.

Vow No. 20: Those living beings who believe in me and the World of Utmost Joy will receive guidance when they are dying.

These favorable conditions have evolved into the convenient dharma that leads to the World of Utmost Joy after death. Because this method is easy to practice with a higher chance of success, and all sorts of advantages are offered at the World of Utmost Joy, many Buddhists now have adopted the Pure Land Dharma.

A soul flies at the speed of light (the speed of light is three hundred thousand kilometers per second; the distance traveled at the speed of light for one year is called one light year), and the distance from our world to the World of Utmost Joy is 44.58 billion light years. If we travelled to the World of Utmost Joy at the speed of light, we would have to travel 44.58 billion years. It takes only one quarter of a second, however, for the Dharma Body of Amitabha Buddha to travel from the World of Utmost Joy to our world. This is why we request for his escort by chanting his holy name.

One can fly at a superluminal speed after achieving Nirvana. It may look slow when compared with the speed of Amitabha Buddha, but the speed still allows such a person to arrive at the World of Utmost Joy in a short period of time. This is the difference between "self-power" cultivation and "other-power" cultivation.

The will sent by the human brain travels at the speed of light, at which speed the message of Buddha-chanting can never reach the World of Utmost Joy. Such message, however, can be received by the Deva of Buddha Institute in our world. This institute, together with the Deva of Yin-Yang United Institute, will make the final decision about where this soul will be going.

"The immense Deva net has no leak." The great number of administrative agencies suggests that the management of all souls is very stringent. No living being should seek for relief through luck. "Deva has eyes that see everything."

Although those who have already attained Nirvana can be reborn into the World of Utmost Joy after death by chanting "*Amitabha*," not everyone else who chants "*Amitabha*" will. Each case needs to be analyzed for its actual circumstance. The World of Utmost Joy is a place that adopts and cultivates only elite practitioners, not inferior souls. It is the place for the good people to enjoy their "blessed retribution," not a trash can or recycling station. A bad-hearted person, who has committed all kinds of bad karmas, who requests guidance to the World of Utmost Joy when dying by chanting "*Amitabha*" will be disappointed. Such a person is disqualified. Even if the Deva of Buddha Institute agrees, the Deva of Yin-Yang United Institute will not agree. On top of that, the Buddha Institute is an institute that knows what is right and what is wrong.

The souls that arrive at the World of Utmost Joy by following the guidance provided by Amitabha Buddha or Bodhisattva will be born from lotuses (through metamorphosis). Their bodies consist of Spiritual Light. There is no pain but only happiness for them. They can command the landscape, objects, and everything they desire (with certain restrictions applied). Their bodies and other aspects, however, are classified according to the cultivation levels in the Saha Land.

There are three major levels and nine classes for birth through metamorphosis. This category system is also called the Nine Grades of Lotuses.

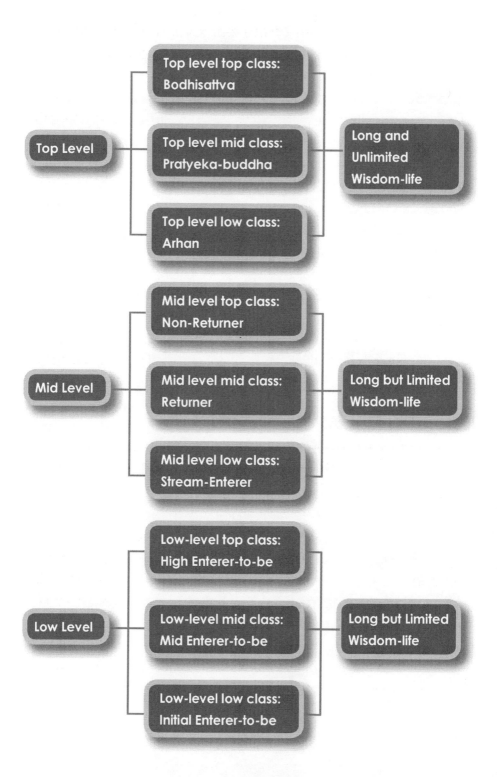

The bodies of those of the low level, low class are entirely luminous with light colors; they are mostly white. The bodies of those of the top-level top class are also entirely luminous, but the color is gold. The bodies of those of other levels and classes give out light that varies on a spectrum between white and gold.

Their bodies may have different colors but not like the material bodies in the Saha Land. They have no materials of composition from the material realm, such as flesh, blood, and bone. They do not have problems of cold, hot, pain, and itching. They do not have gender differences. Their gender features exhibited are, on one hand, controlled by the will power of Buddha and Bodhisattva and, on the other hand, controlled by their own wish and need. When they gather for meetings, they universally exhibit the features of one sex, but when they act alone, they can change gender features at will.

The ground of the World of Utmost Joy is paved with gold. All the buildings there, pagodas or houses, are constructed with the Seven Treasures. The landscape of the entire kingdom is clean and smooth, and the climate is mild and pleasant. There are beautiful lotus blossoms everywhere. The palaces are magnificent and solemn; everything is luminous. All trees are tall with golden branches and jade leaves. These leaves come in different shapes: triangle, pentagon, heptagon, octagon, or nonagon. Flowers fall from the sky; trees play music. All birds are beautiful and sing wonderful songs. Some birds have one head; some have two or even more. Some have two wings; some have four. Some even have several pairs of wings. They fly freely with no predators of any kind. In addition to lotuses, there are all kinds of exotic plants and flowers that have no names. Their blossoms come in all seasons. In this place, the gold on the ground is softer than the carpets used in the human world, and all plants and flowers emit refreshing, mind soothing, aromatic scents that cannot be found in the human world.

People here are all good looking and possess super-natural powers. They can travel through spatial obstacles. They can go to rallying points instantly; tens of thousands of people can gather together without colliding or touching. People of the same level wear the same clothes and are the same age. Everything is the same for the same level, and every level has its distinctive features. Everyone has a living space as big as his or her own lotus, and the spaces of their lotuses may vary according to their respective levels. The differences in the sizes of lotuses can be dramatic. Smaller ones may be dozens of square meters; larger ones may be tens of thousands of square kilometers. Again, the sizes are determined by the respective levels of attainment cultivated by them in the Saha Land. A lotus may be so big that it, itself, is a Little World that has everything from palaces to pagodas and houses; all luxuries can be contained inside.

People leave their lotuses during the day to attend group events or Bodhisattva's lectures about dharma. They also sing, dance, and play games. Some take trips to worship Buddha, some read Buddhist scriptures, and some just practice meditation. When it is time to rest, they go back to their respective lotuses to sleep or sit with legs crossed. Some travel in their dreams. Because this is the

World of Utmost Joy, people's dreams come alive on their respective lotuses and dissipate when they wake up.

For example, when they think of their relatives living in the human world, the images of their relatives will appear in front of them. It is not that their relatives really come to them, and their relatives do not know that someone is thinking about them. In the World of Utmost Joy, all images are projected through the supernatural power of Amitabha Buddha. Within the scope of Amitabha Buddha's supernatural power, their imagination comes into "reality," but when the people here stop imagining, the "reality" disappears right away. This phenomenon is not like a dream in the human world. A human's dream only comes during sleep. But here, people can dream without going to sleep. Everything they have in mind can be brought to "reality" through the "dharma power" of Amitabha Buddha. What has been brought into "reality" will disappear when the imagination changes. This phenomenon is also a way that Buddha enlightens people: imagination does not last for long and only the practice and cultivation of Nirvana gives an eternal life.

In the World of Utmost Joy, what is reality and what is hallucination?

Those dim images that appear and disappear at the command of one's will are hallucinations. Those brilliant and permanent images that do not appear and disappear at the command of one's will are reality. To tell what is what in the World of Utmost Joy, just take a quick look at the shine.

In the Saha Land, when a person begins to chant "*Amitabha*" (while practicing the Pure Land Sect), the Deva of Buddha Institute will relay all information of such a person to the administrative institute in the World of Utmost Joy. That institute will arrange a lotus appearing in the Lotus Pond. If such a person is doing well with cultivation in the human world, the size of the lotus will increase with a stronger shine, and the color of its light will change gradually from white to gold.

If a person stops cultivating or falls from virtue, the shine of his or her lotus dims, and the flower withers accordingly.

People of the low level must have committed some bad karmas in the Saha Land and are, therefore, denied access to the World of Utmost Joy. They, however, still have good conditions; their badness is overwhelmed by their goodness. Because they have "good natures" (善根) and believe in and practice Pure Land Dharma, the kind and pitying Buddha and Bodhisattvas will still offer guidance and training for them to enter the Way of Nirvana quickly, allowing them to go to the World of Utmost Joy after their deaths and be placed in the low level through "reincarnation by metamorphosis."

Because these people are of the low level, they have more problems with deluded conceptualization and receive less blessed retributions than the top-level people. Their bodies are smaller, too. Their lotuses are smaller in size and inferior in shine and color. They do not have higher-level functions and cannot play supernatural games the way they would like. Despite being in the World of Utmost Joy, there is still discrimination in terms of pleasure. It is like the enjoyment of blessed retributions in the human world; some people have more, some people have less. But, there are no mundane problems in the World of Utmost Joy.

In the World of Utmost Joy, the idea of discrimination is quite obvious. Lotuses of the same level and class gather together in one lotus pond. The top level, top class lotus pond is for people of top level, top class to live in. People of low level, low class have to live in the low level, low class lotus pond. Such a social class system is provided to motivate and inspire people to cultivate harder in the Saha Land.

The top level, top class lotuses and lotus ponds are much better than the low level, low class lotuses and lotus ponds. There are bigger and better lotuses, people, and palaces.

In the lotus ponds of the top level, top class, there are grand pagodas as big as mountains that shine with tens of thousands of colors. The ponds have refreshing scents and pleasant views. All bridges and buildings are wonderful. The size of these ponds is so big that their edges seem limitless. In the ponds, the lotuses blossom. Jeweled canopies sparkle in the sky. The lotuses, exclusively for the Bodhisattva, have countless layers. Each layer has pagodas and houses constructed with the Seven Treasures. The Bodhisattvas shine like gold; they wear extremely luxurious clothes and radiate light in the full spectrum of colors.

All of the people of the top level, top class have attained the stage of Bodhisattva. While they were in the Saha Land, they thoroughly realized the true meaning of the universe and life, cultivated relentlessly, made significant progress, saved and converted many living beings, engaged in charity actively, and accumulated "meritorious virtues" for decades, and in the end, they attained the "stage of Bodhisattva of the top level, top class."[37]

These Bodhisattvas have purified six sensing organs and are at the level of Dharma Body. They can still mutate at will and "play in their supernatural powers" (遊戲神通) even when they leave the World of Utmost Joy. In contrast, when low level people leave the World of Utmost Joy and go beyond the scope covered by the dharma power of Amitabha Buddha, they lose all joy.

Even the people of the top level, top class have to repeatedly transmigrate and reincarnate to the Saha Land and practice the Way of Bodhisattva until they have achieved Nirvana without Remainder if they wish to attain Buddhahood.

Not only does the attainment of Buddhahood require reincarnation to Saha Land, the people of the low level, low class must also reincarnate to the Saha Land to upgrade their level to low level, mid-class before they are allowed to live in the low level, mid-class lotus pond and be given the lotuses and bodies of the matching class.

Reincarnating to the Saha Land is not an easy task. First, an application must be filed for approval by the administrative institute of the World of Utmost Joy. This institute will contact the administrative institute of the Saha Land to make appropriate arrangement concerning the reincarnation, such as the place, country, ethnic origin, language, family, gender, religion, acquaintances, social group, religion cultivation, karmic retribution, and so on. The Ministry of Reincarnation and Transmigration will then take over the case. After the serving of the amnesia drink, the person is ready for reincarnation.

On the journey of dharma practicing, do not attempt to take any advantage that you do not deserve. It does not matter which dharma you practice; if your level of cultivation is high, then you will be able to keep the level wherever you go, and vice versa. Any living being in any world must cultivate. If a person deviates from the practice of dharmas higher than the human category, then what is waiting ahead is nothing but falling from virtue or even Hell.

Many Buddhists today believe that anyone may be reborn in the World of Utmost Joy after death by chanting "Amitabha" several times; some even believe that the chanting can be done by other people and the deceased will be reborn in the World of Utmost Joy as well. That's not all. When an animal dies, it too can be "redeemed" (超渡) and reborn in the World of Utmost Joy. They treat the World of Utmost Joy as a garbage can and recycling station; they think it will take any soul, and they do not care if the soul is acceptable to that world. All they know is chanting Amitabha.

Many believe that Sakyamuni Buddha is in charge of everything, including this world. This is totally incorrect cognition. In fact, Buddha has nothing to do with the normally functioning material realm (if Buddha interferes with it at will, he will violate *the Law of Deva*). Buddha is only responsible for the Great Bodhisattvas who convert living beings. Neither do the Bodhisattvas do administrative tasks. All administrative tasks are handled by the respective administrative agencies. For example, mundane people are managed by the mundane people management institutes; Heaven People are managed by the Heaven People management institutes; deities are managed by the deity management institutes. The same applies to ghosts, Deva Kingdom, and Hell. No Buddha or Bodhisattva has jurisdiction over these administrative agencies. All living beings are equal in front of the *Law of Deva*.

Therefore, Buddha is not omnipotent, nor is Amitabha Buddha. They have no right to supersede the command of these administrative agencies and accept any living being from the Saha Land at their choice. Here is a metaphor that can explain this even better. The entire material realm is a big incarceration cage; anyone who has not yet attained Nirvana has to stay in the cage, like inmates, for repetitive transmigrations. These inmates have to serve time in the cage until they are released (attaining Nirvana). This cage is run by an administrative agency, and no one may release an inmate who is not qualified for release; illegal release is a violation of *the Law of Deva*.

Both *the Law of Deva* (天條) and *Dharma Body Management Regulations* (法身管理條例) are stipulated by Buddhas. The legislators are not necessarily the law enforcers, and the law enforcers are not necessarily the legislators. Buddhahood requires full compliance with the law; Buddha is highly law-abiding and will not challenge the law.

Many people in our world have been released from the cage by attaining Nirvana and are, therefore, relieved from transmigration. For some reason, they return to this world again. For example, they realize that their relatives, friends, or people connected with them are still going through transmigration in the cage unaware of how nice the realm of "Non-transmigration" can be. Due to their "commiseration" and "kindness and pity," they choose to give up pleasure and apply for reincarnation in the Saha Land. It's like a group of people who are lost in a desert and have run out of water. They send two members to find an oasis. The two do find an oasis; one chooses to stay without being concerned with the lives of the other members waiting out there, and the other one chooses to go back immediately to find the other members and bring them to the oasis. The one who has chosen to stay is like an Arhan at Nirvana, and the other one who has chosen to go back and bring everybody to the oasis is like a Bodhisattva, who has also attained Nirvana.

Those who already have attained Nirvana and choose to go back to our world and rescue people from the cage have hearts of the Bodhisattva. The heart of Bodhisattva alone, however, is not enough; one must also possess the capability of fulfilling the way of Bodhisattva. This mundane world is like an ocean of pain. A rescue mission on the ocean of pain requires a boat, tools, swimming skill, sailing skill, and a self-contained material body. Otherwise, the rescuer will risk starvation and drowning.

Driven only by impulsive bravery, the rescuers jump into the ocean of pain with very limited capability and lose direction soon due to the effect of the amnesia drink. Their

Yang souls do not understand the current situation, and their subconscious is anxious. Without the knowledge of original soul cultivation, their original souls cannot take care of activities and, therefore, can only influence their Yang souls unobtrusively and imperceptibly. With insufficient capability, their Yang souls can only sense certain things that are not clear. Thus, although these people have the motivation for cultivation and to save and convert people, they do not know how. Therefore, they bump around in a clueless manner.

In the end, many choose the Pure Land Sect. They mistakenly think that the Pure Land Dharma is easy to learn and that once they are "reborn into the World of Utmost Joy" (往生極樂), they will "extinguish births and deaths" and eventually become Buddhas regardless of the levels of their cultivation.

Little did they know the Pure Land Sect is a Convenient Dharma specifically designed to accommodate low-level practitioners. For those who have already attained Nirvana in their previous lives, choosing this sect will be like a college graduate who has chosen to attend an elementary school instead of going up to pursue a master degree or applying for a job.

That is the way of cultivation; one must pursue one stage of attainment after another upward to integrate the stage of attainment of the present life with that of the previous life.[38] Pursuing a stage of attainment that is lower than that of the previous life cannot relieve one from transmigration (depending on the result of the mission). The result of the mission is also a criterion for "stage appraisal." A mission poorly executed earns a low stage of attainment, and that is the way it is. An incomplete mission or a failed mission will result in the continuation of transmigration.

Those who have attained Nirvana already have Dharma Bodies that are "neither born nor ended" (不生不滅); they can enter and exit the World of Utmost Joy freely without the need of escorting from Buddha or Bodhisattvas. If they can walk by themselves, they do not need an escort to hold their hands.

Those who have already attained Nirvana and chosen the Pure Land Sect for cultivation are high stage holders seeking the lower stages of attainment. As the number of such practitioners increases in this mundane world, the Correct-Dharma Proportion Composite Index will drop. Therefore, the popularity of the Pure Land Sect is also one of the standards for identifying the Degenerate-Dharma Period.

III.

WHY ESTABLISH BUDDHA-TO-BE RELIGION?

The Deva of United Enlightenment has several divisions dedicated to the management of different religions. Every religion has its primary purpose and secondary purpose. The primary purpose of a given religion is the correct method or correct dharma, and the secondary purpose is the convenient dharma for saving other living beings. Every religion has its correct method and a chart of the Correct-Dharma Proportion Composite Index, which is further divided into the past chart, present chart, and future chart. The past chart presents historic data, and the present chart and future chart present the dynamic status that constantly changes according to the data provided by the Ministry of Karma Force Registration.

The Deva of United Enlightenment predicts the future Correct-Dharma Proportion Composite Index according to the past and present data. According to the future data, it must file an application for the reincarnation of the designated dharma preacher with the concerned agencies 100 to 150 years in advance. Upon approval of such application, the concerned agencies begin to discuss and plan the related matters jointly (e.g., the facial features (genes) inherited from parents, ethnic origin, country, language, etc.). These matters also include highly complicated "karmic retribution editing," such as the learning period, dormant period, the time of the end of dormant period, the time for dharma preaching, the potentialities and conditions for dharma preaching, when such potentialities and conditions will mature, and so on.

Filing an application 100 to 150 years in advance allows for the preparation of matching parents for early reincarnation. If there is not enough time, then the Deva of United Enlightenment must file an application for a "pardon order" from the Kingdom of United Nebulae to allow *the Law of Deva* to be bent slightly, provided that the circumstance is reasonable. That will allow the Ministry of Reincarnation and Transmigration to execute their missions more easily.

(A)   BUDDHA-COMMISSIONED SPECIAL-DHARMA REPRESENTATIVE (佛敕奇法人)

More than twenty years ago, my master asked me, "Have you ever heard of the Kingdom of United Nebulae?"

I answered, "No, I haven't."

The master then said to me, "If you fly east outside the Solar System for about 112 trillion light years, you will find a very beautiful world; it is called the Kingdom of United Nebulae. It is truly a City of Ten Thousand Buddhas and is a Buddha Kingdom.

"Our Solar System is actually a Little World that exists in

a nebula, which is a Great Chiliocosm. Three thousand Great Chiliocosms comprise an integrated body. This integrated body is the Kingdom of United Nebulae (星雲內外聯合王國).

"The borderless universe has countless organizations like the Kingdom of United Nebulae. This Kingdom of United Nebulae may have three trillion suns and countless living beings, but it is still a piece of dust when compared with the vast universe. Therefore, the king of the Kingdom of United Nebulae can only be addressed as the King of Ten Thousand Buddhas.

"The King of Ten Thousand Buddhas is a great Buddha; however, the vast universe has countless kings like this one. If there is only one Buddha in one nebula, then the Kingdom of United Nebulae has three thousand Buddhas already (excluding the Buddhas in Buddhas' Pure Lands). There will not be only one Buddha, however, in one nebula. Therefore, this King of Ten Thousand Buddhas is the leader of more than ten thousand Buddhas.

"The Kingdom of United Nebulae is the place for Buddhas to hold meetings. It is also the place for the legislation and administration of the three thousand nebulae and the training site for the Great Bodhisattvas.

"The King of Ten Thousand Buddhas attained Buddhahood countless Kalpas ago. He is the mentor and leader of Buddhas. Amitabha Buddha and Medicine Buddha, as you have already known, and myself are all administered by the King of Ten Thousand Buddhas.

"All right, seeing is believing. Tonight, I will take you to the Kingdom of United Nebulae and meet the King of Ten Thousand Buddhas."

That night I followed the master's instructions by lying down with a blanket drawn and loosening up. Soon, I felt as though I was sleeping. The difference from the usual sleep was: everything that happened was clear as if I were not sleeping, but the material body had lost its awareness and become immobile. Even today, the experience is fresh in my mind.

My "Dharma Body of the present life" (External Body) took the Three Souls into the sky. When looking down, I saw my own material body lying flat like a corpse.

"Let's go!" came the master's voice from behind.

I turned around and saw the master sitting on a giant lotus. I could not help myself but looked down and saw that there was also a lotus under my feet. Of course, the lotus was much smaller than the master's, and the color and shine were incomparable.

The interesting thing was that the lotus underfoot could change according to my will. It went up or down and moved or stopped as I desired. It changed shape according to whatever I desired. It was like an ever-changing pagoda in the air.

I kneeled to the master on the lotus.

The master said, "Let's go! I shall present you to the King of Ten Thousand Buddhas."

In a split second, I saw a colossal luminous sphere below us.

One hundred and twelve trillion light years? Were we there already? How incredible that such a cosmic distance could be reached just like that! There was no feeling of movement at all; it was as if we still stood where we had been.

It was so hard to understand that kind of time and space; it was like science fiction or some kind of drunken talk. With my very limited wisdom, I cannot explain clearly. There are many questions that I still cannot answer thoroughly. But, what I saw and experienced are absolute facts.

I, indeed, could not realize the master's state of Dharma Body. If I could have, then I would have succeeded in the attainment. It seemed that being unable to understand was quite normal.

As we hovered in the sky, the master said to me, "Here we are. The colossal luminous sphere below us is the Kingdom of United Nebulae. The Law of Cause and Effect is maintained right here. The principles of 'birth, aging, sickness, death,' 'formation, existence, decay, disappearance,' 'creation, destruction, change, variation,' and others are also being controlled right here. This is also the place where Buddhas meet for discussion and decision-making.

"Never assume that Buddhas are limited to only one level; Buddhas can have many levels, but that subject does not concern you, and you only need to have a general idea about that.

"Don't worry about your material body; I have arranged dharma guardians for you; there will not be any problem.

"Follow me down there."

At the moment he finished his words, we had already landed, and the beautiful lotuses disappeared. In front of our eyes was a grand, solemn and dazzling palace with four Chinese characters written on the front that meant the Palace of the King of Ten Thousand Buddhas.[39] The palace was entirely decorated with the Seven Treasures and emitting golden light.

The world in front of us was exotic; there was no sun or moon. Everywhere we looked was bright. Everything here shined and lit up the entire sky.

I followed the master and walked on the gold-paved ground toward the palace.

All of a sudden, I had an overwhelming feeling of humility. Without any reason, the author felt guilty and ashamed. The universe is beginningless and endless, edgeless and borderless, and has countless sentient beings. The number of high-level sentient beings is also immeasurable. A lifetime lasts for only a few decades and goes swift as a bird; compared to the vast universe, a lifetime is only a short-lived spindrift in an edgeless ocean. Is there any obstacle that cannot be conquered?

As I was wondering, we had arrived at the main hall.

I kneeled to the King of Ten Thousand Buddhas.

With a closer look, I found out that the King of Ten Thousand Buddhas was extremely good looking. He wore a crown embedded with gemstones, a cloak decorated with golden and silver stars, and a pair of black boots. He was dashing and refined with an extraordinary temperament. By all means, he had the perfect image of a Buddha.

I could tell from the conversation between the master and the King of Ten Thousand Buddhas that they had a close relationship.

Later on, the King of Ten Thousand Buddhas led us to the rear hall and had us sit down in a smaller room that looked like a reception room, evidenced by its layout and decoration.

The moment we had sat down, a woman wearing a cheongsam with a tea tray in her hands entered the room. She stopped in front of me and kneeled down on one leg. She placed the tea set on a stand and said, "Please enjoy the tea."

"Thank you," I replied.

That woman was gorgeous to a degree rarely seen in the human world. Her pretty face and lovely expression were beyond description.

Unexpectedly, when I was looking at her, she returned a flirtatious look.

I then wondered how such a solemn and pure place had such a frivolous woman.

I turned my eyes to the master and the King of Ten Thousand Buddhas, but strangely enough, they did not seem to be bothered; they just ignored us.

How could the great Buddha ignore this happening in front of his eyes? I called the master in desperation.

The King of Ten Thousand Buddhas got the message and uttered to the woman, "You sinful animal, get lost now!"

The woman obediently retreated to the corner of the room. There was a cage, and the woman squeezed herself into it.

The king waved his hand at the cage, and the cage door was padlocked just like that. At the same time, the woman turned into a green-faced, long-toothed, and red-haired terrifying beast.

This intense sequence of events stunned me.

The king understood my mood and said to me, "Don't be afraid. It has a good nature, or it would not be so lucky."

The king paused and went on, "It is a goblin that I captured recently from an immature world. It was not easy for this goblin to achieve this level. It violated *the Law of Deva* by showing off its supernatural power and playing with its dharma power in the mundane world. It really had some talent, and it fought relentlessly with the law-enforcement officers. I happened to be there and stepped forward to capture it. Then, I decided to bring it back to be tamed. Before it was completely tamed, you arrived. It looks like you were destined to meet it. Would you like to take it home as your ride?"

I was surprised but declined, "No, no. But I do appreciate Your Excellency's kindness."

Then, I smelled the aroma of tea. I raised my tea cup and saw only one small piece of tea leaf in the cup. The liquid had no tea color to it and looked like plain water. I wondered, "Why does a great place such as this serve such inferior tea? Are they running short of tea here?"

I took a sip and found the taste so refreshingly sweet that it instantly drove away fatigue. It made my entire body relaxed and comfortable. That tea must be hard to find, I had to have some more.

The king said, "Well, that's all right. In our level, there is no gender difference. The 'manifestations of supernatural powers' (神通變化) depends only on your mind. All you need is to keep your mind neutral.

"If a goblin can perform such supernatural power, imagine what a Buddha can do.

"Your master brings you here to give you the chance to learn more and understand more, which you may apply in the future. Your master's presence is required in a meeting with other Buddhas. Meanwhile, let me show you something that is useful to you. Now, follow me."

I followed the king out of the main hall, and the lotuses reappeared under our feet. In a split second, we arrived at the front door of another palace on which a sign said: Qingyang Zang.

The lotuses automatically disappeared again at the moment of our arrival at the front door. I followed the king, went through the main hall, and entered a room.

That was a big room with all sorts of bizarre objects with unknown uses; I had never seen any of them before. On the other side of the room was a bookshelf where books on different subjects were placed in an orderly fashion. There was a big screen at one corner of the room that looked like movie screens I had seen in the mundane world.

The king said to me, "Qingyang Zang is the training base for the Great Bodhisattvas, and it has a tremendous amount of data. If the books at Qingyang Zang were an ocean, then the books you see in this room would be one drop of water in the ocean.

"Qingyang Zang includes all the cultures of this Kingdom of United Nebulae. The term 'this Kingdom of United Nebulae' is used because the vast universe has countless nebulae, and there is more than one Kingdom of United Nebulae. You will understand this concept when you have reached a certain level of cultivation.

"We also have *The Deva's Books* as mundane people call them. *The Deva's Books* are the ordinary collection at Qingyang Zang.

"Counting the books here is a difficult task already, let alone reading them. However, these books are already in your master's head; at any time and place, he knows which paragraph or sentence to apply and what objectives can thus be achieved.

"Buddha knows all cultures and speaks all languages.

"I don't think you know that I visit you very often. You Chinese have a saying: 'By memorizing all three hundred poems of the Tang Dynasty, anyone can be a poet.' Memorizing only three hundred poems can make a person a poet. These Buddhas, whom your master represents, not only memorize but master all knowledge in the Kingdom of United Nebulae. How can a mundane person ever compare? That is why we don't compare ourselves with the mundane people no matter what, since living beings are pathetic.

"You can only read books written in Chinese, but we can read any book written in any language. Focus on your cultivation. One day you too will be able to achieve the same level.

"Let's go over there."

The king led me to the screen and said, "This is the Nebula Internal and External Information System. All information inside and outside the nebula can be displayed here according to your will. There is audio, numeric, picture, and text information. Its functions are comprehensive. For example, if you want to see a world, that world will be displayed like a grain of sand. You can zoom in layer by layer simply by thinking it.

"Now let's look at your world for a demonstration.

"Turn on the screen. Here is the Solar System. Now, it is the Earth, and then the YangZi River, the Great Wall, the Yellow River. Now, this is an ant colony, a group of ants, one ant, and an ant's egg.

"You see that?"

"Yes, I see them. It's amazing."

"That's normal; when you sit inside a well and look at the sky, the sky is only as big as the well opening.

"Now let's move on. Look at you. QingYang County, Jiou-hua Shan, and a mountain cave. Now, through your skin into your stomach. Now look at your childhood. How's that?"

"That's incredible!"

"With this system, you may know the past, present, and future of anyone, including you, me, and your master. It even tells you exactly what animals we've been in past lives.

"It can show you the past, present, and future of any world.

"You have very limited time, and you need something simpler and faster.

"All high Dharma Bodies, like your master, have one screen like that in their brains. That is why Buddha can access any information, adapt to any circumstance, and accommodate any change.

"Buddha is ancient, modern, and futuristic.

"Going forward can be going backward; going forward can be ancient. The present is the past, the past is the future, and the future is the past, because everything is developing in a repetitive pattern. It applies to Buddha, too. The paths you have taken, Buddha has been there many times already. In the eyes of Buddha, the happenings of all things are natural, destined, and expected. Nothing is accidental; nothing is unexpected.

"Buddha has to adapt to all circumstances like human beings have to sleep. It is a normal necessity.

"To adapt to all circumstances, countless methods are improvised. That's why it's said that 'there is no limitation to Buddha Dharmas.' There will always be an alternative method (dharma). The method to be applied is determined as the situation requires. As long as a conversion method serves the purpose of converting living beings, well, it is a correct method.

"You cannot understand Buddha by one single 'image;' you cannot explain Buddha with one single form; and you cannot achieve Buddhahood with one single method. Everything of Buddha changes constantly as the situation calls for it. The existence of any dharma is the result of the adaptation to existing circumstances. All 'prescriptions' are given according to the category of the situation. Buddha has to adapt to changing circumstances in order to successfully realize his goal of converting living beings, and living beings have to adapt to the changing circumstances in order to successfully accomplish their life journeys.

"That's enough for the time being. Your master wants you to know more about *Dharma Body Management Regulations*.

"Dharma Bodies, as mundane people, are classified into many classes, and the differences can be significant.

"We can't go through the vast number of clauses, but you can remember these principal ones first: Dharma Body that has lost its material body may not show its presence or exhibit its supernatural power in the mundane world without authorization.

"Regardless of class, Dharma Bodies may not breach the Law of Cause and Effect[40] of the universe; may not breach *the Law of Nature*[41] by altering any person, thing, or object of the mundane world; may not change the karma force by exercising supernatural power; and may not damage the supernatural power of the Dharma Bodies of lower levels with the supernatural power of the higher Dharma Bodies.

"When reincarnating to the mundane world to save and convert living beings, a Dharma Body must use the 'branch soul' to reincarnate into the mundane fetus and then rely on the mundane fetus. Without special authorization, the task of saving and converting living beings cannot be completed or fulfilled using the form of Dharma Body. Otherwise, if all Dharma Bodies go to the mundane world to save the people they are connected with, then there will be no difference between confusion and enlightenment. To believe or not to believe and to be enlightened or not to be enlightened depend solely on the 'mind power' of the living beings, and a Dharma Body cannot intervene forcefully. If the real image is shown on the grounds of convenience, then it will be a violation of *the Law of Deva* and subject to punishment.

"All Dharma Bodies may not violate *the Law of Nature* for any reason. All Dharma Bodies, at any level, may not speak of things that they are not supposed to speak of during certain restricted periods of time. Violators will be held responsible for any and all consequences.

"There are still many clauses; I think that's enough for you right now."

"If there are such regulations, then why did I and my master—"

"Oh, that. All things that happen between you and your master are ordered and pardoned by Buddhas. These clauses are not stipulated by one single Buddha but by buddhas collectively for immeasurable Kalpas. These are the clauses, namely the law, which all Dharma Bodies have been following for their slow and difficult progress on their ways to Buddhahood.

"This law was originally quite simple. However, time in the universe has no beginning and has no end. There have been many eras during this very long time, and each era has different problems that cannot be handled by only one method. To handle these problems properly, frequent amendments to this law according to the changes that happen in different eras must be done. This law, therefore, becomes bulky. Regardless of the era, whether formation, existence, decay, or disappearance, there should be a law for the Dharma Bodies to follow.

"The law in the past may not be applicable in the present time. That is how it is in Buddhism; it is all about 'emptiness' (空), namely 'change' (變). There are infinite methods to pursue the one and only truth.

"If your master was still teaching Buddhism today exactly the same way that he had done some two thousand years ago, then it would be a terrible mistake. Times have changed, and the teaching must change as well. This is the mission for you to complete in the future, and this is the reason why you have reincarnated to this mundane world.

"What is Buddhism and what is not? Everything is Buddhism, I can tell you. The practitioners are practicing Buddhism, and the non-practitioners are practicing Buddhism, too. Some people are cultivating upward; some are cultivating downward. Some are cultivating neither upward nor downward but horizontally. The bottom line is that they are all cultivating. That is a process by which a living being moves toward the way of Buddhahood, and it will be a very, very long one that may take countless Kalpas to complete.

"That is also a representation of 'there is no limitation to Buddha Dharmas.' The only difference is practicing Mundane Dharma or practicing Supramundane Dharma.

"Since every living being is cultivating, then why do they still need to be saved and converted? Saving and converting gives the living beings guidance and helps them develop correct cognition and views, so they may adjust and help themselves. It is about saving living beings from confusion and converting them to their enlightenment; there can be less trial and error, broader paces, faster steps, earlier achievement of correct stages of attainment, and earlier relief from the ocean of pain. Therefore, practicing the Supramundane Dharma should be the primary purpose.

"Follow me."

We stopped at a bookshelf. The king took a thick book with curly and twisted characters written on it, which I did not understand.

The king looked at me and said, "This book is written in Sanskrit, which comes from one of the richer cultures and is a frequently adopted language in the Dharma Realm. It is a language too complicated for pervasive application in the world of the mid-class human beings. There is a cultural gap between the Chinese words that you have learned and these alphabetical words.

"The name written on the cover of this book says *Buddha-Commissioned Special-Dharma Representatives*, which is also the title."

As the king was explaining, he opened the book somewhere in the middle and continued, "This book has recorded all Buddha-Commissioned Special-Dharma Representatives of the Kingdom of United Nebulae. It mentions that you have been commissioned by the Kingdom as one of the Special-Dharma Representatives, and you have been issued with 108 Order Cards (令牌), but I will not disclose the details to you because it is not yet the time for you to know such confidential information. Anyway, you have been charged with the mission of saving and converting living beings. Therefore, focus on your cultivation and wait patiently. When the potentialities and conditions present themselves, your master will tell you what to do next.

"Okay, our time is up. You are finished here for this time. You may visit here more frequently. If you have any questions, you can refer to your master because he knows everything. Listen to your master, and stay away from bad karmas. If you commit bad karmas, then no one can save you. Don't accuse us of being apathetic toward you. You have been clearly briefed, and you and you alone will be responsible for what to do next. We may choose to tell you or not to tell you, and you may choose to do or not to do. Go on and be your own captain.

"Now let's meet your master."

I and my master parted from the king, stepped onto the lotuses, and headed for our solar system.

(B) LEADING "THOSE WITH DUE CONDITION" TO RECTIFICATION

Cognition and view is critical to both learning dharma and practicing dharma. Without correct cognition and view, there will be no correct direction and specific goal, and consequently no chance of successful attainment.

Due to the effect of the amnesia drink, living beings can

somehow sense the necessity and motivation for practice and cultivation, but they just do not know where and how. They are desperate and lost, and that is pathetic.

People who do not know the method (dharma) for the relief of pain and acquisition of joy exploit the goodness of living beings to serve their interests in fame and money by teaching pseudo-Buddhism in the guise of some holy and prestigious figures. That is regrettable.

It could not be any easier to get hold of a book on Buddhism today. It does not take long to realize that most of these books borrow indiscriminately from each other and do not make any sense at all. They are mostly incomplete dharmas. Some authors of these books cannot even understand some terms in their own books. These books at their best are well-intentioned; they are not legitimate Buddhism scriptures.

Many Buddhist groups have turned Buddhism into a monopoly charity. Some temples know nothing but chanting scriptures, conducting redemption services for the deceased, releasing living animals, and having vegetarian meals. They do not have any idea about how to cultivate themselves for Nirvana at all. Many Buddhists know nothing but worshipping Buddha statues and asking for blessing and protection.

The worst fallacies come from books. These books waste money, resources, and time. Some books that are regarded as treasures by some readers are full of mistakes. Many of these books mention that "among the universe," "within the universe," "inside the universe," "outside the universe," and "the entire universe," which are all incorrect expressions.

As early as 2,500 years ago, Sakyamuni Buddha had already told his disciples that the vast universe has no beginning or end in terms of time and no edge or border in terms of space.

The term "universe" means unlimited time and unlimited space. The vast universe is comprised of countless numbers of worlds.

The term "world" means limited time and limited space.

A world has its edge and border and its beginning and end, but the universe does not.

If there is no edge or border, then there will be no inside or outside. If there is inside and outside to a universe, then there should be an edge or border for the universe as there is for a world. If there is an edge of the universe, then what is outside the edge? A Buddhist cannot explain Buddha Dharma with a view of the cosmos that is against Buddha.

Some talk about the "entire universe." The universe has no edge or border and, therefore, there is no such a thing as entirety. Describing the universe as an entirety suggests there is an edge or border to it.

On the contrary, it is perfectly correct to say "among the world," "within the world," "inside the world," "outside the world," and "the entire world," because the world does have an edge and border.

How could a practitioner who does not have the ability to communicate with Buddha or Bodhisattva possibly be able to understand the universe? First, by looking; second, by listening; third, by imagining; and fourth, by the ghost or goblin that possesses the practitioner's body. With a simple arrangement of the combination of these four factors, anyone can be a prophet.

Prophets of this kind frequently and selectively exaggerate as dramatically and mysteriously as they can. This world is too small for their appetite and talking about the universe is more attractive to them. It is not necessary, in fact. If they can thoroughly comprehend the world, then they should be able to attain the way of Nirvana.

Many people tend to search first for answers from somewhere far out instead of their backyard. They are eager to understand other worlds while their own world is rarely explored. It is not necessary to refer to the universe when this world perhaps has the answer already.

Without correct cognition and correct view, there will be no correct way and correct result. Many people have wasted a tremendous amount of time and money bumping around amidst general fallacies, and they are reluctant to admit such a problem when someone else points it out to them. They may become very defensive and eager to prove that they are correct by employing all kinds of excuses. A mistake is a mistake; the sooner you get out of the general fallacies, the sooner you may succeed. There is nothing wrong with admitting one's own mistake. Stop tangling with the past; stop tangling with the mistakes. Free yourself, and let go of your ego. Correct the mistake, relax and move on; rectification requires humility.

General fallacies are like a maze; the exit is hard to find if there is no guide. Practicing religion is like solving a maze; if you refuse the directions offered by a guide, then you will never find the exit. Even if you are pulled out of the maze coercively, you will go back into it again. One must become aware that this maze is not enjoyable; if you play with it, you are wasting your time and life. You must have the desire to get out of the maze and never go back again in the first place for the guidance to work effectively on you.

Buddhism literatures are overabundant already, and the author is publishing his book lecturing about Buddhism; does that make any sense? If the readers may change or enhance their cognition and views by reading this book, then it does make sense. The correct cognition and view can change a person's concept, which may change life's results. That is why the Buddha-to-Be Religion is being established. It helps the living beings whose conditions are mature enough to part from the general fallacies and accelerate their self-cultivation, creating unlimited wisdom lives within their limited life time.

(C) THE CREATION OF BUDDHA-TO-BE RELIGION
All dharmas exist because the causes and conditions are mature. In response to the coming of a new age, living beings' needs, and more than one hundred years of preparation by the Deva of United Enlightenment, the Buddha-to-Be Religion was created in 2008.

Despite the potentialities and conditions being mature,

the tasks to be done in the Mundane World are just beginning and need the support of believers whose conditions are also mature to bring the correct dharma to the mundane world properly.

Birth is not worthy of celebration because birth is followed by death. An infant may die easily and prematurely if it lacks protection and care. Therefore, birth can also mean death, and the only difference is the length of life.

A seed that germinates is a happy thing, but how strong is it in terms of viability? We must not wait and see; we must nourish it by providing proper temperature, humidity, water, fertilizer, and proper light. We must also eliminate insects that are unfavorable for it. That is the way for the seedling to grow strong, blossom, yield fruit, and reproduce. Otherwise, it may just die.

The business of Buddha-to-Be Religion is not the author's personal business; Buddhism cannot be promoted by one person only. Buddha-to-Be Religion is a business that concerns everyone; it is a joint business of all practitioners and involves collaboration among multiple spaces.

Commanding a great ship of dharma,
ferrying between the Mundane and Supramundane
  Worlds.
The task of transporting countless numbers of pas-
  sengers
cannot be done only by one person.

How big is this great ship of dharma? It is big enough to hold all living beings onboard. Is it possible for the author to steer the ship alone? Not at all. There are too many things to be done on this ship, and the author must concentrate on steering the wheel. Other tasks on the ship have to be shared by other people. That is how we depart from material realm and arrive at the Nano Space.

The creation of the Buddha-to-Be Religion has changed the concept of many dharmas. Some people cannot accept this fact, particularly some celebrity Buddhists. They have studied, cultivated, and preached Buddhism their entire lives, and they have published many books and articles. Suddenly, someone comes forward and argues, telling them something is wrong, and they find it difficult to accept. They cannot admit that they are wrong. They irrationally defend their ideas and criticize the Buddha-to-Be Religion. These results are all natural. One weakness of humans is ego. People do not like embarrassing spots on their faces and will do anything to save their "faces." If a practitioner may overcome this weakness, then success is not far.

Many people have realized that they have taken some wrong ways; they feel resentful and regretful. It is not necessary. Think about it; is there any driver who has never taken the wrong way? We all have done the same. In religious cultivation, every living being has taken the wrong way before. Life is a journey from birth to death. The right ways and the wrong ways are all preparing and perfecting us for the future.

The Buddha-to-Be Religion cannot guarantee living beings will never take the wrong way, but it is our purpose

to provide a satellite navigation device for religious cultivation that allows the living beings to make fewer mistakes
and arrive earlier.

Those who are already on the wrong way do not have
to be upset. When we appraise your stage of attainment,
your mileage accumulated on the wrong way will be tak-
en into consideration in the calculation of your point of
cultivation.

The Buddha-to-Be Religion is silently and peacefully
created in this way. Let us nourish her with actions and
allow her to grow strong to enable her to benefit living
beings, like the "holy infant" bearing mother who
cultivates countless wisdom lives.

ESSENTIALS OF VOLUME TWO

28. Buddha Responding to the World (佛應世)

In ancient times, there was no Buddhism, and no one knew that there was Buddha because the "potentialities and conditions" (機緣) of living beings had not yet matured enough. When living beings' "potentialities and conditions" were mature, the Deva of United Enlightenment (聯合教化天) arranged a "Virtual-Enlightenment Bodhisattva" (等覺菩薩) to reincarnate to the human world to establish Buddhism. At the moment that the branch soul of "Virtual-Enlightenment Bodhisattva" entered the human womb, it turned into a "Marvelous-Enlightenment Bodhisattva" (妙覺菩薩). If a "Marvelous-Enlightenment Bodhisattva," who came to the human world to establish Buddhism, called himself a Bodhisattva, he would not be able to establish Buddhism; he has to call himself Buddha.

In fact, it was the "Marvelous-Enlightenment Bodhisattva," not Buddha, that responded to (the condition of) this world and introduced Buddhism. The "Marvelous-Enlightenment Bodhisattva" had to complete his mission with success, abstain from "fundamental ignorance" (根本無明), and enter Nirvana without Remainder (無餘涅槃) before he could attain supreme correct enlightenment (無上正等正覺) for his Dharma Body. After having been appraised and certified by the United Kingdom of Nebulae, this Dharma Body may then be called Buddha.

In response to the need to cultivate the living beings and establish Buddhism, the Kingdom of United Nebulae especially granted the title of "Buddha" to the "Marvelous-Enlightenment Bodhisattva" in his mission to introduce Buddhism; it was not a real Buddha who responded to the world.

The real Buddha has permanently lost his "retributive body" after his attainment of "Nirvana without Remainder" and will no longer reincarnate. Besides, there are countless "Virtual-Enlightenment Bodhisattvas" (等覺菩薩) waiting in the queue for their Buddhahood. The kind and pitying Buddha will not reincarnate anymore and will not occupy a quota, resulting in one less Buddha in the Dharma Realm.

Although it was the "Marvelous-Enlightenment Bodhisattva" (妙覺菩薩) that responded to the world, not Buddha, most people still believe he was Buddha, and that is also how the Dharma Realm has ruled. Buddha-to-Be Religion follows suit and goes along with the ancient people without making any change but discloses this fact as a measure to enhance the cognition and view (知見) of the practitioners.

The "Marvelous-Enlightenment Bodhisattva" is the final stage among the fifty-two stages of Bodhisattva. Therefore, after one more death of his "retributive body," he shall attain Nirvana without Remainder and become a Buddha.

29. Nirvana through the Present Body (即身涅槃)

Many modern Buddhists believe that they can achieve Buddhahood in their limited lengths of lives. This idea is a big mistake and an obstacle to the attainment of enlightenment. Buddhahood through the Present Body is impossible, and a wise person should know that.

While Buddhahood through the Present Body is impossible, Nirvana through the Present Body is possible. Buddhahood through the Present Body is "Nirvana without Remainder," and Nirvana through the Present Body is "Nirvana with Remainder." Buddha-to-Be Religion is an advocate of Nirvana through the Present Body in the form of "Nirvana with Remainder," and the level of such attainment of Nirvana ranges from Arhan up to "Virtual-Enlightenment Bodhisattva." If specified expressly, "Nirvana without Remainder," or "Final Nirvana" (究竟涅槃), means the Nirvana of Marvelous-Enlightenment Bodhisattva, namely the Nirvana for Buddhahood.

30. Eighty-Four Thousand (八萬四千)

Eighty-four thousand implies a huge quantity. Sometimes, the number eighty thousand also implies the same. For example, the term "eighty-four thousand troubles" actually describes many types of troubles, and the term "eighty-four thousand Dharmas" (or eighty thousand Dharmas) is an expression of the complexity of Buddhist doctrines. Buddha is praised as having eighty-four thousand looks, each of which is noble and wonderful and emits eighty-four thousand beams of light. Hell spans across eighty thousand yojanas (1 yojana is about 9 English miles; 踰繕那, 由旬) and has eighty-four thousand types of instruments of torture and is, therefore, called the Eighty-Thousand Hells. A human body has countless pores, and the term "eighty-four thousand pores" is used as a metaphor. A body with extensive wisdom life (慧命) has a lifetime of eighty-four thousand Kalpas.

In all, the number eighty-four thousand is simply a description of a huge number and was commonly adopted by the people of ancient India. When Buddha was teaching Buddhism a long time ago, he used this number that was familiar among the disciples to denote a huge quantity, which is not exactly eighty-four thousand.

31. Philanthropy (博愛)
Philanthropy ≠ "Kindness and pity" (慈悲)

Many Buddhists in modern times believe that kindness and pity as mentioned by Buddha is equivalent to philanthropy, and philanthropy is kindness and pity. This is a false conception.

The phrase "kindness and pity," as used in Buddhism, is a combined term with two meanings.

"Kindness" (慈) is giving dharma joy, utmost joy, and great joy. In other words, it is the fulfillment of the Supramundane Dharmas (出世間法) that allows the living beings to attain a Nano Body and enter the Nano Space, where there is permanent and ultimate joy, the Nirvana Joy.

"Pity" (悲) is removing pain; it is the fulfillment of Supramundane Dharmas (出世間法) that allows living beings to be relieved from the pains of transmigrations and their roots of pain to be removed, whereby the living beings receive permanent, true ease and happiness.

"Kindness and pity" means a Bodhisattva who knows the dharma of pain and joy and generously teaches the dharma (method) of avoiding pain and receiving joy to living beings. Such dharma is Supramundane Dharma that allows living beings to alienate the material realm (色界) and be relieved from transmigration.

Philanthropy is the great love, widespread love, and the love that benefits the public. The human world needs love; this world could be wonderful if everyone contributed a little love. Love is dignified. Love is to give, not to take. Love is altruistic, not egoistic. The love that is for oneself is selfishness and selfish desire.

While philanthropy is dignified, sexuality is nonetheless an inseparable part of it. Sexuality is one of the many kinds of love. There are many Buddhist precepts. One stipulates that: "monks must forbid sexuality and lust; the rest of the practitioners must forbid evil obscenity."

The first stage of attainment (果位) in extinguishing birth and death is Arhan. A living being must forsake affection for the material realm if he wishes to be released from the "prison" of the material realm. Affection for the material realm is an important cause and condition for transmigration. The shackle of affection drives living beings into transmigration. The return to the mundane world to save and convert living beings after breaking away from the shackles of affection and the Three Realms (三界) is motivated by the heart of commiseration and the "Heart of Kindness and Pity," not by philanthropy.

The distinction between philanthropy and "kindness and pity" is obvious. Philanthropy is a Mundane Dharma, and kindness and pity is a Supramundane Dharma. One can plainly see that philanthropy does not equal kindness and pity.

In the human world, any heart of love is good. At the high level doctrine, however, differentiating philanthropy from kindness and pity is to remind all practitioners not to forget about the relief from transmigration and extinguishment of birth and death while keeping the practice of love through dedication. The practitioners will then be able to live up to the "Heart of Kindness and Pity" of Buddhas and Bodhisattvas. The "Heart of Kindness and Pity" is the heart to give joy and remove pain.

32. Good Karma with Leakage (有漏善)

The heart of goodness is the foundation of Buddhist practice; without it, there will be no "long but limited wisdom life" (長壽有限的慧命). Forbid badness and practice goodness is the basis for Heaven through metamorphosis (化生). Accumulating virtue by doing good deeds is the sublimation of personality.

Goodness is an indispensable virtue for mankind. Good karma, however, can be further divided into Good Karma with Leakage (有漏善) and Good Karma without Leakage (無漏善) from the point of view of cultivating the way of Nirvana.

Retribution for a person's good karma leads to admittance to Heaven, where a long but limited wisdom life can be enjoyed. It also allows reincarnation into mankind to enjoy great "blessed retribution." Such good karma does not save one from the ocean of pain of transmigration, and it is, therefore, a Good Karma with Leakage. Even though one's life may be as long as eighty-four thousand Kalpas, transmigration still waits at the end of life.

Retribution for good karma by people pursuing Nirvana is admittance to the Nano Realm (納界) and the attainment of the Nano Body (納身). Such good karma is Good Karma without Leakage, with which one may be saved from the ocean of pain and never again be subject to coercive transmigration. One may earn a "long and un-limited wisdom life" that never ends.

Any good karma is good. In the high level of doctrine, the Good Karma with Leakage and the Good Karma without Leakage are separated as a measure to warn Buddhists not to forget the relief from transmigration and extinguishment of births and deaths.

33. Dhyana with Leakage (有漏禪)

Dhyana is a delicate effort, a state. To be more precise, dhyana is a combination of delicate effort and state. Dhya-na is divided into Dhyana of Life, Dhyana of Wisdom, Dhya-na of Life and Wisdom, Dhyana of Tolerance, Dhyana of Pre-cepts, Dhyana of Enlightenment, Dhyana of Rebirth-in-Pure-Land, Dhyana of Wisdom Life, and Dhyana of Non-Rebirth.

[1] Dhyana of Life (命禪)

Dhyana of Life is a practice in pursuit of physical health and long life. The currently popular Qi Gong (氣功), Hard Qi Gong (硬氣功), one-finger Chan (Chan is the Chinese translation of Dhyana), two-finger Chan, Tai-Ji, and a variety of Kung Fu are all examples.

The practice of Dhyana of Life may extend the length of life by enhancing the functionality of meridians, harmony of Qi (氣) and blood, circulation of Qi, elimination of clogs, restoration of damaged tissues, and self-adjustment of physiology.

Dhyana of life is divided into static Chan and active

Chan. Static Chan aims to promote the circulation of true Qi among the internal organs, and active Chan strengthens the tendons, skeleton, and skin. The three elements of static Chan are body adjustment, aspiration adjustment, and heart adjustment. Static Chan concentrates primarily on the Lower Dan-Field (in the lower abdomen; 下丹田) with will power, and heart adjustment is the key.

[2]   Dhyana of Wisdom (慧禪)

Dhyana of Wisdom is a practice whose "primary purpose" is the development of physical potentiality. For example, opening up the Deva eye (開天眼), hypnosis (which is a scientific term that has appeared in the past two hundred years yet has existed throughout human history), psychics, underworld trips, and soul departure.

Practicing Dhyana of Wisdom may increase wisdom, activate paranormal functions, and develop potentiality. It gives insight into physiology, life, and the universe, allowing people to work toward enlightenment and eventually attain the great wisdom and enlightenment. Practicing Dhyana for enlightenment may upgrade a soul's "residence."

Dhyana of Wisdom is divided into Independent Dhyana of Wisdom and Dependent Dhyana of Wisdom. Attaining wisdom with one's own effort is Independent Dhyana of Wisdom, whereas attaining wisdom through external assistance is Dependent Dhyana of Wisdom.

Heating (火侯) is as critical to the practice of Dhyana of Wisdom as it is in culinary technique. Heating is the key element that distinguishes good chefs from the ordinary chefs. It is the same in the practice of Dhyana of Wisdom;

heating is a critical element.

Heating in practice is divided into Mild Heating (文火) and Intense Heating (武火). Most of the modern masters teach only the external form instead of the right heating; some only teach Mild Heating. Many of them do not even know the right heating in practice. If the Spiritual Qi runs into the wrong direction when teaching Intense Heating, a misfire occurs in which case a master must do corrective intervention.

Dhyana of Wisdom primarily concentrates on the Upper Dan-Field (in the head; 上丹田) using will power.

[3]   Dhyana of Life and Wisdom (命慧雙修禪)

Practicing both Dhyana of Life and Dhyana of Wisdom at the same time both guarantees health and long life and develops wisdom. It is Dhyana of Life and Wisdom. When practicing both, will power is used to allow the Spiritual Qi inside the human body to gather, operate, and sublimate. It can, therefore, strengthen our material body, extend life, increase wisdom, purify body and soul, realize potential, perfect body and mind, and achieve the goal of turning confusion into enlightenment.

[4]   Dhyana of Tolerance (忍禪)

Dhyana of Tolerance, also called Dhyana of Pain, is an ascetic practice. Some practitioners leave their families, escape from the turmoil of society, retreat from the turbulent human world, hide in deep mountains or virgin forests, and live a hermit's life to pursue attainment. They have neither ample food nor warm clothing; they ignore everything from the human world. Some make their homes of caves; some reside in remote temples. They "do not respond to mundane matters and concentrate only on practicing the Dhyana of saints and sages."

These practitioners live a life intolerable to the common people to seek attainment. Some others practice "the living dead." It takes three to five years, ten at the most, to gain superhuman functions; seemingly, they are ignorant of mundane issues, yet they do know everything that is going on in the mundane world around them. For example, the practitioners of the "ancient-tome faction" in ancient times dug their own tombs while they were still alive and practiced in the tombs and isolated themselves from the world. Practicing in their own tombs was a constant reminder to them that "life has no certainty but death; why not practice earlier, extinguishing births and deaths forever and ever." They finally succeeded in their practice, passed through the tombs, and attained the status of True Person (真人).

This method of practice differs from that of modern practitioners in temples within bustling cities. In modern temples, there are plenty of supplies. There is also frequent contact with people with ample amenities and inevitable conflicts of interest. It is hard to keep one's mind simple and concentrate on practicing Dhyana of Tolerance. Therefore, fewer and fewer people are able to succeed.

As an adaption to life in modern society, some have brought Dhyana of Tolerance to cities and attempted to reform it, but only a few have succeeded.

[5] Dhyana of Precepts (戒禪)

Dhyana of Precepts relies on stringent precepts to achieve a high level of Samadhi in dhyana. For example, the Esoteric Sect, founded in accordance with the

Surangama-sutra (楞嚴經), requires its disciples to comply with its precepts with no tolerance of violation. No alcoholic beverages, no meat, and no lust are the major precepts.

The stringent precepts allow the practitioners to maintain a peaceful mood, simple thoughts, a calm personality, and a clear mind.

Time is limited for a human life. Time is occupied with school, having meals, and cooking. Time is also spent on sleep and livelihood. Time is also needed for love affairs, taking care of family, children, aging parents, relatives, and friends, attending social occasions, working-out, reading newspapers, browsing the Internet, and watching television shows. In one's life span, there is not really much time left for religious practice.

Dhyana of Precepts removes the addictions and hobbies that compete for time with religious practice, and the practitioners are disciplined to focus on successful attainment.

[6]   Dhyana of Enlightenment (悟禪)

Dhyana of Enlightenment is also called "penetrating thoroughly with meditative insight" (參禪). That means "to attain enlightenment by penetrating thoroughly with meditative insight" (參悟, 參禪悟道).

Dhyana of Enlightenment is "sitting in meditation" while musing on one subject until a clear enlightenment is obtained regarding such a subject. Once a subject has become clear, another subject follows.

Dhyana of Enlightenment may also be referred to as

"penetrating the source of a word before it is uttered" (參話頭). As a training measure, a master asks the disciples a question for which an answer is already in place. If the disciple answers correctly, then the master asks the next question; if not, the disciple will be sent to meditation to figure out another answer, with which the disciple returns to the master. If the answer is wrong again, then the meditation resumes until the correct answer arrives.

[7]   Dhyana of Rebirth-in-Pure-Land (往生禪)

Dhyana of Rebirth-in-Pure-Land, also called Dhyana of Pure Land, is a meditation in which a practitioner constantly chants *"Amitabha"* or *"Namo Amitabha."* One of the primary goals of the practice of Dhyana of Pure Land is to be born, after death, in the World of Utmost Joy. The other one is to suppress the chaotic mind with a single thought that replaces all other thoughts, so that a practitioner may enter into a state beyond emotion or thinking in meditation.

[8]   Dhyana of Wisdom Life (慧命禪)

Dhyana of Wisdom Life is a practice that pursues the extension of wisdom life or the attainment of a long but limited wisdom life i.e., a middle or low Dharma Body. For example, the achievement of a Deva fairy stage of attainment.

Taoist dhyana practice that aims to cultivate the Yang Spirit (陽神) requires the gathering of the five Spiritual Qi (五氣朝元): metal, wood, water, fire, and earth. Each represents west, east, north, south, and center, respectively. The intercourse of Yin and Yang results in nidation (of a holy infant). After ten months of maternity, three years of nursing, nine years of wall-facing, and ten years of further cultivating the Yang Spirit to eventually obtain the External Body (Yang Spirit exiting the material body), a long but limited wisdom life can be obtained.

Buddhism has the same practice as well. After one hundred days of foundation establishment, three years of transition, five years for "little achievement," and ten years for "great achievement," the "Four Stages of Hearer" (聲聞四果) (Enterer-to-Be, Stream-Enterer, Returner, and Non-Returner) and a long but limited wisdom life can be obtained. Then, one, after death, may live in the Realm of Liberation of the Refined Space (精維空間) or be reborn in any Pure Land of Buddhas.

The length of time mentioned above applies to independent study. With the guidance and instruction of a good master, however, the process can be accelerated.

[9] Dhyana of Non-Rebirth (無生禪)

Dhyana of Non-Rebirth focuses on extinguishing births and deaths and attaining Nirvana through the Present Body (即身涅槃). "Non-Rebirth" means there is no more need of birth into the mundane world; it is the evidence that a long and unlimited wisdom life has been attained, and, therefore, one is exempt from mandatory transmigration. One may independently decide, however, on the need for reincarnation in the future.

The practitioner of Dhyana of Non-Rebirth must follow a certain sequence. Correct cognition and view must be obtained, and obsession over material realm must be abandoned. The Twelve Links of Dependent Origination (十二因緣) and the Four Noble Truths (四聖諦) must be understood. The Eight Correct Ways (八正道) must be followed. Finally, a prescribed method of dhyana practice must be observed. Then, one may achieve the "fruit" of being non-reborn.

Dhyana of Non-Rebirth is a combination of "cognition and view" and "dhyana method;" both are required.

The nine dhyana practices are briefly described above. Each has its own features. In conclusion, any dhyana practice that allows its practitioner to attain the wisdom life is "Dhyana without Leakage," whereas all others are "Dhyana with Leakage."

34.   Mundane Dharma (世間法)

The material realm is the mundane world, where transmigration of the living beings takes place. The "long but limited wisdom lives" (middle Dharma Bodies, low Dharma Bodies, and Heaven People) are also included. Any dharma, or doctrine, that cannot relieve the living beings from reincarnation is Mundane Dharma. Only the dharma that allows the living beings to leave this world and stop reincarnating may be called a Supramundane Dharma.

35.   Contextual Priority (依義不依語)

When learning doctrines (dharmas) or reading scriptures, a practitioner should not limit the understanding to the linguistic or vocabulary meanings. Otherwise, the true meaning can be obscured and debates over the verbal explanations may rise. Do not be obsessed with formality, but pursue the inner, authentic, and profound contextual meanings. Let them resonate deep in the heart; seek for the central ideas and true essences. That is the only way for us to dig deep into the scriptures and attain wisdom as vast as the ocean.

If a practitioner can study the doctrines using such a method, then this practitioner is fulfilling the contextual priority.

36. Fundamental Ignorance (Sanskrit: *Mulavidya;* 根本無明)

The pain that one suffers in the present life is caused by karmas committed in previous lives due to ignorance. Therefore, ignorance is the root of all troubles.

Ignorance, in this case, means a status in which the living beings have not yet realized the true meaning of the universe and life. They are in confusion, do not know where to go, see no light, and are blinded with their own obsession and imbecility. They simply do not have the wisdom beyond humanity; they do not know about the existence of Dharma Bodies and the Dharma Realm in the world; they do not even know that people do have souls that exist permanently and may rise or fall according to the karma force. Because of all kinds of fallacies, they are obsessed with a pseudo-self by mistaking the material body as the true self and material realm as the real world. They commit all sorts of "karmic causes" just to satisfy the desires of the pseudo-self.

Because they cannot see through life, the world, and self, they call this obscurity "insight." For example, there is a pond of muddy water, and the bottom cannot be seen. There is no way to tell the depth or the aquatic life, if any, unless someone dives into the pond to find out. Standing and speculating at the edge of the pond leads nowhere. That is a manifestation of ignorance.

It is such ignorance that causes the living beings to reincarnate endlessly in material realm and suffer all kinds of pain.

There are two types of ignorance: "derivative ignorance" and "fundamental ignorance."

[1]   Derivative Ignorance (枝末無明)

Derivative ignorance is also called "symptom ignorance" (標無明) as opposed to fundamental ignorance. For example, a practitioner never breaks the precepts, but the precepts are frequently broken in dreams or when meditating. Nonetheless, such a practitioner still qualifies as having abstained from the derivative ignorance.

Depending on the level of enlightenment and practice, such a practitioner is entitled to the stage of "Virtual-Enlightenment Bodhisattva" or the lower.

[2]   Fundamental Ignorance (根本無明)

Fundamental ignorance is also called "cause ignorance" (本無明) as opposed to derivative ignorance. For example, Buddhist precepts stipulate that monks must refrain from sexual lust, and the other Buddhists must refrain from evil obscenity. Some practitioners may be successful at keeping this precept, but in their dreams or meditation, an extraordinarily beautiful woman comes and takes the initiative to flirt, asking for sexual intercourse. Some practitioners will firmly and harshly expel this woman, and some others will comply with this woman. Those practitioners who have complied with this woman are successful only at abstaining from the derivative ignorance, and those who have declined that woman's temptation are further successful at abstaining from the fundamental ignorance.

As a Bodhisattva, the fundamental ignorance must be abstained from at the level of "marvelous enlightenment" (妙覺) to attain the stage of Buddha (佛果). A Bodhisattva with "marvelous enlightenment," however, has been proven to have great wisdom and enlightenment and is, therefore, able to abstain from the fundamental ignorance at the level of "marvelous enlightenment." At this level, all troubles are taken away, Nirvana without Remainder is attained, and the "supreme correct stage of attainment" (無上正果) is granted.

37. Top Level, Top Class Bodhisattva (上品上生菩薩)

A Dharma Body pursuing attainment is like a material body pursuing an academic degree. For example, a person has earned a doctorate degree and received an international dentist's certificate. With such a certificate, this person may qualify as a dentist in any dental hospital. On the other hand, it is impossible for a person without such a certificate to apply for a position as a dentist and can only practice illegally.

In the mundane world, any Dharma Body that has attained the stage of a Bodhisattva will be allowed to choose any Pure Land of Buddha for a domicile.

The top-level superior Lotus Pond is a domicile exclusively prepared for Dharma Bodies who have attained the stage of Bodhisattva. The Bodhisattvas that live at the top-level, top-class Lotus Pond did not attain their stage in the World of Utmost Joy, rather, they have attained it in the Saha Land.

This top-level, top-class Lotus Pond established in the

World of Utmost Joy is only one small example of domiciles for the countless Bodhisattvas in the countless "Pure Lands of Buddhas."

The Dharma Body of a Bodhisattva can travel and reside freely among all Pure Lands of Buddhas.

38.   Integrate the Stage of Attainment of the Present Life with That of the Previous Life (前世果位合一)

Some people already have wisdom lives before reincarnation (轉世). They just do not know from where they came, where they are going, and why they are here in this world, because they drank the amnesia drink (迷魂湯) beforehand. Take, for example, a Pratyeka-buddha (辟支佛) who lives in the World of Utmost Joy and has an endless life. This Pratyeka-buddha wishes to come to the Saha Land to practice the way of Bodhisattva for the purpose of realizing the stage of Bodhisattva. After life has ended, he has attained the stage of an Arhan instead of a Bodhisattva. In this case, he will ask for another reincarnation while combining the Dharma Body of Arhan to enable him to continue to live in the Dharma Realm as a Pratyeka-buddha. If he has attained the stage of Pratyeka-buddha, then he may integrate the stage of attainment of this life with the stage of attainment of the previous life. If he succeeds in the attainment of Bodhisattva stage, then he may combine the Dharma Body of his previous life with the Dharma Body of the present life. Then, his plan is realized, and his Dharma Body shall be a Bodhisattva henceforth.

39.   The Palace of the King of Ten Thousand Buddhas

The author's master once told the author that the

words of "the Palace of the King of Ten Thousand Buddhas" (萬佛王宮) may change. For example, a Chinese, an Englander, and a Spaniard are reading the words of the Palace of the King of Ten Thousand Buddhas at the same time; the words they see are written in a language comprehensible to each of them. That is "Word Dharani" (語言陀羅尼).

If there is a need for a living being to comprehend, then he will be allowed to comprehend; if there is no need for him to comprehend, then he will not be allowed to comprehend. When a living being is not supposed to comprehend, the text will turn into a language not known to him or become blurry. This is the mystery of "Dharani."

40. The Law of Cause and Effect (因果定律)

The Law of Cause and Effect is a law that will never change and has been determined by the collective body of all Buddhas since beginninglessness. Simply put, a bad or good karma will be justifiably rewarded with bad or good retribution, respectively. The retribution may come late, but it will come eventually. When the time is up, the retribution will be administered. People often say, "Growing gourds leads to the harvest of gourds; growing beans leads to the harvest of beans;" "A good deed begets a good result, and a bad deed begets a bad result;" "Practice correctly, and you will receive a correct result;" and "The result now comes from the cause made in the past, and the cause made now will lead to the result in the future."

Enlightenment begins with farmland preparation. One must appreciate the rhythm of life on a farm. A seed planted in spring will grow into ten thousand grains in fall; raise the children and feed the livestock—breeding is about cause and effect, and education, too. If there is a cause, there will be an effect.

Buddhism has been practiced for thousands of years, but it is never easy to learn the cause and effect properly. Thousands of Buddhism scriptures discuss cause and effect. Buddhism can be complex, but it is quite simple; it is all about cause and effect. It is easy to understand but difficult to fulfill and practice. Cause and effect have been discussed for several thousand years, and it is still being discussed now.

The Law of Cause and Effect is set forth by all Buddhas; anyone with paranormal capacity must not take the liberty of exercising such capacity to alter cause and effect without permission.

41. *The Law of Nature* (《自然法則》)

The Law of Nature has been stipulated by all Buddhas since beginninglessness. For example, the birth, aging, sickness, and death of humans; the birth, growth, maturity, aging, and death of creatures; the formation, existence, decay, and disappearance of the world; the decline and growth in "the law of conservation of matter" (one grows while the other declines, and vice veresa; one disappears while the other forms, and vice versa); birth is death and death is birth; the Sun and the Moon; the spring, summer, autumn, and winter; the interchange between Yin and Yang; existence arises from non-existence and fades into non-existence—confrontation versus mutual-dependent unification; existence is non-existence and non-existence is existence; material is emptiness (change), and emptiness (change) is material; Yin and Yang are non-separable, but they are not as one; there are reciprocity and counter-cancellation among people, issues, and objects; there is coexistence between pros and cons; and so on and so forth.

All these rules may help people with enlightenment. In the meantime, *the Law of Nature* gives living beings a certain path to follow. In short, it is the rules of the game, and it inspires people to attain enlightenment.

The Law of Nature is set forth by all Buddhas; anyone with paranormal capacity must not take the liberty of exercising such capacity to alter natural phenomena without permission.

VOLUME THREE

ANALYSIS OF
MATERIAL REALM

I.

SPIRITUAL QI (靈氣)

Since beginninglessness, the vast universe has a form of basic energy. This energy spreads randomly and chaotically across the multiple spaces. When it exists alone, it is in the form of a small micro-particle that cannot be seen by the physical eyes. It has a high penetration capability and may penetrate spatial obstacles.

Ancient Chinese practitioners call this energy Qingticle (炁), which is the building block of the soul and the food for the soul. Some bodies in Thin Space (細維空間) are also composed of Qingticle. Therefore, Qingticle is also called the Spiritual Qi (靈氣). Some alternative terms include True Qi or Pure Qi.

Spiritual Qi is a material that completely differs from the air that is used for a material body's respiration. It is a critical element for material realm; it is the root of birth, destruction, change, and the variations in all things; it is the foundation of human life. Only people with their Deva eye[42] unlocked or senior practitioners can see the Spiritual Qi.

In terms of physiology, Spiritual Qi inside the human body is called inner Spiritual Qi, and Spiritual Qi outside the human body is called outer Spiritual Qi.

Every person and every material is made of Spiritual Qi; not just us, but our forefathers and ancestors too. In terms of chronological sequence, Spiritual Qi can be further divided into Congenital Spiritual Qi and Acquired Spiritual Qi.

(A) CONGENITAL SPIRITUAL QI (先天靈氣)
Congenital Spiritual Qi has two sources.

1. The Soul That Has Existed Since Beginninglessness
It is "a bit of Spiritual Qi" (forming the soul) (一點靈氣). It is also called the Primal Spiritual Qi (原靈氣).

2. Parents
The inner Spiritual Qi inside the bodies of the father and mother are condensed separately and then liquefied. The results are the sperm and ovum (an even mixture of liquid and Qingticle (炁)). The sperm and the ovum engage and fertilize to form a liquid cell. With constant nourishment from the mother, this liquid cell begins to solidify into a skeleton. At this stage, the fetus and the mother are still one entity.

(B) ACQUIRED SPIRITUAL QI (後天靈氣)
After the fetus has matured inside the mother's body, it breaks away from the mother and becomes an independent life form.

After parturition, the sensory organs of the infant begin to make contact with the outside world, and the infant begins to develop consciousness, movement, ideas, emotion, and so on. The infant learns to adapt to and mingle with family and society. It is the time when the bit of "Spiritual Qi" mentioned above becomes acquired.

The acquired Spiritual Qi comes from two sources.

1. Daily Diet
When the fetus is still inside the womb, it is still a part of the mother, and all of its Spiritual Qi is provided by the mother. After birth, the infant becomes independent and satisfies the needs of its own material body.

A material body is a complete "Qingticle-ized" (炁化) system ("Qingticle" is another term of Spiritual Qi) that has five Zang-viscera (五臟), six Fu-viscera (六腑), twelve regular meridians (十二經絡), eight special meridians (奇經八脈), five facial organs and nine apertures (五官九竅), and extremities and bones. This system constantly works with the Spiritual Qi in routine and rhythmic "material movement and change."

People need food; food is crucial for a body to maintain health. Reasonable adjustment of diet may keep sufficient Spiritual Qi, reduce accumulation of waste inside the body, and enhance vitality. This is also one key element in the practice of Dhyana of Life (命禪).

After a practitioner's material body nature has changed to Spiritual Qi (the material body has been "Spiritual Qi-ized"), he or she no longer needs human food, a phenomenon called Bi Gu (辟穀). Bi Gu means the food source is not the common diet, especially grains. A practitioner who has acquired the function of Bi Gu does not consume food through the digestive tract, but absorbs Spiritual Qi with the entire body. Spiritual Qi is a form of energy that works much better than grains. Bi Gu, however, cannot be forced, or it will cause sickness. Therefore, a practitioner should not try Bi Gu recklessly. If a practitioner feels better without eating and drinking, then it is real Bi Gu.

Daily diet is a specialized knowledge as well. Good knowledge in daily diet helps to gather Spiritual Qi, enhance health, and prolong life. Poor knowledge in daily diet will deplete Spiritual Qi and harm physical health. Daily diet includes eating and drinking.

2. Outer Spiritual Qi (外靈氣)

Spiritual Qi is the fundamental energy that forms the sky, the Earth, people, and all things. "Tao generates one; one generates two, two generates three, and three generates all things. All things are comprised of Yin and Yang." The "Tao" is the Spiritual Qi, which is the fundamental material and cosmic energy. The borderless and edgeless universe is full of such energy, which is constantly in motion. From the aspect of time, it has no beginning or end. From the aspect of space, it has no border or edge. It has no top or bottom and no outside or inside. It is countless, but it can be gathered inside the human belly.

Spiritual Qi in space is eternal. It has no birth or destruction; it is not dirty or clean; and it does not increase or decrease. It constantly changes its composition and returns to its original state.

The Spiritual Qi is a cosmic energy that never extinguishes and spreads all over the universe. People may gather it inside their bodies and make use of it by following a certain practice.

The meridians and collaterals inside the material body are channels for Spiritual Qi. The "acupoints" (穴位) on the material body are the gates of the Spiritual Qi. The Spiritual Qi operates inside the material body in a certain pattern. Using certain methods, Spiritual Qi can enter the material body through different acupoints and circulate along the meridians and collaterals in a regular and rhythmic way, which will: enhance the inner force of the material body; dredge the meridians and collaterals; harmonize Qi and blood; replenish "primordial Qi" (元氣); drain away pathogenic Qi; heal disease; promote health; improve muscles, organs, the circulatory system and nervous system, etc. of the material body; increase immunity; excite and suppress muscles in a harmonized and orderly fashion; and trigger and activate the potential functions of the material body.

Ancient Chinese medical theories have already pointed out that the Spiritual Qi is critical to the human body. If it operates smoothly, then there will be no pain. Conversely, if there is pain, then the Spiritual Qi is not operating smoothly. "Smoothly" means the smoothness of meridians and collaterals. The meridians and collaterals have to function smoothly to allow the Spiritual Qi to reach all parts of the human body without resistance. Then, the skin will be moisturized. If Qi is flowing smoothly, the blood will run smoothly, whereas if the blood circulation is clogged, there will be sickness. The term Qi means the Qingticle (炁) or the Spiritual Qi. If the meridians and collaterals are smooth, then the Spiritual Qi may circulate smoothly, allowing the blood to circulate smoothly. On the other hand, if the meridians and collaterals are not smooth, then the Spiritual Qi may not circulate smoothly, causing blood circulation to clog and sickness to attract.

Most of the outer Spiritual Qi is dispersed without order. It can be changed into orderly Spiritual Qi, however, in order to serve human needs.

Here is an example of "order." A construction company is to erect a building on an empty lot according to a blueprint. Workers and materials are scattered in different places (no order). Thereafter, the workers are recruited and given prearranged tasks. Materials from different places are shipped to the construction site according to the sequence of their use. Both workers and materials are put into order. Soon the building is completed. This is the process from no order to order.

Dirt is no order, but a brick built with dirt is order.

There are ten thousand people hanging out on the street on Sunday. These people are not in order. Now, they have learned that there will be an exciting ball game in the nearby stadium. Three thousand of them have decided to go to the game. They go to the stadium, line up to purchase tickets, enter the stadium, find their seats, and sit down. These three thousand people have transformed from a state of no order to a state of order.

The practice of outer Spiritual Qi requires a certain method to turn the Spiritual Qi with no order into the Spiritual Qi with order. Then, it will be condensed and changed to raise our level of energy class. The practice in this life will raise the energy class to a new stage.

The Outer Spiritual Qi that the material body absorbs comes from three sources:

(a) Self-Power (自力)

This is a practice by which a certain method is learned to gather the dispersed, chaotic Outer Spiritual Qi into the material body completely independently. The core courses may be the Dhyana of Tolerance and the Dhyana of Precepts, which can be practiced separately or concurrently. After intensive practice over a long period of time, the practitioner may increase the level of energy class.

(b) Other-Power (他力)

"Other-powers" can be classified into two types:

- In the mundane world, a person of low energy may follow a master who has a high-energy class. This high-energy master somehow injects Inner Spiritual Qi into the body of the disciple. There is a phrase: "Water always flows to the low ground." If this disciple is already a high-energy class but has chosen a low-energy class celebrity master due to a lack of wisdom, the disciple's energy will inadvertently flow against the master when the master tries to inject the energy. "Birds of a feather flock together." Practitioners of low-energy class hanging around other practitioners of high-energy class will naturally raise their own energy class. One practitioner of the Spiritual Qi will benefit the entire family.

- In the multiple spaces, there are countless highly intelligent living beings with high-energy class. These living beings exist in the space in all kinds of forms and are in motion and changing constantly. For example, we human beings depend on oxygen for life, but the "human beings" on other planets do not necessarily depend on oxygen. If they come to Earth, they have to carry gas cylinders to support their lives. Similarly, if we are going to other planets, we must carry oxygen cylinders to support our lives. The color of the sky on the Earth is blue, and the colors of the skies of other planets may vary. There are other "human beings" who depend on breathing the Spiritual Qi to live. Therefore, this type of human beings is not constrained by time and space and enjoys a lifestyle apparently more leisurely and carefree. Some other "human beings" exist in the form of light, wave, Qingticle, magnetic field, or electric field. The worlds they inhabit and the materials they use also exist in the form of light, wave, Qingticle, magnetic field, or electric field. These spaces are only visible to successful practitioners. Those phenomena regarded as mysterious by common people are actually the life materials in the multiple spaces.

There are countless lives living in the multiple spaces who possess high energy. If we somehow have developed connections with some high-energy beings during our past or present life, then it is very likely that these high-energy beings will inject Outer Spiritual Qi into our material bodies.

(c) Meritorious Virtue (功德)

As we have learned, karmas are committed throughout one's lifetime, and there are good karmas, bad karmas, and unrecordable karmas. Good karma can be "with Leakage" or "without Leakage." Committing Good Karma with Leakage is like farming a "field of blessedness" (福田), which will be rewarded in the future life (lives) by being a person full of blessedness or becoming a Heaven Person. If the present life is the spring, then the future lives will be the fall. "If you plant a seed in the spring, you will enjoy a good harvest in the fall." Talking about farming, one must (1) examine the land quality, (2) take care of the field diligently (you cannot simply plant the seeds and ignore them unless you have someone else to do it for you), and (3) be aware of natural and manmade disasters that may destroy your farm. There is a phrase: "Keep farming and you will have your harvest sooner or later." If you commit diligent labor without asking for harvest, your efforts will repay you with a great harvest eventually.

The above description, however, is about "blessed virtue" (福德) as opposed to "meritorious virtue" (功德). Then, what is meritorious virtue? This is a frequently asked question. Meritorious virtue concerns the Supramundane Dharma, and blessed virtue concerns Mundane Dharma.

Blessed virtue is Good Karma with Leakage, and meritorious virtue is Good Karma without Leakage.

Blessed virtue will be rewarded in future lives, and meritorious virtue will be rewarded in the present life.

A Great Bodhisattva on a mission to save and convert living beings in the mundane world must possess the ability to "convert karma,"[43] converting a living being's blessed virtue into meritorious virtue. The "karma conversion" (化業) first requires knowledge of the methods and procedures for inquiring, changing, and balancing this living being's deserved retribution brought by the karma force. (Such Bodhisattva must present the "pardon order" (特赦令) issued by the Kingdom of United Nebulae in order to make direct inquiry with the concerned agencies for the information of the karma force and submit the change result to the concerned authorities for approval and documentation.) Secondly, the living being has to have the blessed virtue at an amount sufficient enough to be worth the trouble of the karma conversion procedure.

A practitioner who begins to cultivate for the Spiritual Qi from childhood and continues until the end of life, excluding the time spent on daily trivial things, can only have a maximum of a few decades of "attainments" (道行). The "attainments" that have been through the process of karma conversion, however, may become as high as thousands of years, tens of thousands of years, or even hundreds of thousands of years.

The meritorious virtue will be rewarded in the present life because (the following are all prerequisites to the attainment of Nirvana and a long and unlimited wisdom life): (1) The meritorious virtue can be directly converted into Spiritual Qi and injected into the body of a practitioner as Inner Spiritual Qi (With sufficient Inner Spiritual Qi, a practitioner may further cultivate the Five-Qi Concentration [五氣朝元] to achieve a Holy Fetus [聖胎] that will develop as the "present-life Dharma Body" [今世法身], which will then become an External Body [身外身] of the practitioner); (2) If the Inner Spiritual Qi is injected directly into the External Body of a practitioner, such External Body may instantly heighten his energy class (If the practitioner has significant meritorious virtue, then such practitioner may instantly upgrade the level of External Body or even the stage of attainment); and (3) Those who do not have the "present-life Dharma Body" may have the Spiritual Qi injected into the "previous-life Dharma Body." If the previous-life Dharma Body was a long but limited wisdom life, then either the length of life can be extended or the stage of attainment can be upgraded. In the case of a long and unlimited wisdom life, then either the energy class can be heightened or the stage of attainment can be upgraded. (The soul will make a decision to choose from the three options above.)

Accumulating meritorious virtue is, as the above suggests, exceptionally important for those who cultivate Spiritual Qi, supernatural power, and Dharma Body for the attainment of Nirvana. All practices must be set on the ground of meritorious virtue; the higher it is, the higher the supernatural power and the stage of attainment will be.

In the World of Endurance with Five Impurities, a master with high supernatural power is difficult to find. As long as the practitioner's meritorious virtue is high enough, however, such master's Dharma Body will find him anytime.

Meritorious virtue accumulated through Good Karma without Leakage gives living beings an advantage to come closer to the way of Nirvana and achieve Nano Body rapidly, as well as achieve Nirvana through the Present Body in some cases. Meritorious virtue may stop the leakage of the sailing boat and allow the arrival at the coast of wisdom and ultimate joy, attaining eternal and true "ease and happiness." Therefore, it is Good Karma without Leakage.

(C) CHANGES OF SPIRITUAL QI

There are changes of Spiritual Qi. In terms of state, it can be gaseous state, liquid state, and solid state. In terms of property, it has physical changes and chemical changes.

1. Physical Changes

All things in the world exist in one of the three states; there are three states in chemical changes and three states in physical changes.

Tearing one piece of paper is a physical change. It changes from large to small, entirety to parts. But, it is still paper, and there is no change in chemical properties.

Water, in the liquid state, becomes vapor (gaseous state) after being heated and becomes ice (solid state) after being frozen.

Similar to water, natural gas also exists in one of the three states. It is one of the primary sources of energy in the twenty-first century; it is cooled to minus 162° Celsius to allow liquefaction for easier storage and transport. Liquefied natural gas has a volume at 1/165 of its gaseous state.

The same applies to Spiritual Qi. It also exists in one of the three states and shares the same physical properties of other material. Spiritual Qi exists in gaseous state and drifts randomly in the world. It can be gathered into the human body as Inner Spiritual Qi through particular methods. Inner Spiritual Qi circulates constantly inside the human body along the meridians and collaterals in a gaseous state.

Practitioners with high energy have Dan (丹) at Dan-Field (丹田). As implied by the name, "Field" is the place that grows all things, and "Dan-Field" is the place that grows "Dan."

Dan is an energy mass and is the highly condensed product of the combination of Inner Spiritual Qi and Outer Spiritual Qi. Taoists call it Dan, Confucians call it Ren-Yi (仁義; benevolence and justice), and Buddhists call it Sarira

(舍利子).[44] Spiritual Qi in high density produces Dan in a gaseous state, which can become liquid with further condensation. Upon exiting the human body, it loses the pressure exerted by the Dan-Field and meridians and collaterals, and it becomes gaseous again and disseminates in the atmosphere. It is like a transparent cigarette lighter; you can see the liquid content inside, but the content becomes gaseous when it is released from the lighter into the air. A material's liquid state is the result of its condensation from a gaseous state. Once it loses the ambient pressure, it returns to a gaseous state.

Humans can cultivate Spiritual Qi, so can many animals. They cultivate their Dan every night during the Zi period (11 p.m. to 1 a.m.) by capturing the Spiritual Qi scattered in the atmosphere (天地之靈氣) and the "essence" of the Sun and the Moon (日月之精華). When they cultivate Spiritual Qi, they adopt the "respiration technique" (吐納法) in most cases. Many animals become fairies through tough practice and cultivation and later on become human beings through reincarnations.

The physical property of Spiritual Qi is: solidifying through condensation and gasifying through diffusion.

2.   Chemical Changes

Chemical change is about change in the material's property.

If a piece of paper is burned, it becomes smoke and ash. The burning changes the material's structure, causing the property of this piece of paper to change. This is chemical change.

Products of chemical changes can be seen everywhere in the technologically advanced twenty-first century. Petroleum (liquid state) or natural gas (gaseous state) can be turned into solid material through chemical processing to produce products for all kinds of applications, such as synthetic fiber, synthetic rubber, plastic, chemical fertilizer, dynamite, cosmetic products, and synthetic detergent.

Dan can be formed at many locations of the human body if it is highly condensed. Of course, after a practitioner dies and his or her material body is cremated through a certain method, there will be chemically changed Dan (Sarira) in the remaining ash. Such chemical change takes place through burning at an extremely high temperature. The chemically changed Dans are crystal clear; some are bright with many colors and very beautiful.

The Sarira obtained through cremation is the legacy of a practitioner. It is not a precious commodity, and it does not have to come from an enlightened practitioner. Any person who practices Spiritual Qi may leave Sarira in his or her ash after cremation through a certain method; the only differences are in size and color. Other things left behind, such as bones, cannot be regarded as Sarira.

Chemically changed Sarira cannot disseminate into the atmosphere in a gaseous state like physically changed Sarira.

The chemical property of Spiritual Qi is that it can become a material of the Coarse Space if burned with a high heat.

II.

SPIRITUAL LIGHT (靈光)

Spiritual Light is a form of high-grade energy produced through the change or sublimation of Spiritual Qi. Compared with Spiritual Qi, Spiritual Light is more refined, vibrant, and full of variations and energy.

"Nano Space" is a space of Spiritual Light. "Nano Bodies" consist of Spiritual Light, and the Pure Lands of Buddhas are created with Spiritual Light as well. The World of Utmost Joy in the West created by Amitabha Buddha, the World of Lazurite in the East created by Medicine Buddha, and the Kingdom of United Nebulae are all created with Spiritual Light.

The halo around the head of a high Dharma Body is actually spherical Spiritual Light and is an extension of the Upper Dan-Field Spiritual Light. Looking at it from any angle, it is spherical. Spiritual Light is an indication of a stage of attainment, which can be concealed or exposed according to circumstances.

Because Spiritual Light results from a change in or sublimation of Spiritual Qi, its quantity is much lower than Spiritual Qi, which can be found virtually everywhere. Spiritual

Qi is like the dirt on the Earth; it is there when material realm is created. Spiritual Light, however, is like a rare element extracted from dirt. Spiritual Light results from a change in or sublimation of Spiritual Qi and is not a natural material. It is a form of high-grade energy available only to sentient beings dedicated to practice and cultivation.

Deity Light and Buddha Light are all highly condensed Spiritual Light, each of which has different functions.

In the world of Spiritual Light, all humans and materials are created with Spiritual Light. Because Nano Space consists of Spiritual Light, Spiritual Light is also referred to as Nano Light.

Spiritual Light also has physical changes and chemical changes. These changes are controlled by Dharma Bodies and are beyond the control of material bodies.

Spiritual Light penetrates spatial obstacles better than Spiritual Qi. Under certain conditions, Spiritual Light may be transformed into Coarse Space material.

In religious cultivation, normal people only know body building (including sports and all kinds of Dhyana of Life). When they reach a higher level, they begin to learn and practice the absorption of Spiritual Qi. Toward yet another, higher level, they begin to search, learn, and study the theory of External Body and even put it into practice. Toward yet another, higher level, they begin to cultivate External Body and cultivate Spiritual Light with External Body. Toward yet another, higher level, they begin to cultivate Spiritual Light with their material body and External

Body concurrently for the purpose of Nirvana.

The cultivation of Spiritual Light involves the level of Dharma Body. In the beginning, the Dharma Body of the present life is produced with "Five-Qi Concentration"[45] (五氣朝元) ("Nidation" [坐胎] at the Middle Dan-Field). After leaving the "womb," it transfers to the Lower Dan-Field for cultivation. After the cultivation at the Lower Dan-Field is completed, it transfers again to the Upper Dan-Field for cultivation. After the cultivation at the Upper Dan-Field, the Dharma Body will exit from the Bai-Hui Acupoint (百會穴) at the top of the head, becoming a pure body (External Body). The color of the Spiritual Light of the Dharma Body determines the energy level of this Dharma Body. The cultivation at this stage is far from completion; it will take a long journey of cultivation to achieve Nirvana.

The Dharma Body collects Spiritual Light in high density and administers Samadhi True-Flame[46] to the highly condensed Spiritual Qi. Different temperatures and compounds with other materials produce different Coarse Space materials.

A high Dharma Body may produce inward spinning and outward spinning of Spiritual Qi and Spiritual Light. Inward spinning is a centripetal whirlpool and outward spinning is a centrifugal whirlpool.

The inward spinning formed by both Spiritual Qi and Spiritual Light is very powerful. Because it cannot be seen by a material body, it is called a "dark particle stream." It is an invisible force. A large whirlpool can produce tremendous amounts of gravity, enabling it to absorb one entire

Solar System easily. When the matter absorbed by this dark stream accumulate to a certain volume, the "dark matter" will transform into "light matter" and begin to "release"--

III.

ANALYSIS OF MATERIAL REALM

The material realm is itself a complete Little World where there are a Sun, a Moon, and the Earth on which human beings and animals may live and breed; there are also "multiple spaces" for Heaven, Hell, etc. Following the development and use of these spaces, there must be thorough administrative systems that include executive organizations, legislative organizations, and judiciary organizations. In general, from souls to material bodies, from ghosts to Heaven People, from low Dharma Bodies to high Dharma Bodies, and from animals to "Deva devils" alike, there must be "rules" to follow and "organizations" proceeding under hierarchical management. That is how a Little World functions normally and provides a true "grand examination site" for the living beings.

As a practitioner, one needs to understand how this "grand examination site" operates in order to enrich one's "cognition and view."

The structure and operation of this "grand examination site" is analyzed in three aspects: Yin-Yang Space, Yin Space, and Yang Space.

(A)   YIN-YANG SPACE (陰陽間)

People have believed since ancient times that the world in which human beings live is the Yang Space and have frequently referred to it with this term. In fact, it is an inaccurate idea. The Earth upon which our lives depend is a world of half Yin and half Yang, and people and animals are also creatures of half Yin and half Yang. For example: sleeping is Yin and waking is Yang; inside is Yin and outside is Yang; female is Yin and male is Yang; moon is Yin and sun is Yang; and night is Yin and day is Yang.

The Earth rotates and its criterion of Yang is the Sun. Yin pulls in when the Sun goes down, and Yang comes when the Sun rises. When dark clouds block the Sun, it is Yin; when the clouds subside, it is Yang. In short, being not exposed to the Sun is Yin, and being exposed to the Sun is Yang; the side beyond the reach of sunlight is Yin, and the side under sunlight is Yang.

Seemingly, the connotation of Yin and Yang is merely the phenomenon of sunlight movement. After exploring the multiple spaces in depth, however, one will find that the connotations of Yin and Yang are actually abundant.

In the movement mentioned above, there is Yin within Yang and Yang within Yin. When Yin prospers, the Yang recedes, and vice versa. Yin, in its extreme, yields to Yang, and vice versa. Things will develop in the opposite direction when they become extreme; reciprocal transformations do exist, and a result serves as the cause of the result.

Our material bodies live on the Earth. From the viewpoint of the material body, this form of Yin-Yang transformation makes human beings live among Yin and Yang. That's why we call the space we live in the "Yin-Yang Space."

The living beings living in the Yin-Yang Space include human beings, animals, and low Dharma Bodies.

1.   Human Category (人道)

There are countless Little Worlds where human beings exist, and these worlds are at different levels. Our world is in the middle level. Most of the people who are planning to pursue religious cultivation choose the world of middle level for reincarnation because a world of middle level allows people to attain enlightenment easier and is ideal for human beings to cultivate religious practice.

The human category on Earth is a middle category, which is a category of half-pain and half-happiness. The statistics for living beings who have attained enlightenment in different worlds suggest that the majority attained enlightenment in the middle level worlds, and most of the "Marvelous-Enlightenment Bodhisattvas" have attained their Buddhahood in the middle level world.

Enlightenment, religious cultivation, and doctrine propagation are all closely related to the general environments and the life realms where living beings exist. An extremely painful realm, such as Hell, is not suitable for religious cultivation. An extremely foolish realm, such as low-class animals, has no knowledge of religious cultivation. An extremely joyful realm, such as Heaven People, gives no motivation for religious cultivation.

In our Saha Land, for example, it is easy for any person who has normal intelligence, does not pursue extreme joy, and does not suffer extreme pain to achieve enlighten-ment provided the conditions are mature enough.

The human category is a realm in the Coarse Space, a realm where sinners and saints mingle together, a realm where everybody wears a mask, a realm of dramas, a realm where "causal stages" (因地) and "resultant stages" (果地) co-exist, a realm where all kinds of "effected ret-ributions" (果報) co-exist, a realm where contamination and decontamination co-exist, a realm where the soul sublimation and degeneration take place, and a realm that happiness and sadness, joy and sorrow, rejoicing and anger, affection, hatred, adoration, resentment, and all other emotions are tangled together.

The human category is a giant platform where every-one writes his or her own script and performs his or her own role. "Being poor, rich, prestigious, or despicable" or "having a painful, happy, or long life or a premature death" is already in the script written in one's previous lives. In the meantime, everyone is also writing his or her own scripts and the roles to play in the future lives. Therefore, everyone is a script writer and a great actor; everyone is solely responsible for writing the development of the plots of his or her future lives and determining the roles to play in the dramas.

2.   Animal Category (旁生道)

The animal category is a giant organism. Saha Land is a religious cultivation realm created for human beings who are the primary subjects to be saved and converted. Therefore, the living creatures living "next to" human beings are called "next lives" (旁生) or, in this case, the animal category.

The levels of the animal category in the Yin-Yang Space are great in number and can be a complex system. The animals breed in three categories of moisture-birth, oviparity, and viviparity.

The animal category also has its own rules of practice and cultivation. It has to follow the hierarchy of souls and work upward in a progressive, step-by-step manner. An animal must accumulate "attainments" (道行) of at least five hundred years before it may apply for reincarnation as a human being to the competent authority. After receiving such an application, the competent authority will dispatch an inspector to review, and then a decision will be made. The disqualified will be rejected, and the qualified will be issued with a certificate of candidacy, waiting in queue for the quota.

Of the forms of breeding, the level of moisture-birth is the lowest, followed by oviparity. Viviparity is the highest.

In terms of the level of soul evolution, (1) moisture-birth comes first; (2) moisture-birth is followed by oviparity (which comes in high and low levels as well, depending on the length of life; some with long lives may end up with low Dharma Bodies); and (3) oviparity is followed by viviparity (in which animals come in high and low levels as well; the higher the level, the better the animals understand humanity).

An animal must earn its mammal level before reincarnation as a human being may be allowed. To change from a furry, horned animal to a human being, an animal must evolve from multiple pregnancies annually to a single pregnancy annually, from multiple fetuses per pregnancy to a single fetus per pregnancy, from multiple nipples to two nipples, from short pregnancy to long pregnancy (except those animals for which pregnancy lengths are longer than human beings, such as dolphins and whales), from small animals to larger animals, from legless to multiple-legged or two-legged animals, from multiple-legged or two legged to four-legged (four-limbed) animals, from animals living in deep mountain or virgin forest who have no contact with human beings to domesticated animals, from cave dwelling animals to ground-lair animals, and so on. These processes are a part of the training that readies these animals to become human beings. Without the training, they may not survive in this World of Endurance with Five Impurities because they would not be able to compete with those who have been human beings longer.

Animals have to transmigrate constantly in this manner. Some animals that have already progressed to higher-level animals may be downgraded to lower-level animals in the next reincarnation, circulating up and down many times. Anyway, no matter what level of animals they may become through reincarnations, they have to complete the bottom-up procedure. It is not a problem if an animal is reversed back down after one complete procedure. Whatever the level at the end, an animal with five hundred years of "attainments" may apply for reincarnation as a human being to the competent authority.

Why is a complete bottom-up procedure mandatory? It is a process of accumulating "attainments" and is a predetermined procedure for the animal category. Nevertheless, it does not mean an animal that reincarnates to become a human being must be an animal of high level. For example, animal A has progressed to a high-level animal but does not qualify as a human being at its end of life. It moves on to another reincarnation. In this life, it becomes a low-level animal B and has accumulated five hundred years of "attainments." Therefore, it files an application to become a human being. The application is approved, and it subsequently obtains the quota. The human being it has become will have an appearance more related to its previous animal-life. In each reincarnation as a human being, such a person's appearance will become more and more perfect. In short, a living being will go through the animal appearance, fairy appearance, deity appearance, Arhan appearance, Bodhisattva appearance, and, eventually, the Buddha appearance.

In conclusion, how good or bad a person's appearance looks is determined by the cultivation and evolution through countless Kalpas.

3.   Low Dharma Body Category (低法身道)
Most of the low Dharma Bodies come from the animal category. Most of them live in deep mountains, virgin forests, caves, seas, and oceans.

Low Dharma Bodies have many levels. Due to *the Law of Deva*, they must adopt an "invisibility technique" (隱身術) and be invisible to mundane people.

Some low Dharma Bodies work as institutional agents in the Thin Space and are very busy every day. Some do not have work to do and are free and at leisure in the human world. Some of those without work want to save and convert people; they often look for human subjects to possess so they can "open mouth" to talk. This, however, must be approved in advance by the competent authority to avoid violating *the Law of Deva*.

Most of the low Dharma Bodies living in the Yin-Yang Space are at leisure and seeking to convert people. Some of them need to use "body possession" to fulfill their missions of producing "appearance dharma" to convert living beings. Through the phenomenon of "body possession," living beings will believe in the existence of souls, deities, supernatural powers, transmigrations, and so on. People will then spread the news through word of mouth and inspire higher and deeper levels of thinking, eventually resulting in deeper enlightenment.

(B)   YIN SPACE (陰間)

Yin Space is a world created within the Thin Space where all objects and lives, such as buildings, foods, and "ghost bodies," consist of Spiritual Qi or its variations.

Yin Space is pretty much like a cloudy day in Yin-Yang Space, hazy and dim. Everything, however, is still visible. Because it never changes, there will never be a sunny day or sunshine. That's why it's called Yin Space.

Yin Space is as complex as Yin-Yang Space. There are many countries but not as many as in Yin-Yang Space. Actually, the so-called countries are living areas divided according to different religions, ethnic groups, and cultures (e.g., the Chinese Area and the Caucasian Area).

Each area has its unique culture and life style; two areas are not allowed to develop a relationship. Entering into a different area can only be done in three situations:

1. Relying on karma force
2. Applying for immigration
3. Relying on dharma powers (supernatural powers; including "other-power" and "self-power")

There is no other method than the above.

Each area has its own executive institute, legislative institute, and judiciary institute. If a person immigrates from a Caucasian Area to a Chinese Area, all his or her files in the Caucasian Area must be transferred to the Chinese Area along with this person.

Any life inhabiting Yin Space, regardless of the category, has the "supernatural power of reading minds" (他心通), which is a normal body function.

The analysis of material realm by the Buddha-to-Be Religion focuses on the Chinese Area in this material realm. Other areas are quite different from the Chinese Area. Since the Chinese Area is more complex, the reader can learn other areas through analogy. It is more than enough for a practitioner to understand the situation in the Chinese Area thoroughly. The desire to know more is merely curiosity.

The executive, judiciary, economic, cultural, and educational centers in the Chinese Area are located in Feng-Du City, and this "country" is ruled by the Yin Space Central Authority. The life of "ghost citizens" is peaceful and stable; everything operates in an orderly fashion under the thorough justice system.

There are large and medium buildings of government agencies at the center of the city. These buildings are solemn and glamorous. Around the central city are many satellite cities inhabited by "ghost citizens" and Dharma Bodies separately.

A large residential area is designated to the souls and Dharma Bodies of the human beings living in Yin-Yang Space; it is called the "Destiny Village" (本命莊園) in which "Destiny Houses" (本命住宅) are scattered. These residences are located in nine different villages according to people's levels in Yin-Yang Space.

These nine villages are:

1. Saint Village
2. Noble Village
3. Wisdom Village
4. Rich Village
5. Superior-Class Village
6. Candidate Village
7. Middle-Class Village
8. Low-Class Village
9. Despicable People Village

The Saint Village is the best, followed by the Noble Village, then the Wisdom Village, and so on. The Despicable People Village is the worst. Even though the Saint Village is the best, it too has classes with different "blessed retributions" (福報). The same applies to other villages.

The author has a disciple named Yong-zhong Liou. When he first followed the author for religious cultivation, he lived in the Superior-Class Village. After a few years of cultivation, his Destiny House was relocated to the "Noble

Village." After a few more years of cultivation, he was moved again to the "Saint Village."

Qiang Lu (alias) used to live in the Noble Village. He had inherited millions of U.S. dollars from his parents in Yin-Yang Space. He did not, however, cherish his "blessed retribution" and cultivate his own "field of blessedness" to cause his "dharma wealth" (法財) to grow. Instead, he insatiably spent his wealth and committed countless bad karmas, and eventually his Destiny House was moved from the Noble Village to the Despicable People Village. Qiang Lu's life style in the human world led him to bankruptcy and imprisonment for drug dealing.

Everyone's Destiny House has a "wealth vault" (財庫) where a certain amount of money is deposited. People will earn money as "blessed retributions" in Yin-Yang Space, but the money in the wealth vault will be reduced accordingly. When the deposit in the wealth vault decreases to a certain level, the Destiny House will be ordered by the administrative institute to relocate to the next-level village. The wealth vault is directly linked with the Central Bank of Yin Space, which directly links to the administrative institute. Therefore, the administrative institute may review wealth information at any time. If people spend a small portion of their wealth in Yin-Yang Space in cultivating their respective "Fields of Blessedness" (福田), convert this small portion of wealth into "meritorious virtue" (功德), or use the amount of money originally for luxurious items on accumulating "blessed virtue" (福德), (regardless of whether the accumulated virtue is blessed or meritorious) the wealth in their respective wealth vaults will increase accordingly. When the deposit in the wealth vault has increased to a certain level, the

Destiny House will be upgraded to a higher-level village.

A Destiny House is a place for the soul and Dharma Body to rest. In a situation where the "original soul" and "Yang soul" cannot leave one's body, only the "Yin soul" or Dharma Body may visit the House frequently. The "appearance" of a Destiny House represents the general situation of a person's life. It tells whether one's life is good or bad. If the general condition of a Destiny House is good, then the person's general condition is good. If the general condition of a Destiny House is bad, then the person's general condition is bad.

People must go through Time-Space Tunnels (時空隧道) to arrive at the Destiny Village. The tunnels are classified into past time-space, current time-space, and future time-space. Different tunnels lead to different scenery of buildings and daily commodities. Therefore, one should choose a Time-Space Tunnel wisely.

The residents in the Saint Village live an extremely comfortable life. The courtyard is big; some are as luxurious as a palace and are decorated with plenty of trees, flowers, small bridges, and ponds. Goods and materials are bountiful; there is plenty of food, and the population is thriving. They often give away food to the poor. Those who are religious have their private chapel or church in their own residence.

The Destiny Houses in the Despicable People Village are very small; the largest has only three rooms, and the smaller one has only one room. Some residents there do not even have a house and are forced to live on the streets. No luxury goods can be seen in the Despicable

People Village.

The level of virtue (德行) cannot be seen in Yin-Yang Space. But, in the Destiny Village, it is easy to differentiate who has great virtue and who lacks virtue because the residence levels are determined according to the amount of virtue. High virtue may receive a house upgrade, whereas low virtue will be subject to a downgrade. This will also directly affect the person living in Yin-Yang Space accordingly.

There is a big forest in the Destiny Village called Destiny Forest (本命樹園) where every tree represents a man, and it is the Destiny Tree (本命樹) of that man. Destiny Trees can be many species; some are not even recorded yet. The number of trees here is innumerable, but none of them are identical to another. They may come from the same species, but their heights, diameters, and conditions are never identical. Some people have their respective Destiny Trees planted in their own courtyards of their Destiny Houses.

The growth condition of the tree reflects the general condition of a person's life. Some trees lack fertilizer and irrigation; the twigs are fragile and leaves browned. Some are over-fertilized, causing broken bark and attracting worms. Some are bent, collapsing, with roots exposed. Some have cracks throughout the trunk. These signs suggest the owners have health problems.

The tall and flourishing trees reflect great men. Trees with large trunks represent social nuclei and celebrities. Ordinary trees represent ordinary people. The rotten, bored, and decayed trees represent the rascals, hooligans, and scum of society.

If the tree withers and dies, then the man in Yin-Yang Space must be dead, too. If the Destiny Tree's trunk is broken in the middle, then the man will have an unexpected calamity.

There is a giant garden in the Destiny Village called Destiny Garden (本命花園). Its flowers represent women. In other words, these are women's Destiny Flowers (本命花). Some women have only one flower, while some others have plenty. Destiny Flowers are of so many species that many of them do not even have names.

The Destiny Garden is extremely large. It has flowers of beautiful colors in many species. There are flower buds, blossoming flowers, withering flowers, and dying flowers.

The health condition of each flower plant represents a person's physical health and fortune.

Famous flowers like peony, magnolia conspicus, tulip, rose, etc. represent wealthy and highly privileged women of high-rank officials or business tycoons. Lotus, orchid, narcissus, corn poppy, chrysanthemum, and violet represent chaste, noble, and graceful female doctors, masters, professors, etc. with exceptional achievement in academic or art fields. Morning glory, delphinium, saffron, oleander, Chinese rose, etc. represent women in special businesses. Poppy flower represents attractive, popular women with great social and public relation skills. Epiphyllum represents talented but short-lived females (with sad lives usually). Ordinary flowers like lily, marigold, garden balsam, flowering crab apple, viola, bellflower, rose, jasmine, rainbow pink, etc. represent the ordinary women.

A flourishing Destiny Flower indicates a woman enjoys good health and a great career. A flower lacking fertilizer or irrigation or suffering blight indicates the woman is sick in Yin-Yang Space. A Destiny Flower surrounded with bees or butterflies indicates the woman is having problems of multiple relationships in Yin-Yang Space.

The Destiny Flower also tells how many children a woman has. A white flower represents a boy and red represents a girl. The number of flowers represents the number of children. The hidden flower bud suggests the largest possible number of children in a lifetime or no child at all. A bud represents an unborn child. A fallen bud or flower represents miscarriage or premature death of a child.

If a Destiny Flower withers and dies, the lady in Yin-Yang Space will die.

There are countless Flower Guardians in the Destiny Garden working relentlessly for these flowers.

The above description cannot properly explain the meanings of these multifarious flowers in the Destiny Garden. These flowers can have so many meanings that they cannot be thoroughly described.

1.   Ghost Category (鬼道)
A ghost is a "person" living in Yin Space. Like the people in Yin-Yang Space, a ghost may be an adult or a child, male or female, young or old, and pretty or ugly.

Ghosts, like human beings, have emotions, sentiments, and troubles of all kinds.

After death in Yin-Yang Space, a person "reincarnates by metamorphosis" (化生) to become a ghost because of the traction of karma force. Because a ghost originates from a person's "reincarnation by metamorphosis," his or her appearance, speech, behavior, and habits are the same as he or she was in Yin-Yang Space.

The life of ghosts is well organized. On the streets, they wear a diversity of clothes of different ancient dynasties or different modern periods. They do not need to ask the price when shopping; they simply take the item they want and leave the correct amount because they all have "the supernatural ability to read the minds of others" (他心通).

Justice in Yin Space is impartial and clear. The author once went to court in Yin Space for an investigation. The defendant on trial was an old ghost who had injured a young ghost's leg with an air gun. The court found the old ghost meant no harm and ordered only a punitive fine of thirty thousand Yin dollars without imprisonment.

The differences between ghosts in the ghost category and humans in Yin-Yang Space can be observed in four aspects:

(a) Different composing materials
(b) Ghosts have the telepathic function (the supernatural ability to read the minds of others).
(c) Ghosts do not need to take the amnesia drink.
(d) Ghosts are born through metamorphosis and cannot breed.

"Ghost bodies" are not affected by the amnesia drink; their souls are sober, and they all know about religious cultivation. Because they cultivate their Spiritual Qi and practice in sobriety without needing "awakening," however, their speed of attainment is much slower than human beings in Yin-Yang Space.

The author once visited a ghost who served as an officer in the "under government" (地府). He told the author, "I practice religion down here, too, only I progress much more slowly than you do in Yin-Yang Space. It is dark in the ghost category; practice and cultivation go slowly. Even though there are ghosts that have 'blessedness' to enjoy, we still would prefer to be human beings instead of ghosts. However, Buddhism in Yin-Yang Space is in its chaos stage. We call it the chaotic era, and, therefore, we don't want to reincarnate at this time. We are waiting here in Yin Space for the right time to arrive in Yin-Yang Space. Then, there will be many ghosts applying for reincarnation. But again, the quota will be small then."

Many living beings regard being ghosts as a transitional period: (a) Some have died without achieving wisdom lives and have had no wisdom lives before or have exhausted previous wisdom lives; and (b) some do not want to be human beings for now, have no reincarnation quota, are not qualified to be human beings, have no mature "potentialities and conditions," and so on. Under such situations, many living beings become ghosts.

A common saying is "Be the best, alive or dead." People's karmic retributions can be very different and cannot be identical. Similarly, ghosts do have different levels. If a person has done well in religious cultivation, then such a person will enjoy blessedness when he or she becomes a ghost. Because people have different "karma forces," ghosts, like humans, have many different levels. There are rich ghosts, poor ghosts, good ghosts, bad ghosts, full-stomach ghosts, hungry ghosts, noble ghosts, despicable ghosts, suffering ghosts, happy ghosts, long-life ghosts, short-life ghosts, scraper ghosts, dissolute ghosts, living ghosts, dead ghosts, mountain ghosts, water ghosts, smart ghosts, stupid ghosts, clever ghosts, dumb ghosts, healthy ghosts, weak ghosts, male ghosts, female ghosts, old ghosts, young ghosts, tough ghosts, loser ghosts, thief ghosts, sick ghosts, lazy ghosts, diligent ghosts, alcoholic ghosts, lewd ghosts, great-virtue ghosts, virtue-lacking ghosts, helpful ghosts, harming ghosts, and so on.

Modern Buddhism only talks about the hungry ghost category, which is not sufficient. Hungry ghosts are only a part of the ghost category.

As long as there are human beings, there will be jails. All countries with a well-founded justice system have jails. The same applies to the ghost category; it has a well-organized justice system and naturally has a jail. Differentiating the jails in Yin Space and Yin-Yang Space is for the convenience of preaching doctrines of Buddhism in Yin-Yang Space; the jail in Yin Space is thus called Hell, which is a part of the justice system in the ghost category.

Modern Buddhism has singled out the hungry ghost category in order to emphasize the retributions for bad karmas and thereby deter bad acts. That approach, however, completely ignores the ghost category and falls short of the general view of the material realm. In terms of the completeness of religious cultivation, it is a fallacy that causes "confused views" and misunderstanding about all the spheres after death among the living beings. Some people are afraid of ghosts because of that and regard ghosts as "dirty things." A ghost is a life living in another space and does not bother those living in other spaces. A common saying is "Humans take humans' way and ghosts take the ghosts' way." Both have their own respective environments and will not interfere with each other.

Ghosts and Hell are both governed by the government of Yin Space. To differentiate the government of Yin-Yang Space, the government of Yin Space is called the "under government." Both good and bad ghosts are subjects to the laws of Yin Space; those sentenced will be incarcerated in Hell.

A soul may become a hungry ghost through metamorphosis due to the traction of karma force. Retribution to a hungry ghost is much easier than the painful retribution to a ghost in Hell. That being said, only the punishment of hell is worse than the pain suffered by hungry ghosts in Yin Space.

The poverty and "disappointed hope" (求不得) suffered by hungry ghosts are caused by their greed and miserliness in previous lives. Perhaps, they were rich people unwilling to give alms to the poor, taking pride in wealth, pursuing insatiable desire, and committing all kinds of bad karmas. Or, they were people who were talented but would not help the less talented to learn and, instead, ridiculed them. These may become hungry ghosts through metamorphosis after death.

Some people have greed in their minds and seize other people's property or spouses with unjust measures; some people are jealous about other people's achievements, defaming and sabotaging them; some people cannot acquire something and will try to prevent other people from succeeding. These people, too, have sowed the seeds (cause) of becoming hungry ghosts in future lives.

The hungry ghosts who end up in the ghost category through metamorphosis will be subject to retributions of different levels according to their respective karma forces. They will be denied what they desire; they will suffer poverty and insufficient clothing and food; they shall be helpless.

There are many types of hungry ghosts and each shall suffer different "painful retributions" (苦報). For example, needle-mouth ghosts have large abdomens and, therefore, will always be hungry no matter how much food they eat. They have narrow esophagi that cause difficulty filling their hungry stomachs. They will see all kinds of gourmet foods but will not be able to satisfy their desire; they are usually unbearably hungry and thirsty. It is not difficult to imagine what kind of "painful retributions" they are going through.

The ghost category is a mixture of saints and ordinary souls. Whether saintly or ordinary, as long as this soul is going through transmigrations in the material realm, receiving a ghost body is not unusual.

2.   Animal Category (旁生道)

Yin Space is itself a "world," and, naturally, there are all kinds of lives in it.

Yin Space is an environment established for ghosts; all animals in the space live around the ghosts. These animals, like the ghosts, consist of Spiritual Qi.

These animals in Yin Space obtain their bodies through metamorphosis and are, therefore, unable to breed.

Most of these animals are waiting for their chance to reincarnate to the Yin-Yang Space. The time they spend in Yin Space is considered a transitional period; their hope is to enhance their "attainments" (道行) and reincarnate to be human beings.

3.   Low Dharma Body Category (低法身道)

The low Dharma Bodies living in the Yin Space are a large group, most of which are workers. Among them, the "earth fairies" (地仙) are the most active.

The low Dharma Bodies are under the direct governance of the Fairy Category Administration that is stationed at the Tusita (兜率天). A low Dharma Body will be transferred to and governed by a designated unit once a task is given.

These low Dharma Bodies work at different units and are waiting for the appropriate conditions to "branch their souls" and reincarnate as humans. They are practicing religion while working to raise their Dharma Body levels.

◆   Yin Space government

The "underworld government" (陰朝地府), as referred to among the public, is actually the "Yin government" (陰府), more commonly called the "under government" (地府). The under government is the government that rules the Yin Space. It is also a collective term for all agencies under the Ministry of Yin Space Central Authority. Some call the under government the "Yin Justice" (陰司), which however is only the justice institute of the under government. A court of law in the Yin Space, for example, is one of the many justice agencies of the justice institute.

The justice system in Yin Space operates independently. The well-planned laws cover all kinds of crimes. The administrative operations in the entire Yin Space are all controlled by the Ministry of Yin Space Central Authority, and all "ministers" are chosen by the Ministry of Yin Space Central Authority.

The "under government" includes ten major departments: the Ministry of Yin Space Central Authority; the Ministry of Qingyang Enlightenment; the Ministry of Reincarnation and Transmigration; the Ministry of Karma Force Registration; the Ministry of Yin-Law Justice; the Ministry of Hell Administration; the Ministry of Land Administration; the Ministry of Soul Administration; the Ministry of Security Enforcement; and the Ministry of Diplomatic Contact.

(a) The Ministry of Yin Space Central Authority (陰間 中央極權院)

The Ministry of Yin Space Central Authority is the highest administrative institute for the Chinese "under government." It leads the other nine ministries to make sure that the Yin Space operates properly.

The Minister of Yin Space Central Authority is also the president of Yin Space or the king of the "Yin Kingdom" (陰 國). He is commonly called Yan Wang (literally "King Yan"; 閻王) by the public.

During the earlier part of history, Yan Wang was a king in the Yin-Yang Space and a person of integrity, justice, and righteousness. He and his army often fought the evil powers. He created many heroic dramas throughout his life. He also swore that he would fight against evil in his future lives.

His integrity has earned him the "deity" stage of attainment, and he has been chosen to be the president of Chinese Yin Space to ensure the normal operation of Chinese Yin Space.

Because Yan Wang's deity stage of attainment is a long but limited wisdom life, he is relentlessly "soul-branching" to reincarnate into Yin-Yang Space for continuous cultivation whenever the potentialities and conditions are appropriate. His objective is to achieve the correct stage of attainment (正果) and obtain a long and unlimited wisdom life sometime in the future.

Yan Wang has applied for reincarnation many times since he took the office of the king of "Yin Kingdom." In one of his lives, his family name was Bao and was called BaoGong (Lord Bao) and Just Judge Bao by the people.

Yan Wang also has many other names: YanMoLuoShe; YanMoLuoWang; YanLuoTianZi; YeMoLaoZi; YanMoWang; YanLaoZi; YanWangYe; YanLuoWang; YanMo; YanWang; YanLao;YanMo; and others.

To properly manage reincarnation for souls and cultivation for living beings, the Ministry of Yin Space Central Authority has installed the "world information module" (世界全息儀) for many of its subordinate agencies.

The world information module is an educational tool for the use by living beings and souls in Yin Space and has a variety of functions. The most frequently used functions are tracking, home view, home return, and prediction.

- Tracking function (追測功能)

A user stands in front of the world information module and conveys, by itself or a proxy, the intention to the module of tracking the past of a certain living being. The module screen displays the karma makings in that living being's previous life. For example, a user inquires about how the bad karmas were made in the previous life, and the screen shows the details and what crimes were committed.

Some living beings may be dissatisfied with the arrangement of karmic retributions or the court judgment delivered. The tracking function can help the living beings recollect the past and make them sincerely convinced and ready to accept the arrangement or judgment.

In some cases, a living being's karmic retribution gets mixed up with another living being, and they have to reincarnate and live together. The tracking function may explain to the dissatisfied party what karmas they have done and that they have to live together to settle such karmas.

- Home View function (望鄉功能)

Due to a low level of "temperament" (心性), many souls after their deaths still worry about their family and friends in the Yin-Yang Space.

The Ministry of Yin Space Central Authority has pity on such souls and offers the home view function for them.

A user stands in front of the big screen of the world information module and thinks, "I want to see my home." The big screen will then display the current situation of the user's friends and family or particular persons regardless of whether they are in Yin Space, Yang Space, or Yin-Yang Space.

This function can also reveal the "karmic retribution" connections between the user and the user's friends and family—how a "field of blessedness" was grown to receive blessed retribution and how bad karmas lead to deserved punishment.

As the most frequently used function, the home view function is singled out by the public, and the world information module is improperly called the home viewing station.

- Home Return function (回鄉功能)

The residents in Yin Space and the souls that have just lost their material bodies may apply for a home visit, subject to the approval from the competent authority.

There are two situations for home return: a need to request friends or family in Yin-Yang Space to perform something, or, out of awakening after losing his or her material body, a need to save and convert friends and family in Yin-Yang Space.

A soul that is given a home-return "order card" (令牌)

and is about to visit his or her home stands in front of the big screen of the "world information module" with the "order card" in hand and thinks, "I want to go home." Then, a column of light will appear in front of this soul. The soul walks into the light column, and he or she will be beamed instantly back to his or her friends and family. The physical eyes of the friends and family cannot see the soul next to them unless a person with Deva eye happens to be there. A person with Deva eye may communicate with the soul and understand the intention of this visiting soul.

If a person with Deva eye is not available, the visiting soul will do whatever possible to serve his or her purpose. Provided the "order card" allows it, such a soul may try bodily possession or appearance in dreams.

Some visiting souls have a great grievance left in the Yin-Yang Space and must come back to settle scores. It will be major concern for the debtor because there can be a disaster coming. Examples of a disaster include an accident, sickness, or even a life threat.

No other institute may issue this type of "order card." Other institutes can only forward an application for it to the Ministry of Yin Space Central Authority, where the application, if approved, will be further forwarded to the president for final approval. Such an "order card" is called the "black card;" it allows free passage to and from Yin-Yang Space, and all law enforcement or protection officers must honor it. It cannot be interfered with by Dharma Bodies of any level. Even a Great Bodhisattva with a "pardon order card" (特赦令牌) cannot interfere with the debt collection in Yin-Yang Space sanctioned by the "black card." Violators shall be punishable by *the Law of Deva.*

Not even Buddha may interfere with the debt collection of a "black card" holder. Issuance of such an "order card" follows the regulations provided by the Deva of Yin-Yang United Institute. A Great Bodhisattva with a "pardon order card" promoting Buddhism in Yin-Yang Space has only two options when in contact with a "black card" holder: (1) mediation by giving a lecture on the true meaning of the universe and life; or (2) "karma conversion" for both concerned parties by making the debtor grow the "field of blessedness," followed by converting the "blessed virtue" into "meritorious virtue" (or without conversion), and then transferring such meritorious virtue (or blessed virtue) to the creditor until the debt has been settled. The creditor may demand an additional amount (such as interest) from the debtor, and the debtor must repay more to settle the debt.

• Prediction function (預測功能)

A living being in Yin Space who wishes to reincarnate to Yin-Yang Space, or a soul about to reincarnate to Yin-Yang Space, may learn the details of the future by using the prediction function of the "world information module." These details may include future parents, relatives, friends, karmic retribution relationships with them, self's growth, the parents' aging and deaths, how the good and bad karmic retributions will be sustained, and how self's birth, aging, sickness, death, etc. will happen.

A soul that must go through "mandatory transmigration" may not refuse such transmigration even when such a soul has learned that extremely bad "karmic retribution" is waiting in the next life. If such a soul does not accept the result and wishes for an alteration, it may file an appeal within a given period.

Some of those with choices (such as ghosts) may have realized that human lives are short and do not want to transmigrate unceasingly. They may choose not to rein-carnate to Yin-Yang Space and remain in Yin Space in-stead to practice religion until such time as they have accumulated "enough" meritorious virtue for direct pro-motion to the Deva or Rebirth in Pure Lands, such as the World of Utmost Joy, through the "redemption service" (超渡儀式) held by people in Yin-Yang Space. According to the level of meritorious virtue, they may even attain the stage of fairies (仙) or deities (神).

The above are the four major functions of the "world information module." There are many other functions that are less utilized, such as visiting the Deva Realm and visit-ing the Nano Realm. These functions will not be covered in this book.

(b) The Ministry of Qingyang Enlightenment (青陽教化院)

The Ministry of Qingyang Enlightenment is the place where Di-Zang Bodhisattva (地藏菩薩) performs his official duties and educates the living beings in Yin Space. The Di-Zang Bodhisattva at "the Ministry of Qingyang Enlight-enment" is a Duplicated Body of his Dharma Body and is responsible primarily for ideological education.

There is no "Great-Sun Buddha" in Yin Space. That means that no Buddha appears in Yin Space because Buddha symbolizes the Sun. Di-Zang Bodhisattva brings Buddhism to Yin Space as though reflecting sunlight and shining on the minds of living beings in Yin Space. That light drives away the shadow that blinds living beings' minds in Yin Space, allowing them to see a bright future. These living beings, taught by Di-Zang Bodhisattva, practice religion relentlessly and are one by one emerging into the way of Buddhism. Qingyang, literally meaning Green Sun, is a gigantic spherical object (group of workers) that shines by reflecting the sunlight; it symbolizes the meaning and function of the Ministry of Qingyang Enlightenment.

In Yin Space, Yan Wang is in charge of administrative tasks and Di-Zang Bodhisattva is in charge of education and rehabilitation. They have different stages of attainment and duties, but their purposes are the same: to save and convert more living beings in better, faster, and more efficient ways.

Di-Zang Bodhisattva is the "religion founder" of Yin Space. He is also called the religion founder of Nether World. As a religion founder, he must teach and promote Buddhism. To do so, Di-Zang Bodhisattva has set up a great auditorium in the Ministry of Qingyang Enlightenment where scheduled keynote speeches are delivered constantly to the living beings of Yin Space.

In addition, Di-Zang Bodhisattva also "imprints memory" (授記) onto the souls that have been to Hell and are about to reincarnate to Yin-Yang Space, to make sure that they remember the suffering in Hell and commit more good karmas and less bad karmas after reincarnation so as to avoid coming back to Hell again. At the same time, Di-Zang Bodhisattva will arrange for those who are about to reincarnate to have the conditions for contacting and studying Buddhism in their next life.

The Ministry of Qingyang Enlightenment is the head-quarters of education and rehabilitation, and it has many subsidiaries and personnel. In addition, Di-Zang Bodhisattva has a large staff. These subsidiaries and personnel are constantly busy educating and rehabilitating living beings. Like other agencies, the Ministry of Qingyang Enlightenment is a busy agency.

(c) The Ministry of Reincarnation and Transmigration (轉世輪迴院)

When the material realm formed, the World of Matter (the natural world; 器世間) came first, which was then followed by the World of Sentient Beings (有情世間). It was the beginning of the Existence Period, and human beings appeared and began to prosper. It was during this time that the Ministry of Reincarnation and Transmigration was established in Yin Space.

Since then, every soul that wishes to go to Yin-Yang Space through reincarnation must go through this institute regardless of where the soul comes from or its status or position. Even the soul of a Virtual-Enlightenment Bodhisattva coming down for Buddhahood must go through the Ministry of Reincarnation and Transmigration to avoid violating *the Law of Deva*. A soul committing unauthorized reincarnation will be punishable by *the Law of Deva*.

Souls waiting for reincarnation in Yin Space shall first report to the Ministry of Soul Administration for registration and residence arrangement. They will be there waiting for the result of soul evaluation and "karmic retribution editing" (業報編輯). When the result becomes available, they will be sent to the Ministry of Reincarnation and Transmigration where they have access to a diagrammatic explanation of the "karmic retribution editing" result. If there is any dispute, the soul in question may file an appeal to the basic court of the Ministry of Yin Justice, and to save time, the court will sit immediately. If the case cannot be judged there, or the court judgment is not accepted by the soul, it may appeal to the Appeals Court of the Ministry of Yin Justice or directly to the Ministry of Yin Space Central Authority.

The time between a soul's departure from its previous body (residence) and the possession of its next body shall not exceed forty-nine days. In special situations, an extended period of no more than one hundred days may be requested. A soul must rely on a body and cannot exist independently over a long time. Therefore, the appeal against the "karmic retribution editing" must be filed and judged as soon as possible.

The Ministry of Yin Space Central Authority also has its court in Yin Space, and its court is the final tribunal. Once the judgment is delivered, it will be the final decision and will be executed by the Ministry of Security Enforcement who will escort the soul in question to the Ministry of Reincarnation and Transmigration, where the amnesia drink will be served followed by reincarnation to Yin-Yang Space. Therefore, souls filing an appeal "are not afraid of Di-Zang Bodhisattva but are of Yan Wang."

All souls must read the diagrammatic explanation of "karmic retribution editing" before reincarnation. If a soul has no objection, or if an appeal is overruled, then the amnesia drink will be served before the soul is sent to the place where it will reincarnate.

The administrator of the amnesia drink will prepare the

drink in a container according to the average designated volume, and the subject soul must drink it voluntarily. Some souls have been through reincarnation many times and think they are smart enough to spill some of the amnesia drink purposefully. They may succeed if the administrator pretends not to see it. Sometimes, the administrator will pour some more and force it into the soul.

Some souls of great significance (such as a Great Bodhisattva) will continue to serve as a role model for the rest and be keen to take the amnesia drink to the last drop.

Once the amnesia drink is served, a soul will become muddled, and maintenance of judgment will entirely rely only on the soul's "mind power" (心力).

(d) The Ministry of Karma Force Registration (業力登 記院)

Transmigrations of living beings are simply formed by "karma commission" and "karmic retribution," and this is the relationship between cause and effect. Good karma and bad karma are reflected in good karmic retribution and bad karmic retribution, respectively.

The Law of Deva is fair. "Karmic effect" (業果) comes from "karmic cause" (業因). Although some souls do not believe it, all arrangements are fair. The task of transmigration administration is well-documented by records of good and bad karmas supporting the transmigration decisions.

The Ministry of Karma Force Registration only keeps records of the karmas that have "force" to cause good or bad situations to souls (the karmas without "force" will not be recorded). That is why this ministry is called karma force registration. The karma that produces neither a good nor bad result is called unrecordable karma (無記業).

A soul will automatically keep record of all karmas, but the administration cannot simply rely on these records because some souls may cheat on such records. Furthermore, it is too complicated to look for the soul to investigate and verify everything.

The Ministry of Karma Force Registration has a tremendous amount of responsibility; it must periodically supply the concerned agencies with reports. These concerned agencies' plans for future works rely on the reports provided by the Ministry of Karma Force Registration. For example, the Deva of United Enlightenment relies on the reports supplied by the Ministry of Karma Force Registration to produce the Correct-Dharma Proportion Composite Index.

Every time a new soul is born in this world, the Ministry of Soul Administration will create a file for it, and a duplicated copy will be transferred to the Ministry of Karma Force Registration where the file will be kept and a specialist assigned to record karma force on a daily basis.

The Ministry of Karma Force Registration has a large staff consisting primarily of "earth fairies." They are tightly organized with clearly defined tasks. They work diligently every day to ensure that they do not miss any karma force.

The tasks of the Ministry of Karma Force Registration can be divided into office tasks and field tasks. The field agents work in two shifts of day and night (in Yin-Yang Space). They are dispatched outside to gather their subjects' karma force records and bring the records back to the office staff for further processing. The office staff is responsible for registering, data sorting, file managing, statistics generating, tabulating, chart drawing, and supplying information to the concerned agencies.

The office staff of the Ministry of Karma Force Registration has contact only with data and will not contact the souls and bodies of living beings, whereas the field agents must get close to the souls and bodies.

When the author presents an "order card" (a "pass" or "file access permit," which is not necessary if trust has been established) to access data, only the office staff will be contacted. They will find the data for the author. There are restrictions according to the levels of permission. Some are only allowed to access regular files and are not allowed to access critical files. Such access is determined by the grades of the "file access permits."

The Ministry of Karma Force Registration is an important agency; its job determines the fates of living beings, and there is no margin for error. The Yin government has a large group of "earth fairies" for this job to ensure that the registration task is properly done as it is responsible for every living being.

All ministers of the other nine ministries of the Yin government, other than the Ministry of Qingyang Enlightenment, have the deity stage of attainment (神果).

(e) The Ministry of Yin Justice (陰律司法院)
The Ministry of Yin Justice is also an important agency that holds the power to kill or to spare. It is a giant agency

with large numbers of subsidiaries and staff members. All disputes or lawsuits concerning economic, civil, and criminal cases among living beings in Yin Space are settled at the Ministry of Yin Justice.

The living beings in Yin-Yang Space communicate with Yin Space through their Yin souls. All cases concerning a living being in the material realm shall be governed by the laws of the material realm and will concurrently be filed with and ruled by the Ministry of Yin Justice.

Contrary to the common understanding, not every living being has to stand trial. If there is no dispute, then it is not necessary to report to the court. After all, it is an agency of law; why would anyone go to court if there was no case to be tried?

Some cases have already been processed by the Yin soul while one is still alive, which makes the arrangements much easier after death. Some living beings' Yin souls, however, cannot handle the case, and the case must be taken care of by the trinity of souls (三魂合一) after death, a process which will be much more complicated.

Every case is first processed at the basic court. All cases will be first received by the reception office where the files will be reviewed, categorized, and distributed according to their respective courts. Upon the distribution of the cases, the respective court will schedule the proceedings. Every basic court is established for a particular type of case; there are as many basic courts as the number of types of cases. Currently, there are ten courts. Court for A type of cases takes only cases of A type, and court for B type of cases does not take cases of A type. In other words, every basic court is a specialized court. For example, a court specializing in cases of personal assault can only process cases of personal assault. The court and its presiding judge have no jurisdiction on the matters beyond their respective specialization. Otherwise, it will be a violation of the law and punishable by expulsion of public office.

After the proceedings at the basic court, the case may be appealed.

The court of appeals of the Ministry of Yin Justice is a general court that does not discriminate on types of cases. Upon receipt of an appeal case, the Ministry of Yin Justice will soon schedule a trial, and the plaintiff will be made aware of the judgment while at the court. If the plaintiff still has any dispute, such soul has one last chance to appeal to the Yin Space Central Authority. If the second appeal is overruled and the judgment affirmed, the plaintiff must accept the ruling. Those who must go through reincarnation shall reincarnate, and those who are condemned to Hell shall go to Hell.

The Ministry of Yin Justice stipulates that no case may be placed on hold, and, therefore, the basic courts are very busy. In fact, they are constantly in session. Some cases have to be put on suspension due to a lack of evidence, and such suspensions may have to continue for an extended period of time. Some other cases cannot be put in suspension because a soul must reincarnate within forty-nine days after death, and the case concerning such a soul must be processed at a fast pace to meet the tight deadline.

There is a saying: "no plaintiff, no trial." If no living being or law enforcer files the case to the reception office, the

Ministry of Yin Justice will not take the initiative to interfere in any matter. Therefore, the Ministry of Yin Justice also results from the causes and conditions of living beings.

The judgment of the Ministry of Yin Justice is not delivered solely at the discretion of the concerned presiding judge. All presiding judges of the Ministry of Yin Justice are carefully screened and trained. They must have a heart of goodness, integrity, and honesty, and must have memorized every clause of "Yin law." Only a judge of this caliber is competent to serve in such an important office.

(f) The Ministry of Hell Administration (地獄管理院)

Hell is the jail of Yin Space and is established for the souls in Yin Space. All inmates are ghost bodies. To be more precise, Hell is the jail specifically designed to incarcerate ghost bodies in Yin Space.

A soul cannot be incarcerated in Hell independently; it must have a body on which to depend. Hell is established for the living beings in Yin Space, and, therefore, the souls being incarcerated shall first have ghost bodies.

If all bad karmas were to be settled by "bad retributions" after reincarnation, the human world would turn into a "bad world," and the Yin-Yang Space would become a Hell for human beings because there are too many bad karmas of living beings.

While the ghost bodies in Yin Space must settle their karmas by going through Hell, some other people having bad karmas that are independent and concern no one else do not need to settle these karmas through reincarnation. To allow such a living being to suffer less bad retributions after reincarnation in the human world and to live a better life, such a living being may become a ghost through metamorphosis and be incarcerated in Hell first to sustain painful retribution specifically so that the living being may settle the karmas.

Some bad karmas concern other living beings and are too complex to be settled independently and, therefore, must be addressed through reincarnation. Some other karmas may also concern other people but are quite simple; such karmas may be independently settled by going through Hell, provided the concerned parties agree. If the concerned parties do not agree, then karma settlement in Hell will not be an option. The karma can only be settled by karmic retribution involving the concerned parties after reincarnation. Therefore, the reincarnations of all parties must be arranged within a relatively short time span. This is also one of the major ways of karma settlement.

Because the bad karmas of the living beings are so complex, to allow thorough karma settlements among the living beings, there must be dedicated resources. A jail cell will be established specifically for a type of bad karma; whenever a new type of bad karma evolves among the living beings, Hell will establish a new jail cell specifically for it.

The number of karmic retributions corresponding to the bad karmas of living beings is so big that Hell has become a gigantic organization with a huge staff, and the forms of karmic retributions have also evolved in complexity and diversity. From small rooms to large rooms, from a small cell to a large cell, from small Hell to middle Hell, from middle

Hell to large Hell, everything is managed in an orderly fashion. That was exactly why the Ministry of Hell Administration was created.

Like the Ministry of Yin Justice, the Ministry of Hell Administration is a passive agency that waits for other agencies to send in the subjects with bad karma and then follows the due process. Other than that, they have no other tasks to do.

The massive amount of bad karmas of the living beings makes the workers in Hell extremely busy. Prior to their job assignment, the workers are intensively trained. Complete settlement of the bad karmas of the living beings who have sinned requires meticulous calculation and planning; the intensity of punishment and length of incarceration must be precisely and appropriately measured.

The Ministry of Hell Administration has a reception office. All living beings serving time in Hell must first stand trial at the Ministry of Yin Justice, and the executors of the Ministry of Security Enforcement will escort the inmates to the reception office of the Ministry of Hell Administration to deliver the court judgment and sign off the inmates. The turning over of the inmates is now completed.

After receiving the sentencing papers, the reception office of the Ministry of Hell Administration begins to review the documents immediately and assign the inmates to their bad retribution cells according to the descriptions in the sentencing papers. The inmates will sustain the respective karmic retribution at a designated cell until the karmic retribution is exhausted, and then move onto the next designated cell for another count of karmic retribution.

During the karmic retribution, the instruments of tortures are not used all at once. They are supposed to be used slowly and evenly across and throughout the time span of the sentence.

After the inmates are released, they may remain in Yin Space and continue to be ghosts and wait for the right time for reincarnation, or they may apply for reincarnation immediately.

After the sentence has been fully served, the officers of the cells will turn the inmate along with the associated documents to the reception office where the documents are reviewed. The inmate will then sign the release document. After identification has been verified, the inmate will be released.

The names of the cells and the instruments of torture in Hell are so many that they are beyond describing in detail one by one. It will be enough if a religious practitioner understands how it operates. After all, it is not a place to which we want to go.

(g) The Ministry of Land Administration (管轄土地院)

The Ministry of Land Administration is an administrative agency in charge of the land in Yin Space and is responsible for all administrative tasks of administrative areas, for example, metropolitan development (including construction, protection, management, and maintenance of public facilities), allocation and use of land, postal service, banks, markets, diet supply, and civic life and welfare.

In Yin-Yang Space, the administrative areas are nation, province, city, county, area, township, and village, which are headed by minister, governor, mayor, magistrate, area chief, township chief, and village chief, respectively.

In Yin Space, Ministry of Land Administration is the center for land management. Its Minister is "Great Land Deity," who supervises subsidiaries like City Deities (Chenghuang), Little Land Deities, all the way down to Land Lot Master that is in charge of a small piece of land.

The Ministry of Land Administration works jointly with the Ministry of Karma Force Registration to supervise the household management tasks through a management hierarchy. The household management extends as far as the individuals in every household. They work very hard to prevent any oversight.

The Ministry of Land Administration demands all Land Deities be familiar with all details of their respective land. If they are called upon, they must answer immediately and precisely. They must know every link and detail.

The job title of Cheng-huang is equivalent to a mayor in Yin-Yang Space. A Cheng-huang has a busy daily itinerary and supervises all of the subsidiaries handling matters in Yin Space.

(h) The Ministry of Soul Administration (靈魂管理院)

The Ministry of Soul Administration is an important administrative institute under the leadership of the Ministry of Yin Space Central Authority. In addition to managing the souls in Yin Space and Yang Space, it manages the souls in Yin-Yang Space. These souls add up to a huge number, and it is, therefore, necessary to have an agency dedicated to the management of these souls and the comprehensive and vigorous training of the staff. The Ministry of Soul Administration exists for this purpose.

The Ministry of Soul Administration is in charge of complex tasks, among which one is particularly important. It has to constantly evaluate the level of every soul under its management, thereby categorizing the souls, and provide reports to the concerned agencies.

The unit in charge of this task is "the Soul Level Appraisal Division" (靈魂層次評審部), which is under direct supervision of the Ministry of Soul Administration. The Division undertakes the tasks of statistics, examination, evaluation, and conclusion. They first acquire firsthand data from the Ministry of Karma Force Registration, then examine past data stored in the original soul and produce all kinds of indices. The indices will be transcribed to the Soul Level Conversion Table (靈魂層次換算表) to display the level of the soul.

An animal with five hundred years of "attainments" (道行) may become a human being through reincarnation.

After balancing the karma force indices of all types of souls, some souls will be men, some will be women, some will be poor, some will be rich, some will have long lives, some will have short lives, some will be good people, some will be bad people, and so on.

The control of the reincarnation quota and the balance of reincarnation types require meticulous arrangement and design. When there are not enough types, they can be found at the "Original Soul Palace" (原魂宮). In the Original Soul Palace, there are all types of original souls beyond imagination. When the other world decays and disappears, this world is created, and the Original Soul Palace at the other world is relocated to this world. When this world is annihilated, the other world is created, and the Original Soul Palace at this world will be relocated to the other world.

A soul must go through the Ministry of Soul Administration regardless of whether the soul is: entering or exiting the material realm; being born or dying in the material realm; being born through metamorphosis, viviparity, moisture, or oviparity; becoming human, animal, Deva fairy, or ghost; going to Heaven or Hell; and so on.

The existence of the "Life and Death Book" (生死簿) in Yin Space is frequently referred to in folklore. It is the "soul karmic retribution file" (靈魂業報檔案) edited and produced by the Ministry of Soul Administration for the souls going through reincarnation. Every time a soul goes through the Ministry of Soul Administration, a file is generated, and all such files are stored in the account of the soul for inquiries by concerned agencies from time to time. When a soul is transferred from the Ministry of Soul Administration to the Ministry of Reincarnation and Transmigration, the karmic retribution file of the soul will be copied and transferred as well. Therefore, the karmic retribution file can be found at the Ministry of Reincarnation and Transmigration. Copies of this file can also be found at some other agencies, such as the Ministry of Security Enforcement. The Ministry of Security Enforcement must know when the life of a soul's body will end and arrange for the law enforcer to escort the soul to where it should be to ensure that the soul will not be left straying.

The Ministry of Soul Administration is the highest authority in administering souls in Yin Space. It has many subsidiaries in soul management. Notwithstanding the importance of the diligent management of the souls and "soul files" in the "Original Soul Palace" (原魂宮), the editing of "karmic retribution program" (業報程序) is even more important. The "karmic retribution program" is very complicated. For example, it is concerned with whether a soul will be born as a male or a female, what kind of family it will be in, what family members and friends it will have, the place of birth, what schools to attend, what education to take, what pain to suffer, what pleasure to receive, how many tribulations to go through, how many worries to have, when to be sick, when the teeth should go bad, when to meet whom, and so on. It is so complicated that mundane people can never imagine or understand. This is a "life program."

The evaluation of the level of a soul is also a complicated task. Despite the fact that all souls are the same in that they have no supernatural power and cannot exist independently over a long period of time, their levels can be dramatically different. It can be observed which souls are of entry level, which are of middle level, which are of high level, which are twisted and perverted, which are ferocious, which are soft and kind, which are stringent, which are loose, which are smart, and which are stupid. To properly perform soul evaluation, one must learn to observe and categorize.

The souls at entry level have spent a shorter period of time being human. Some have just become human and lack life experiences. They are like tender seedlings, some of which are childish like children. Souls at the middle level have spent a longer time being human. They already have some life experiences. They are passionate, pushy, and keen to learn and excel like young people, but they have not matured enough. The high-level souls have extensive life experiences over a long period of time, even countless Kalpas. They are very mature, stable, wise, and experienced like the elderly. They are highly matured souls; they will have sufficient "mind power" (心力) after reincarnation.

Both the number and levels of souls are countless and complicated, and the karma forces can vary. Entry level, middle level, and high level are not enough to describe them. A brief description is provided for a general understanding.

Soul management looks like punishing the bad and rewarding the good. In fact, its essence is "cause-and-effect retribution." A good cause leads to a good result, and a bad cause leads to a bad result.

The staff of the Ministry of Soul Administration, like the living beings in Yin Space, frequently goes to the preaching lectures of Di-Zang Bodhisattva at the Ministry of Qing-yang Enlightenment. Because of this, they know very well that their job is critical to every living being. In addition to arranging normal "cause-and-effect retribution" during "karmic retribution program editing" (業報程序編輯) for living beings, they have to arrange as many chances as possible for contact with and enlightenment of dharma without violating the "Yin law."

(i) The Ministry of Security Enforcement (安全執法院)

The Ministry of Security Enforcement is the administrative agency in charge of police, military, special police, bailiffs, and jail guards. Its responsibility is making sure its subsidiaries properly perform the role of basic law enforcement and maintaining public safety to ensure that Yin Space may function normally in accordance with law.

In folklore, there are two major "ghosts" that specialize in claiming lives and escorting souls to the "underworld government" to face "karmic retribution" The one who works the day shift is called BaiWuChang (literally "white impermanence"), and the one who works the night shift is called HeiWuChang (literally "black impermanence"). They are collectively called Hei-baiWuChang. The two of them are the law enforcers of the "Material Body Life Termination Division" (色身壽結部) of the Ministry of Security Enforcement. The Ministry of Security Enforcement has many law enforcers, and Hei-baiWuChang represent them. Because of the extraordinary appearance of Hei-baiWuChang, anyone who ever sees them is deeply impressed, and that is why they are frequently mentioned in folklore.

There are jail guards in Hell; there are patrol police on duty in Yin Space; there are special police escorting souls; there are bailiffs protecting the court; and so on. In all, the law enforcers of the Ministry of Security Enforcement are everywhere in Yin Space.

All legal cases in Yin Space are the jurisdiction of the Ministry of Security Enforcement. The law enforcer of the Ministry of Security Enforcement, upon receiving a case report, will appear at the scene to arrest the suspect, if necessary, and the case is then reported to the "Ministry of Yin Law Justice" for indictment according to case details. The ruling and sentencing will be left to the discretion of the "Ministry of Yin Law Justice." In other words, the Ministry of Security Enforcement is responsible only for arrest and release and has no authority in judging and sentencing.

(j) The Ministry of Diplomatic Contact (外交聯絡院)

Compared with other agencies, the Ministry of Diplomatic Contact is relatively small. It is not as big as the Ministry of Soul Administration because its workload is smaller.

This ministry is responsible for all matters concerning foreign affairs in Yin Space, such as immigration and document exchange.

The Ministry of Diplomatic Contact frequently attends meetings, delivers documents, and receives documents in the Deva Realm. It also visits other "countries" in Yin Space on official business. Sometimes, it also visits other worlds if living beings are involved. If a case concerns other worlds, then it must contact these worlds.

The staff of the Ministry of Diplomatic Contact often goes to "the Devas of High Dharma Body Institutes" (高法身機構天) to deal with matters regarding stage appraisal. For example, many souls already have "long and unlimited wisdom lives" and reincarnate again to Yin-Yang Space to be human beings. When their material bodies die, there will be some matters that concern "the Devas of High Dharma Body Institutes." The needed files will be copied and submitted to the Ministry of Diplomatic Contact, the staff of which will take over and conduct the process. The result will be reported back to the document sender.

Let us assume there is a Chinese in Yin-Yang Space who has been living and working in a Western area for a long time. When his material body dies, this person's soul is escorted by the law enforcer of the Western country of Yin Space to the Western under government, but this person's previous-life files are still stored at the under government of the Chinese area. If this soul is to be reviewed by the Westerner under government, then the Ministries of Diplomatic Contact of both sides must collaborate to take care of the case. If the soul wishes to be reviewed by the Chinese under government, then the law enforcers will turn this soul along with the soul's "karma force registration book" (業力登記簿) for the present life in Yin-Yang Space to the Ministry of Diplomatic Contact. Similarly, a Westerner living and working in a Chinese area of Yin-Yang Space shall follow the same pattern.

After the under government has reviewed a soul, if, due to the traction of "karma force," the soul must reincarnate by metamorphosis to become a Heaven Person to savor blessed retribution in Heaven, reincarnate to another world, or must be reborn in a Buddha's Pure Land through metamorphosis, then this soul must be handled by the Ministry of Diplomatic Contact.

(C) YANG SPACE (陽間)

Yang Space is always full of light, and there is no night or a cloudy day. From a broader perspective, a space that matches this description can be called Yang Space.

The Deva Realm of the material realm is also a Yang Space.

In regard to the concept of "multiple spaces," both Refined Space and Nano Space have only Yang Space, and Thin Space has both Yin Space and Yang Space.

No objects have any shadow in Yang Space; it is full of light everywhere.

Similar to Yin Space, Yang Space in the material realm is divided into Chinese Deva Kingdom (華人天國), Westerner Deva Kingdom, and so on. This book only discusses Chinese Deva Kingdom.

Some may argue that Deva Realm is an aggregation of many layers. It is not so. Deva Realm is divided into many different domains, each with a different environment.

In Chinese Deva Kingdom, the core institute is "the Deva of Deva Kingdom Central Authority" (天國中央集權天), which supervises justice, administration, wisdom life management, and other institutes. These institutes allow the Deva Kingdom to function normally in accordance with the law.

Chinese Deva Kingdom is divided into twenty-eight areas, and they are collectively called the Twenty-Eight Deva Domains.

Chinese Deva Kingdom has developed two spaces: the Yang Space portion of the Thin Space; and the Refined Space.

Yang Space is also a place shared by residents of different levels, including high Dharma Bodies, middle Dharma Bodies, and Heaven People. Heaven People are the primary residents in Deva Realm and have a great range of levels. The bodies of human beings, ghosts, and Heaven People are inhabited by souls of mixed levels. Regardless of the levels in previous lives and the stages of attainment before reincarnations, these souls will receive the same type of bodies if they arrive at the same sphere through reincarnation.

The Deva Realm situation is introduced below according to the order of the Realm of Desire, the Realm of Disassociation, and the Realm of Liberation.

1. The Deva of Dharma Guardians (護法天) (Four Deva Domains)

The Deva of Dharma Guardians is the Deva domain that is the location of the military, police, and security guard institutes led by "the Deva of Material Realm United Authority" (the highest administrative institute of material realm; 色界聯合集權天). The law enforcers of the Deva of Dharma Guardians are charged with the great responsibility of protecting the material realm. They not only must guarantee internal peace among the living beings in the Deva Realm, but more importantly, they must defend against the Deva Enemies (intrusion and interference from other worlds).

The Deva of Dharma Guardians is a large and busy agency. It never rests in its role of defender to make sure material realm functions normally.

The Deva has eight commands. They are collectively called Deva Dragon Eight Commands (the eight divisions of Deva, Dragon, etc.; 天龍八部).

All officers and soldiers of the Deva Dragon Eight Commands are officially commissioned as deity stage. Their bodies are all at the Dharma Body level, and all have "long but limited wisdom lives."

They all have supernatural powers; the functions of their Dharma Bodies are beyond those of Heaven People, humans, and ghosts.

The details of the Deva Dragon Eight Commands are:

(a) The Deva Division (天部)

The Deva Division is the command core of the "dharma guardians." It is the general command and reports directly to "the Deva of Material Realm United Authority."

In the Chinese country in Yin Space, all institutes are exclusively owned by the Chinese under government. It is different, however, in Deva Realm. Some institutes are exclusively owned by the Chinese Deva Kingdom, while some others are jointly owned by all countries. For example, The Deva of Dharma Guardians is jointly owned by all countries. The highest administrative institute of material realm is the Deva of Material Realm United Authority (色界聯合集權天), and the Deva of Dharma Guardians, like the United Nations' Peacekeeping Force or Interpol, constantly protects the security of the material realm.

For convenience of management, the Deva of Dharma Guardians has divided the material realm into four areas: east area, south area, west area, and north area, which are separately administered by four Deva Deities. They are called the Four Great Deva-Kings (四大天王).

The Chinese Deva Kingdom is located at the south area, so when Chinese souls enter Deva Kingdom, they first go through the South Deva Gate (南天門).

Each of the Four Great Deva Kings performs the duties independently and guards the respective area of jurisdiction in accordance with *the Law of Deva*. They maintain parallel contact and are colleagues and good friends.

The king in charge of the east area is called ChiGuo Deva King. He has a white face and a "pipa" in his hand.

The king in charge of the south area is called ZengZhang Deva King. He has a blue face and a sword in his hand.

The king in charge of the west area is called GuangMu Deva King. He has a red face, with a purple-golden dragon (snake-shaped), or sometimes a silk cord, in his hand.

The king in charge of the north area is called DuoWen Deva King. He has a gold face with a pagoda, or sometimes an umbrella, in his hand.

These Four Great Deva Kings are all dharma-guardian deities. Therefore, when people build temples, the statues of these four deities are often placed at the front hall.

The other seven divisions are under their jurisdiction.

(b) The Dragon Division (龍部)

The Dragon Division is the marine corps and is responsible for all marine territories, including the oceans. It specializes in amphibian warfare and can shake the rivers and oceans and summon the wind and rain. When Deva Realm is at war with its Deva enemies, however, it provides logistics and is responsible for transportation.

The dragon has a tremendous amount of wealth and is the billionaire of the ocean.

Dragons are animals commissioned as guardian deities and are ranked second among the Deva Dragon Eight Commands. Why do the dragons have such a prestigious status? They have gained significant credit in war.

When Buddha was preaching Buddhism at LingShan (靈山), the Dragon King heard about this and led its sons and grandsons to see Buddha and become Buddhists. The Dragon King invited Buddha to its Dragon Palace as a resident guest.

Buddha accepted the invitation.

Then, the Dragon King built a spacious and stately palace under the sea. The palace was decorated and surrounded with the Seven Treasures. The Dragon King also built three roads paved with the Seven Treasures, which led from the seaside directly to the underwater palace.

Buddha arrived at the palace, sat on the grand seat in the hall, shared wonderful words of wisdom, and enlightened the Dragon King and its offspring.

Later on, Buddhism encountered "devil tribulation" in the mundane world. A Deva devil called PoXun (Sanskrit: *Papiyan*, meaning devil; 波卑緣, 波旬) and other groups that hated Buddhism began to slaughter Buddhist monks and demolish Buddhist temples. As Buddhism was going through this crisis, a Dragon King collected Buddhist scriptures around the world and hid them in an underwater vault.

It was the time when Buddhism was severely challenged, and all Buddhism scriptures were no longer seen in the world.

After a few hundred years, the Dragon-Tree Bodhisattva (Sanskrit: *Nagarjuna*; 龍樹菩薩) came to this world. He acquired the scriptures from the Dragon Palace, and Buddhism was able to reappear in the world again.

(c) The Ye-Cha Division (夜叉部)

Ye-cha (Sanskrit: *Yaksa*) has an absolutely ugly face and great supernatural power.

Ye-cha is under the command of DuoWen Deva King of the north area, but its operation covers all areas. Therefore, Ye-cha's operation includes the entire material realm.

Once upon a time, Ye-cha was a mean character; it loved eating people. Later on, it was subdued by Buddha and was commissioned as a dharma guardian. Because Ye-cha has great stamina and may cover a wide area, it is ranked the third among the Deva Dragon Eight Commands.

Ye-cha has an intimidating look and is agile. It can fly, it can dive into the earth, and it can be stealthy.

Luo-cha (Sanskrit: *Raksasa*; 羅刹), similar to Ye-cha, can fly and dive into earth. It is agile, too, and loves eating people. It, too, has been subdued, commissioned as a guardian, and assigned to the Ye-cha Division. Male Luo-cha has a dark body, red hair, green eyes, and an ugly face; female Luo-cha, on the contrary, is very beautiful.

The mission of the Ye-cha Division is to patrol, to make sure the material realm is not invaded by foreign living beings, and to maintain public safety.

Like other divisions, the Ye-cha Division has a hierarchical structure.

During routine patrol, a patrol unit consists of one leader and four soldiers. Each unit performs its security duty in a designated area. The shift change takes place every two hours.

Five units comprise a squad, including a sergeant and a staff sergeant. There are twenty-five combat personnel in total in a squad.

Four squads comprise a platoon, including a platoon leader and a platoon sergeant. There are one hundred combat personnel in total in a platoon.

Five platoons comprise a company, including a company commander and a deputy commander. There are five hundred combat personnel in total in a company.

Two companies comprise a battalion, including a battalion commanding officer and a battalion executive officer. There are one thousand combat personnel in total in a battalion.

Seven battalions comprise a regiment, including a regiment commander and a deputy regiment commander. There are seven thousand combat personnel in total in a regiment.

Four regiments comprise a division, including a division commander and a deputy division commander. There are twenty-eight thousand combat personnel in total in a division.

Four divisions comprise an army, including an army corps commander and a deputy army corps commander. There are 112,000 combat personnel in total in an army.

(d) The Fragrance Deity Division (香神部)

The Fragrance Deity Division is supervised by Department Three directly under the Chinese "Deva of Deva Kingdom Central Authority." Department Three is established in the Eighteenth Deva domain and is the Internal Security Division. The Fragrance Deity Division is a spin-off from the Internal Security Division and is responsible for the internal security of the Yang Space Deva institutes established by the Chinese Deva Kingdom in Thin Space. The Deva domains under its protection include the Deva of Devil Realm, the Deva of Enjoyment Creation, Tusita, the Deva of Yin-Yang United Institute, and the Deva of Thirty-Three Domains.

In the Deva of Dharma Guardians, they are under the command of the east Deva domain, and the leader of the east Deva domain is ChiGuo Deva King.

In addition to the security and safety of the east area, ChiGuo Deva King is also in charge of the Fragrance Deity Division.

These Fragrance Deities are responsible for internal security during peace time and are combat personnel during war time. They are multi-functional deities that have three major jobs: internal security, music masters, and war deities. That is why they maintain a military organizational structure and operate as an army. Once they receive notice for war readiness, they must leave everything behind and report to their units. All leaves are revoked because nothing is more important than war at that moment.

These deities do not consume meat or alcohol. Instead, they nourish their bodies with fragrance. They inhale fragrance essence, and their bodies release fragrance.

The Fragrance Deities wear octagonal hats. Their bodies are red, and they hold flutes in their left hands and swords in their right hands.

The leader of the Fragrance Deities once led his troops to perform instruments at the Deva of Buddha Institute to pay respect to Buddha. Their music shook the Great Chiliocosm.

Fragrance Deities are great musicians. In the Deva of Thirty-Three Domains, during leisure time when the Heaven People yearn for the human world and the past, they often request the music they used to enjoy in the human world. Any mundane music they request, classical or pop music, Beijing operas or local operas, Fragrance Deities can play very well.

Not only they are outstanding musicians, Fragrance Deities are also excellent warriors. Their weapon is music. The music that they perform in the battlefield causes disturbance, headache, internal organ explosion, aching body, loss of motor actions, and eventually failure to fight on the part of the enemy.

Because of such power, they are given multiple concurrent tasks. They do not want to be this busy, but everyone needs them.

(e) The Asura Division (阿修羅部)

The Asura Division is an army specializing in combat.

Since ancient times, Asuras have been extremely ugly monsters. They are not deities, ghosts, or humans. They are bad-tempered, arrogant, stubborn, jealous, and provocative. They live in deep oceans or caves. Their bodies are similar to ghosts, but they are not ghosts. They have desires and emotions, but they are not humans.

The Division of Asura has four combat groups with formidable fighting power.

The commander of the First Group is PoYa. General PoYa is very brave in combat, and his group, therefore, is often assigned to the front lines.

The commander of the Second Group is KuanJian. General KuanJian has wide shoulders. He can make the ocean surge, and he roars like thunder. He likes charging into the enemy line.

The commander of the Third Group is BaoShi. General BaoShi has nine heads, and each head has one thousand eyes. He has 999 hands and eight legs. He spits fire from his mouth. Due to his super-power, he loves to fight and loves wars.

The commander of the Fourth Group is FuZhang. General FuZhang has big palms, and he makes good use of his big palms. A slap of his palm is like a mountain crushing down. General FuZhang can block the sunlight with his giant palm.

Because Asuras have been invading everywhere since ancient times and brought the world to chaos, Buddha often received distress signals. Later on, Buddha subdued Asuras and converted them into disciples.

Under the teaching of Buddha, they may know the great knowledge of liberation, but their minds are not determined enough. Therefore, Buddha can only assign them to be great "dharma guardians" as the protecting deities of material realm and holy warriors to fight wars.

(f) The Roc Division (大鵬鳥部)

The Roc Division is the security guard division of The Deva of Dharma Guardians (護法天) and is responsible for personal security.

The security guards of the Roc Division are different from the security guards of the Ye-cha Division. The security guards of the Ye-cha Division are primarily responsible for patrolling a certain area, and the security guards of the Roc Division are primarily responsible for protecting certain "bodies." In other words, the Roc Division trains security guards to become bodyguards.

The commander of this division is ChiaLoLuo. ChiaLoLuo is a roc with gold wings. Its feathers are gold. When it opens its wings, the sky can be blocked, and the earth can be covered.

The big roc has a big stomach.

There was a time when poisonous dragons were causing disasters everywhere. The big roc volunteered to take out the bad dragons from the world, so it began to feed on the poisonous dragons. It had to eat one giant poisonous dragon and five hundred small poisonous dragons every day.

Later on, it ate so many poisonous dragons that the poison caused it excruciating pains that prevented it from standing up. Finally, it flew up to JinGangLun Mountain and died there. When it died, the poison inside the roc transformed into intensive fire; it burned day in and day out. The Dragon King was afraid that its treasure mountain might become the fire's collateral damage, and it rose into the sky and made pouring rain to stop the fire. The raindrops were as big as cart wheels.

When the fire subsided, the roc's body had been burned out, and its heart smelted into a gemstone, which became the decoration of the crown of the King of Deva Kingdom.

The roc fed on the poisonous dragons and saved the people, but it died of the poison.

Buddha was moved by the roc's integrity and took it as a disciple.

The kindness and pity of Buddha also moved the roc, and it made a vow that it would sacrifice itself to protect Buddha.

In light of the loyalty of ChiaLoLuo, Buddha granted deity stage to it and commissioned it the commander of the sixth division among the Deva Dragon Eight Commands. ChiaLoLuo then became the great "dharma guardian" of material realm.

(g) The Music Deity Division (歌神部)

The nature of the jobs of the Music Deity Division is quite similar to that of Fragrance Deity Division; it is supervised by "Department Three" during peace time and works along with the Fragrance Deity Division to maintain the internal security of the Realm of Desire (欲界天).

The Music Deity Division is a combat legion. It fights shoulder to shoulder with the Fragrance Deity Division, and the results of their cooperation are exceptionally great.

There are male and female Music Deities. The male Music Deity has the head of a horse and a human body; the females are very pretty and are good at singing and dancing.

During peacetime, Fragrance Deities play musical instruments, and Music Deities dance and sing. Their performance is seamless. They have 84,000 different plays, giving joy to every corner of the Deva Realm.

When the Music Deity Division performs in different places, it, like the Fragrance Deity Division, still maintains its military organization. When they are called to prepare for war, they must leave everything behind and report to the legion to prepare to be shipped out. All leaves are revoked. This is the time when all Music Deities abandon all joys and obey their order to fight.

In combat, Music Deities use their wonderful singing to soften the enemies, making them drunk with ecstasy and eventually losing combat ability.

(h) The Python Division (大蟒蛇部)

The commander of the Python Division is MoHouLuoChia (Sanskrit: *Mahoraga*; great snake), which means a python or a python deity. MoHouLuoChia has the head of a snake and a human body. It has great supernatural power.

In the beginning, MoHouLuoChia was a python. This snake had a giant torso and great supernatural power. Its character was unstable, and it was a hoodlum of the world.

It was later on subdued by Buddha and taken as a disciple. It was commissioned as the commander of the Eighth Command of the Deva Dragon Eight Commands and became a protecting deity of the material realm.

The Deva Dragon Eight Commands as described above is a large defensive force for material realm. One mission of such a large force is to maintain the normal operation of material realm, and another mission is to protect our world against invasion, vandalism, and sabotage from the dark forces or conspirators of other worlds. For example, the people in some other worlds are already highly advanced technologically; their flying vehicles travel beyond the speed of light. They regard humans as low-class animals. There is an evil organization from another planet, which has come to Earth on a spaceship to abduct humans as experimental subjects. When they returned to their planet, they dissected the abducted human subjects. They soaked the brains and internal organs of the human subjects in medical solvent for later research. The remaining meat was refrigerated for food.

A thing like this that takes place among us as earthmen does not concern the Deva Dragon Eight Commands. When this kind of thing happens, our material bodies are under the jurisdiction of the justice institute in Yin-Yang Space, and matters concerning our souls are under the jurisdiction of the justice institute in Yin Space. However, things like these events between planets, such as high-class-life visitors from outer space onto Earth regardless of whether they have a good or bad intention, are under the jurisdiction of the Deva Dragon Eight Commands. An alien that wishes to visit the Earth for the purpose of leisure must first be approved by the Deva Division and be monitored at all times by the specialist assigned by the Deva Division.

The vast universe has countless planets inhabited by human beings. The human beings on Earth are of relatively middle wisdom, shorter lived, technologically underdeveloped, and are not able to compete with high-wisdom human beings. We cannot compete with them in various respects, such as flying vehicles, life spans, body functions, scientific inventions and applications, etc. Their technology and capability can annihilate the Earth completely.

The Deva Dragon Eight Commands are, therefore, established to protect living beings in the material realm. They include "Deva soldiers and Deva generals" as often referred to in folklore.

2. The Deva of Thirty-Three Domains (Sanskrit: *Trayastrimsa*; 多羅夜登陵舍, 忉利天) (Thirty-Three Deva Domains)

"The Deva of Thirty-Three Domains" is also commonly

referred to as "Heaven." "The Deva of Thirty-Three Domains" has thirty-three Deva domains in total, and each of them has its own Deva Lord (天主). The thirty-three Deva domains are thirty-three spheres created according to the blessed retributions of the living beings.

If living beings in both Yin-Yang Space and Yin Space plant the "causal seed" (因種) that leads them to Heaven by embracing charity, growing their "Fields of Blessedness" (福田), abandoning badness and doing goodness, then, when the living beings in Yin-Yang Space die, they may go to "The Deva of Thirty-Three Domains" through metamorphosis (the ones in Yin Space may do so through the redemption services held in Yin-Yang Space) where they shall receive the blessed retributions that they deserve according to the good karmas they have done.

All enjoyments and needs, spiritually or physically, can be obtained as one may wish in happy Heaven. The environment in Heaven is excellent. It is relaxing, clean, happy, and peaceful. All things go as one wishes. Such an extremely comfortable, easy, and enjoyable life is hard to imagine for the living beings in Yin-Yang Space.

The living beings in Heaven may be there to enjoy, but there are still social classes among them, determined according to the quality and quantity of the good karmas they have done. They live in different Deva domains and enjoy different blessed retributions.

Deva Realm is in Yang Space and is divided into the Realm of Desire (欲界天), the Realm of Disassociation (離界天), and the Realm of Liberation (滅界天).

Living beings born in the Realm of Desire have strong desires for mundane sex and diet. They can hardly forget the pleasures they had when they were human beings. The pleasures they yearn for are the satisfaction of all their desires. Therefore, they come to the Realm of Desire through metamorphosis, where their desires can be fully satisfied, to enjoy blessed retributions. In the Realm of Desire, all desirable pleasures are provided in abundance—great diet, gorgeous men and women, gold, silver, jewelry, palaces, and so on. Whatever a Deva Person wishes for will appear on the spot right away.

The living beings born in the Realm of Disassociation have already lost interest in the sex and diet pleasures that they had when they were human beings. They find happiness in spiritual and mental satisfactions—study, learning, music, art, contemplation, and dhyana. They are more satisfied with these things. They live at a high level of spiritual life and savor spiritual joy and dhyana. Even so, they still cannot let go of their attachment to all images, particularly their affection for the material realm and material bodies. The bad habits (bad nature) that they had when they were human beings can still be found among them.

The living beings born in the Realm of Liberation will soon cut off the troubles of transmigration and disconnect from their affections for the material realm and material bodies. Their "spiritual nature" has entered a high level. They no longer persist in having tangible bodies. They may live in a spiritual world without any material phenomena and feel the subtle activities in life with a non-physical mindset, They remain in a happy, relaxed, and peaceful state of meditation, and experience their "selves" in the pure mindset. In general, they have begun to cultivate themselves seriously, allowing themselves to be liberated from material bodies and the material realm and receive "ease" and energy. At the same time, they are constantly enhancing their levels of Spiritual Light, "spiritual energy," "spiritual power," and "spiritual nature." They have established a firm foundation for their future Nano Bodies in Nano Space.

The living beings enter into different realms according to their respective karma forces. Heaven is located in the Realm of Desire, and all kinds of desires naturally exist in it.

"The Deva of Thirty-Three Domains" primarily comprises cities and gardens, and Central City is the center of it. Surrounding Central City are Eastern-cities Deva Domain, Southern-cities Deva Domain, Western-cities Deva Domain, and Northern-cities Deva Domain. Each has eight cities, and there are a total of thirty-two cities. Together with the Central City, there are total thirty-three cities, and they are called the Thirty-Three Deva Domains.

Around the Thirty-Three Deva domains are four large gardens with different functions.

In the Central City is "ShanFaTang" (善法堂), which is a large convention center where Buddhist services have taken place many times. ShanFaTang was also the place where Sakyamuni Buddha's lecture for his mother took place.

The Thirty-Three Deva domains are enclosed by great walls built of gold. The ground in the cities is also paved with gold. The ground is smooth, soft, and comfortable.

In "The Deva of Thirty-Three Domains," the thirty-three cities together comprise a mega fortress with Seven Treasures. In Deva Realm, everyone calls this fortress "Shan-JianCheng" (善見城), which literally means that only the people of great goodness may see or live in this fortress.

The above is the basic plan outline.

Around ShanJianCheng, there are one thousand great, tall gate towers, and each tower is manned with armed guards. These guards are tall, strong, solemn, and formidable.

There is a luxury palace in the Central City. All kinds of precious jewelry can be found everywhere in the palace. The hall of the palace is tall and magnificent. It is the Central Authority Institute of "The Deva of Thirty-Three Domains" and the residence of the General Deva Lord (總天主) of "The Deva of Thirty-Three Domains." The Deva Lords of the other thirty-two cities are supervised by the General Deva Lord.

This central authority palace in "The Deva of Thirty-Three Domains" is so big that it almost occupies the entire Central City. Around the palace are tall walls with 499 large gates and one small gate. Each gate is guarded by Deva soldiers around the clock.

The city has everything—a luxury palace, the treasure ground, music, dramas and dancing, and countless jewels.

The four great gardens outside the mega fortress of "The Deva of Thirty-Three Domains" are the pleasure grounds for the Heaven People of the Thirty-Three Deva cities.

The name of the east garden is ZhongCheYuan in which Heaven People may have various vehicles appear for them according to their respective blessed retributions.

The name of the south garden is CuEYuan. Heaven People discuss all the harsh and bad things in the material realm. When war breaks out, all kinds of armor and weapons will appear automatically according to needs.

The name of the west garden is ZaLuanYuan. Heaven People of the Thirty-Three Deva domains often allow their imperial maids to visit this garden and have fun with Heaven People to the fullest. Heaven People always feel happy whenever they are in this garden.

The name of the north garden is XiLinYuan. Heaven People visiting this garden will feel exceptionally happy because everything in this garden is extremely beautiful, and the desires of Heaven People will be satisfied here. They are never bored with this garden.

Each garden is very big, and each has a pool called an As-Wish Pool (如意池), which is also very big and is filled with "eight-meritorious-virtue water"[47] (八功德水). Exotic flowers, birds, and trees are everywhere in the garden.

The streets in the Deva of Thirty-Three Domains are all straight, and Heaven People's houses are all built with Seven Treasures. The quality of the house and the number of rooms a house has are determined according to their respective blessed retributions.

All main streets in "The Deva of Thirty-Three Domains" are interconnected in an orderly fashion. The trees and streets are also comprised of Seven Treasures and are beautiful and luxurious.

Heaven People in "The Deva of Thirty-Three Domains" have ten special characteristics:

(a) Free to come and go without obstacle
(b) Live their lives with nothing to worry about
(c) No difference between walking fast and walking slow
(d) Leave no footprint when walking and can fly
(e) No fatigue and no scourge
(f) Body has no shadow but has a shape
(g) No urination and no defecation
(h) No saliva, no mucus, and no tears
(i) Body clean and fragrant; no skin, muscles, tendons, veins, body fat, blood, bone marrow, or bones
(j) Body transforms as one wishes, such as length and color; body is beautiful, dignified, and solemn; people enjoy their company

All Heaven People have the ten subtle characteristics described above. In addition, Heaven People are tall and strong. Their teeth are snow white, their hair is neat and shiny, their bodies are bright with supernatural power to enable them to fly and take leisure trips to Yin-Yang Space, and their clothes are luxurious and dust free.

Through practicing dhyana, any living being in Yin-Yang Space may allow his soul to depart from material body and enter Deva Realm (not limited to Heaven only), with "self-power"(自力) or "other-power"(他力), to enjoy the scenic views and take leisure. Through "memory imprint" (授記) made by "other-power", all scenic views, things, and moments will be remembered vividly and never be forgotten.

The quantity and quality of diet of Heaven People is determined according to their respective blessed retributions.

Each of all six Devas in the Realm of Desire has different social classes, such as emperor and subjects, prestigious and humble, and upper class and lower class (also, wife or concubine is allowed). The humble must obey the prestigious; the lower class must obey the upper class. These relationships are determined according to the quantity and quality of blessed retribution.

In the Realm of Desire, there are also animals that are born through metamorphosis, and Heaven People may make use of these animals for leisure purposes. For example, some Heaven People may prefer a ride on the back of an elephant, some may prefer a ride on a horse, some may prefer a ride on a peacock, and some may prefer to ride a crane. They can do so if they desire.

Why are there animals in the Deva Realm? A saying goes, "One man attains the Way, and his chickens and dogs also rise to Deva." That is absolutely correct. In Yin-Yang Space, if a living being attains the Way (achieves Dharma Body), then that person must have accumulated abundant meritorious virtue, possibly even immeasurable meritorious virtue. With such credits, of course, he may practice great filial piety in the mundane world and redeem any living being that are connected with him. Anyone who has ever helped this person in any way to achieve Dharma Body shall also earn credits toward enjoyment of blessed retribution in the Deva Realm through metamorphosis.

The above suggests that the method of converting living beings, the level of such conversion, and the level which the subject of such conversion can achieve are all deeply dependent on the level of "meritorious virtue" of a practitioner.

All Heaven People are born through metamorphosis, and, therefore, they leave nothing behind after death. There will be no need of burial, cremation, or disposition; when they die, their corpses fade away like beams of light diminishing into darkness.

After the blessed retributions of Heaven People have been exhausted, they will be subject to their karma force and be born in other worlds. If the proportion of bad karma is relatively high, then they will be reincarnated in the animal category or in other undesirable categories to sustain painful retribution.

When a Heaven Person is about to die, there will be an omen signaling that the blessed retribution is about to be exhausted completely. It is one of the phenomena that will occur to all living beings who have the "Phenomenon of the Lifespan" (壽者相).

While still alive, many Heaven People will go to lectures on dharma at ShanFaTang to learn about retributions for good and bad deeds. Long before their death, these people will file applications to reincarnate to Yin-Yang Space, where they will continue their acts of goodness to accumulate virtue, extend their wisdom lives, and keep themselves from falling into bad categories.

When Heaven People are about to die, there will be the following signs:

(a) Thinning and withering bodies;
(b) Clothes begin to gather dust and become stained;
(c) Armpits are always sweating;
(d) Facial color changes and body loses glow;
(e) Becoming ill, having incurable carbuncles, scabies, etc.;
(f) Hair shedding, discoloring, and losing of sheen; and
(g) Gradually losing passion for life.

Despite the fact that life in Heaven can be very enjoyable and very long, there is an end to it eventually. Once the blessed retribution has been exhausted, the suffering of transmigration is still unavoidable. Therefore, Heaven, after all, is an incomplete blessed retribution (not just Heaven, but the entire Deva Realm is an incomplete blessed retribution). Only the attainment of Nirvana can give eternal and true blessed retribution.

There is yet another undesirable thing in the Deva Realm: people cannot breed like the living beings in Yin-Yang Space. Some Buddhists argue that, according to Buddhism Scriptures, people living in Deva can breed. The author must seriously tell readers that the material realm is a world specifically created for the material bodies in Yin-Yang Space. Except for the people and animals in Yin-Yang Space, no life may reproduce. This is stipulated by the Ministry of Soul Administration and is one of the clauses of *the Law of Nature*.

In Deva Kingdom, only "The Deva of Thirty-Three Domains" is the Heaven to which people often refer. "The Deva of Thirty-Three Domains" is different from all other Deva domains. For example, although the blessed retribution for the Heaven People is distributed according to their needs, the blessed retribution is like the savings that one deposits in a bank. When the savings are all withdrawn, the blessed retribution stops. It is then time to leave Heaven and earn some more credits to be deposited back in the "Heaven Bank." Deva People living in other Deva domains are different. They may have limited lives, but compared with the Deva People (Heaven People) living in "The Deva of Thirty-Three Domains," their lives are still much longer. Their blessed retributions do not need savings in advance; they produce their own blessed retributions through their supernatural power. The good karmas fulfilled by the Deva People living in "The Deva of Thirty-Three Domains" in their previous lives are the savings in the bank in Heaven or Yin Space; the good karmas fulfilled by the Dharma Bodies living in other Deva domains in their previous lives result in the attainment of Dharma Bodies.

3. The Deva of Yin-Yang United Institute (陰陽聯合機構天)

The Deva of Yin-Yang United Institute is equivalent to the United Nations for the Chinese area in the material realm. This Deva domain is primarily where administrative institutes and large leisure facilities are. The large convention center is one of the major buildings in the Deva of Yin-Yang United Institute. All buildings here are luxurious and are built with the Seven Treasures. The needs for diet of the people coming here for a convention are satisfied.

Yan Wang, the king of Yin Kingdom, has built a large luxurious palace in this Deva. Yan Wang is the chief officer of the "United Kingdoms." When he does not want to live in Yin Space, he will stay in his palace in the Deva Realm to enjoy the blessed retribution of Deva People. Therefore, Yan Wang has another nickname, "Yan Luo, the Son of Deva."

Due to the effect of karma force, a living being shall die and be born repeatedly and transmigrate constantly from Yin Space to Yang Space, from Yang Space to Yin Space, and so on and so forth. There are a considerable number of individual cases concurrently involved with Yin Space and Yang Space. Because of the extreme difference between the natures of these two spaces, the Deva of Yin-Yang United Institute is established to handle such cases.

A massive "soul archive" is built in the Deva of Yin-Yang United Institute, and there is a large staff dedicated to the management of the archive. A person in Yin-Yang Space dies, and the evaluation by the agency in Yin Space has determined that this soul is to be sent to the Deva Realm through reincarnation to enjoy blessed retribution. Such a case will then be sent to the Deva of Yin-Yang United Institute for further handling. A Deva Person in the Deva Realm dies, and, due to the effect of karma force, such a soul is to be sent to Yin-Yang Space through reincarnation. His files will also be sent to the Deva of Yin-Yang United Institute first and then forwarded to Yin Space to arrange reincarnation.

Because of the sheer number of cases and the daunting workload, in addition to a central administrative agency, the Deva of Yin-Yang United Institute also has established other divisions dedicated to all sorts of tasks.

4. The Deva of Fairy Category Administration (仙道管理機構天)

In the material realm, all living beings begin their cultivation at the lowest level and progress toward higher levels. Most of them attain the stage of fairy through the process of cultivation. Therefore, the Fairy Category Administration (仙道管理機構) has been established.

The Fairy Category Administration is established in Tusita (another name of the Deva of Fairy Category Administration; 兜率天). The palaces in Tusita are tall, spacious, and luxurious. They are built with the Seven Treasures. The city's structure consists of office palaces, residential palaces, convention palaces, leisure palaces, and religious practice palaces.

In Tusita, the most distinctive and eye-catching are the four palace clusters: the Mi-Le Bodhisattva palace cluster, the "Deva Worthy of Primordial Beginning" palace cluster, the "Deva Worthy of Numinous Treasure" palace cluster, and the "Deva Worthy of Virtue" palace cluster.

(a) Mi-Le Bodhisattva (彌勒菩薩)

Mi-Le Bodhisattva has already completed the cultivation of Tenth Ground (十地) and attained the stage of "Virtual-Enlightenment Bodhisattva." Now, he is waiting for the perfect time to accomplish his Buddhahood in Yin-Yang Space. In order to enter into the status of Nirvana without Remainder, he is currently in the process of karma settlement; he is settling karmas with a concealed identity while teaching dharma at Tusita to save and convert living beings.

(b) Deva Worthy of Primordial Beginning (元始天尊)

Deva Worthy of Primordial Beginning is also called Yu-

Qing (玉清) or TianBaoJun (天寶君). He holds the highest Taoist power. Deva Worthy of Primordial Beginning holds the stage of attainment of divine fairy, which is also the highest stage of Taoism.

Deva Worthy of Primordial Beginning has two roles and two stages of attainment at the same time. He is the chief officer of the Fairy Category Administration and has the stage of divine fairy, and he is also the Deva Lord of Tusita and has the stage of Deity.

(c) Deva Worthy of Numinous Treasure (靈寶天尊)

Deva Worthy of Numinous Treasure is also called Shang-Qing (上清) or TaiShangDaoJun (太上道君). He is the second highest authority of the Fairy Category Administration. Under the leadership of Yu-Qing, he supervises all divisions jointly with Tai-Qing, making sure everything is functioning in an orderly fashion.

(d) Deva Worthy of Virtue (道德天尊)

Deva Worthy of Virtue is also called Tai-Qing (太清) or TaiShangLaoJun (太上老君). He is a divine fairy and the third highest authority of the Fairy Category Administration.

TaiShangLaoJun is also called Lao-zi (老子) or Lao-dan. His family name is Li and given name Er. His style name is BoYang. He was born at QuRen Village, Ku County, state of Chu during the Spring and Autumn Period, which was 580 BC. He died in 500 BC.

Lao-zi lived like a hermit most of his life. His primary book is *Daodejing* (道德經), which became the scripture of Taoism. Accordingly, Lao-zi is regarded as the founder of Taoism.

The three Deva Worthies, Yu-Qing, Shang-Qing, and Tai-Qing, hold the power of Fairy Category Administration. The Dharma Bodies under them are the "divine fairies," "Deva fairies," and "earth fairies" in our material realm. The Dharma Bodies at the Deity stage of attainment, however, are not under their administration. The Deity stage of attainment is one level above divine fairy and is under the direct jurisdiction of the Material Realm Deity Headquarters (色界神總部).

The three Deva Worthies (天尊) are collectively called the "Tri-Qings" (三清) and are worshiped in the "Tri-Qing Palace" by people. Tri-Qings represent: Deva, Earth, and Tao (Way).

Tri-Qings all live in Tusita. They are the kings of the Fairy Category Administration. TaiShangLaoJun, however, has responsibilities different from TianBaoJun and Tai-ShangDaoJun. Everything that requires direct presence of an official authority will be TaiShangLaoJun's responsibility. Therefore, people are more familiar with the name of Tai-ShangLaoJun.

5. The Deva of Enjoyment Creation (Sanskrit: *Nirmanarati*; 化樂天) (the Deva Devils)

The Deva of Enjoyment Creation is one of the two Deva domains for "Deva devils." It provides devil's tests for people in terms of "material appearances" (色相) and lust. They do not have the liberty, however, to administer any plan. If they do, then they will be violating *the Law of Deva* and subject to severe punishment by Deva Kingdom.

If people wish for utmost and eternal happiness, then they must first attain Nirvana. Achievement of Nirvana, however, must begin with Arhan. A Nano Body is only given to people of or above the Arhan level. Even Arhan, the lowest level among the Four Great Correct Stages of Attainment, must abstain from craving material things. Only by abstaining from this craving can one be qualified for Nirvana. Material desire is greed and love for the material realm, the material body, and lust. A living being who wishes to be liberated from transmigration and freed from the material realm must abstain from greed for material things; only by doing so may one receive eternal and true happiness.

The Deva of Enjoyment Creation means imposing a great challenge in greed for material things to a practitioner. It cancels and diminishes the utmost joy that a practitioner is about to receive—great happiness is reduced to little happiness (eternal, great happiness is reduced to termed, little happiness). If, however, a practitioner can pass the challenge of greed for material things, then his or her little happiness will become great happiness, and brief happiness will become eternal happiness. This is exactly the true meaning of the Deva of Enjoyment Creation.

The organization of the Deva of Enjoyment Creation is as stringent as any other Deva domain. Under the leadership of the Deva Lord of the Deva of Enjoyment Creation, it has accomplished many daunting tasks and achieved great success.

The living beings cultivating themselves to attain stages of attainment of Virtual-Enlightenment Bodhisattva or lower must abstain from "derivative ignorance" and pass the challenge administered by the living beings reincarnated from the Deva of Enjoyment Creation. On the other hand, for the Marvelous-Enlightenment Bodhisattva who is abstaining from "fundamental ignorance" to attain Buddhahood, the living beings of the Deva of Enjoyment Creation need to appear frequently in this Bodhisattva's dreams or dhyana practices.

When Sakyamuni Buddha was contemplating under a Bodhi tree, he conquered the devils he encountered in his hyper-meditation, successfully abstained from "fundamental ignorance," and achieved Buddhahood. Some of the devils he encountered are "fairy ladies" from the Deva of Enjoyment-Creation. These "fairy ladies" were beautiful, nude, and dancing. They tried everything to lure Sakyamuni Buddha into intercourse, but Sakyamuni Buddha proved their efforts ineffective.

Many of the earliest disciples of Sakyamuni Buddha had encountered similar situations. Cultivation for Arhan, however, does not require abstaining from "fundamental ignorance" as Sakyamuni Buddha had to. Instead, it is only necessary to abstain from "derivative ignorance" to succeed.

Among Sakyamuni Buddha's disciples, there was Aniruddha (阿尼盧陀, 阿那律) who was also called the Number One Deva Eye. He had seen the Deva Women from the Deva of Enjoyment Creation with his Deva eye. In addition to being beautiful and charming, these Deva Women performed supernatural powers according to people's demands. Because Aniruddha had a high level of cultivation, he was not perturbed mentally. After dancing in vain, these women retreated in peace.

The "angels" working in the Deva of Enjoyment Creation are at the Deva fairy level. Some made it directly from the animal category in Yin-Yang Space. These Deva fairies have lived in the Devas of Deva fairies of the Realm of Disassociation since they arrived in Deva Kingdom. Because they have very long lives, some of them are at leisure and still have the appetite for sexual union and lust (similarly, some people living in Yin-Yang Space have various hobbies; some love to drink, some love to smoke, some love to play chess, and some love to read). They filed applications to work in the Deva of Enjoyment Creation. If they do their jobs well in the Deva of Enjoyment Creation, they may extend their wisdom lives. It is fun, and they can cultivate and raise their level at the same time. As they have seen too many things between men and women, they become indifferent about such things and gradually lose interest in these things. Thereby, they can enhance their "temperament" (心性) and move up to another level.

Once the requests filed by the Deva fairies are approved, they present the approvals and register at the Deva of Enjoyment Creation. When registering, one may specify preferred gender, and the registrar at the Deva of Enjoyment Creation will make arrangements accordingly, such as one's residence.

All Deva fairies are Dharma Bodies of the Dharma-eye level. When they live in the "Devas of Deva fairies," which is in the Realm of Disassociation, they cannot have desires for sexual union or diet. When they arrive and work at the Deva of Enjoyment Creation, which is in the Realm of Desire, they will then be able to have desires for sexual union and diet.

As Deva devils of the Deva of Enjoyment Creation, when they execute their missions, their bodies and faces change according to their courtship partner's ideas. For example, when a male is having fun with a female, it is not he who controls himself but the other party. Whatever the courtship partner desires, he will change accordingly; he is totally controlled by the other party. However, there is one condition; the demand of the courtship partner must be sincere deep inside, or this function will be lost automatically.

In the material realm, all good and bad karmas will be subject to the traction of karma force. Everything is governed by "the relationship between cause and effect." It is different, however, in the Devil Realm of the material realm. The living beings working in the Devil Realm are commissioned pursuant to special laws. Their actions are done pursuant to instructions and not because of the traction of karma force. There will be no "cause-and-effect retribution;" they are even rewarded if they do a good job. This also corresponds to the saying, "The devil always outsmarts attainments by one inch." If one has a strong will, then all devils will be defeated, and one will receive Nirvana without Remainder. There will be no more devil bothering one's mind and the saying, "The devil always outsmarts attainments by one inch" will be proven wrong. At such a level, there are only attainments and no devil. Therefore, it does not matter how many devils there are in this world. The greatest devil hides in one's mind. For this reason, the practice of religion must focus on cultivating one's own mind.

6.   The Deva of Devil Realm (魔界天) (the Deva Devils)

The Deva of Devil Realm and the Deva of Enjoyment Creation are both parts of the Devil Realm. The "devil tribulations" (魔難) provided by the Deva of Enjoyment Creation, however, is in one type, whereas the "devil tribulations" provided by the Deva of Devil Realm are comprehensive—all "devil tribulations" are provided, except for the sexual desire.

If they are both "Devas of Devil Realm," why are they not established together? The challenge of sexual desire can be extremely complicated; many people are involved, and the process is entangling. In particular, many Deva fairies are willing to provide "devil tribulations" of all sorts except the sexual desire. Furthermore, each of the Devil Kings of the two Devas is specialized in different aspects. Therefore, the Realm of Devils has these two Deva domains established separately.

The Deva Lord of the Deva of Devil Realm is the Great Devil King, and below him are many agencies. Each of these agencies has different tasks and is headed by a Little Devil King. These Little Devil Kings have different specialties, and all are highly experienced.

These Deva devils from the Deva of Devil Realm, like the Deva devils from the Deva of Enjoyment Creation, may not administer any "devil tribulation" at liberty; they can only do so when there is a mission, or they will be violating *the Law of Deva*.

The palace of the Devil King is tall and luxurious and is built with the Seven Treasures. The Little Devil Kings and every Deva devil have their own luxurious palaces, but the extent of the luxury differs. When the Deva devils are not on a mission, they indulge themselves in the blessed retribution in Deva Realm as much as they can.

The living beings who have achieved the stage of Deva fairy and moved to the Devas of Deva fairies can live for a very long time. Some of them find hobbies according to their own preference, and they choose to work as Deva devils. They do not have an appetite for sexuality, so they choose to work as Deva devils in the Deva of Devil Realm.

The services provided by the Deva of Devil Realm are not in the scope of the living beings' karma forces; these services are tests for scoring or level appraising. Once a mission is assigned, they may possess bodies, reincarnate, or execute their mission in the subject's dreams or meditation. Anyway, different choices are made according to the needs of the mission.

These "devil tribulations" are simply tests. The subject being tested will pass one way or the other. Once the subject has passed, the evaluation follows. The mind testing, or "mind tribulation," is the primary test.

The above are the six Devas of Realm of Desire in Yang Space. They are established in the Yang Space of the Thin Space, and are shared by all kinds of souls.

7. The Deva of Stage Appraisal Institute (評定果位機構天)

The Realm of Disassociation begins from the seventh Deva domain. The Dharma Bodies living in the Realm of Disassociation have completely departed from desires for sexuality and diet.

The twenty-two Deva domains, from the seventh to the twenty-eighth, are all established in the Refined Space.

All bodies living in the Refined Space are comprised of Spiritual Light and are of Dharma Body level. They have achieved their stage of attainment through cultivation in other spaces, and they now live in the Deva Realm to enjoy their blessed retributions.

The three Deva domains of the seventh, eighth, and ninth are the agencies established in this material realm by the high-Dharma Bodies (Buddhas and Bodhisattvas).

The Deva of Stage Appraisal Institute is an institute under the guidance of Buddha that appraises living beings' stages of attainment (評定果位) and is headed by a Bodhisattva leading several Dharma Bodies.

In material realm, the level of practice and cultivation of a soul is appraised by Soul Level Appraisal Division (靈魂層次評審部) of the Ministry of Soul Administration, and the appraisal of the level of Dharma Body is done by the Deva of Stage Appraisal Institute.

The Appearance-Dharma Period in every material realm has a Buddha proxy (代理佛). A Buddha proxy is not a Buddha; he is acting on behalf of a Buddha during an interval period when Buddha A already has achieved attainment, and Buddha B is about to achieve attainment; it is a transition period. During such transition periods, the tasks of conversion and stage appraisal (評定果位) in the material realm cannot wait. There has to be a high Dharma Body stationed in the Refined Space of this material realm and taking charge of the tasks of conversion and stage appraisal. These tasks are collectively called "Dharma Propagation and Stage Appraisal" (傳法定位).

The one that is stationed in the Refined Space of our material realm is Di-Zang Bodhisattva (Sanskrit: *Ksitigarbha*; 地藏菩薩). Therefore, the Deva Lord of the Deva of Stage Appraisal Institute is Di-Zang Bodhisattva. This is also a way that Buddha converts a Bodhisattva—by giving a chance to a Bodhisattva to combine theory and practice.

Under the instruction of Buddha, Di-Zang Bodhisattva leads a great number of Dharma Bodies and works relentlessly for the souls that have attained Dharma Bodies in the material realm. He and his staff are appraising the stage of attainment for each and evey Dharma Body achieved in the material realm during the last two thousand years.

After the appraisal is done, the data of the Dharma Bodies is forwarded to the designated administrative agencies where further arrangements are made. For example, a Dharma Body claims that he is a Buddha, but after the appraisal, he is determined a Deva fairy. This Dharma Body will be forwarded to the Fairy Category Administration at Tusita for unified management. If this Dharma Body has any objection, he is given three chances to appeal:

(a) Appeal to the Deva of Qingyang Institute (forwarded by and from the Appeal Division of the Deva of Stage Appraisal Institute)
(b) If overruled, another appeal can be made to the Deva of Buddha Institute.
(c) If overruled again, and the plaintiff believes that he deserves Buddhahood, the final appeal can be made to the Buddha Qualification Authentication Institute of the Kingdom of United Nebulae.

If all three appeals are overruled, the plaintiff must obey the judgment unconditionally. Further complaint may result in imprisonment or other punishment until there is no dispute.

The Deva of Stage Appraisal Institute is very busy. Basically, the tasks are done by its subsidiaries and the allocation of tasks is very delicate. A direct appraisal by Di-Zang Bodhisattva is rare. For example, there are divisions according to territory; there are divisions for water, land, mountain, and forest; there are divisions for human, animal, and ghost. Anyway, the entirety is divided into parts, parts into sections, and sections into points.

The busiest agency is the appeal division. Every Dharma Body believes that he or she has done a good job and is successful. They all believe that they have accumulated more than sufficient meritorious virtue and deserve a high level of attainment. Therefore, many Dharma Bodies are not satisfied with the results of stage appraisal. They can appeal if they are not satisfied. Every appeal may take a long time to process and need extensive explanations; indeed, it is not easy to convince the plaintiffs. In many cases, a Dharma Body may complain that he is much better than someone else, and ask why his level is lower. In such cases, facts and logic must be presented and *Dharma Body Management Regulations* must be cited to justify the result. If this does not work, then the plaintiff may resort to an appeal.

Appeal is encouraged in the Dharma Realm. Such a dispute concerning stage of attainment (果位) is not regarded as greed. Instead, it is regarded as "Pure and

Unadulterated Progress" (精進). Many Dharma Bodies who are not satisfied with the appraisal result will immediately file an application to continue cultivation through reincarnation.

8. The Deva of Qingyang Institute (青陽機構天)

"Qingyang" used here means a young sun, an adolescent sun, a rising sun, or the sun in the morning.

There are differences among Nano Bodies (namely, the Four Great Correct Stages): Arhan, Pratyeka-buddha, Bodhisattva, and Buddha. All Buddhas are white-bearded elderlies. All Great Bodhisattvas who have achieved Tenth Ground or higher stages are young people or adults (in this book, "young people" are considered to be the same as "adults"), while Little Bodhisattvas (of stages lower than Tenth Ground), Pratyeka-buddha, and Arhan are all juveniles. These are not symbols; these are all Nano Body appearances. One may wish for a transformation of solemn appearance like the "dharma appearance" (法相) as seen in Buddhist temples, but one must have a certain level of energy or this transformation will not take place.

In order to save and convert the living beings in material realm who are connected with them, these young Nano Bodies come to work in our world. Their temporary residences and offices are located at the eighth Deva domain.

The eighth Deva domain (which is the Deva of Qingyang Institute) has many palaces for the Great Bodhisattvas.

Many Great Bodhisattvas live here. They remain anonymous and help Di-Zang Bodhisattva with "dharma propagation and stage appraisal." People are only familiar with a few of them, such as Guan-Yin Bodhisattva (觀音菩薩), Wen-Shu Bodhisattva (文殊菩薩), and Pu-Xian Bodhisattva (普賢菩薩). Actually, there are many more Great Bodhisattvas working in our material realm, but people are unaware of it. Knowing too much, however, does not help a true practitioner; an adequate amount of knowledge is enough.

There are many palaces in the Deva of Qingyang Institute. They are large, solemn, beautiful, and are built completely with the Seven Treasures. Every palace is built according to the tastes of its resident. Because all Bodhisattvas have different backgrounds and habits, the palaces here are all different and are not poorer than the Top Class, Top Level Lotus Pond in the World of Utmost Joy. The only difference is that the palaces in the eighth Deva domain are built by the Bodhisattvas themselves, and the palaces in the World of Utmost Joy are all made possible by the power of vows of Amitabha Buddha alone.

The palaces of Guan-Yin Bodhisattva, Wen-Shu Bodhisattva, and Pu-Xian Bodhisattva are all in the eighth Deva domain. Their palaces are built with different features.

These Great Bodhisattvas are here to help Di-Zang Bodhisattva. Most of the cases they work on are appeal cases.

Every palace of the Bodhisattva has a large staff. They work on different tasks relentlessly according to the will of their Bodhisattva.

Dharma lecture halls, administration offices, reception rooms, stage of attainment appeals courts, gardens, Eight-Virtue Pools, and all kinds of pagodas are built inside the palaces in the Deva of Qingyang Institute. Everything is there. The size of a palace is beyond imagination.

The Bodhisattvas in the Deva of Qingyang Institute have no concern for the administrative tasks in Yin Space, Yang Space, and Yin-Yang Space. They are only concerned with stage of attainment appeal cases and converting living beings.

The cases they have completed are transferred to the headquarters of the Deva of Qingyang Institute. The Dharma Bodies who object to the judgment file an appeal with the Deva of Buddha Institute.

9.   The Deva of Buddha Institute (佛陀機構天)

The ninth Deva domain is the Deva of Buddha Institute. Of course, every Buddha lives in the Pure Land that he has created for himself, but their Duplicated Bodies have moved to the Refined Space of this Saha Land and become teachers of the Bodhisattvas in order to help the Bodhisattvas to achieve Buddhahood and complete their jobs.

One can say that every Buddha has his own Pure Land. In other words, each has his own eternal World of Utmost Joy. Therefore, in this vast universe, there are as many Pure Lands as there are Buddhas. In other words, the universe has countless Buddhas and Pure Lands. In this world, whenever there is a new soul that achieves Buddhahood, there will be a new Pure Land instantly in the Nano Space. A Buddha has the power to create his own World of Utmost Joy, a power which is stipulated by *the Law of Nature*.

In the Deva of Buddha Institute, there is a general administrative agency in charge of everything concerning the ninth Deva domain. Currently, the Deva Lord of the ninth Deva domain in the Deva Kingdom is Sakyamuni Buddha.

Many Buddhas have built their own palaces in the ninth Deva domain as their station posts for official business. In addition to the large palace of Sakyamuni Buddha, the Buddhas that people are familiar with have built large and luxurious palaces here (e.g., Amitabha Buddha and Medicine Buddha).

Every Buddha brings his own workers from his own kingdom. These workers live, work, and learn in the palace built by their Buddha.

Spacious, luxurious, grand, and solemn palaces can be seen everywhere in the ninth Deva domain. Every palace has its own unique appearance such that those who are familiar with these palaces can tell instantly by looking at them which one belongs to whom.

In addition to handling the affairs of the living beings who have connections with their respective worlds, these Buddhas are busy handling the appeal cases in this material realm. After they have completed the appeal cases assigned to them, these cases will be transferred to the general agency in the ninth Deva domain for the final judgment.

In fact, there are indeed many appeal cases in the Deva of Qingyang Institute. The number of appeal cases that can reach the Deva of Buddha Institute has been reduced greatly. Appeal cases that actually make it all the way to the Kingdom of United Nebulae are extremely rare.

The Buddhas stationed at the Deva of Buddha Institute have been certified by the Kingdom of United Nebulae. They have been converting living beings for many lives. They all have great wisdom, and they are more than familiar with the process of stage of attainment appraisal. There is virtually no case that they cannot resolve. A living being coming here will basically leave with satisfaction.

The Buddhas stationed at the Deva of Buddha Institute are also charged with the great responsibility of escorting those to be reborn in the Pure Lands. For example, the Amitabha Buddha Institute is very busy. The message of chanting Buddha's name of the practitioners of Pure Land Sect can only travel at the speed of light and cannot reach the World of Utmost Joy. The messages sent by the Buddhists chanting Buddha's name in the material realm shall be received by the palace of Amitabha Buddha at the ninth Deva domain and will be further processed jointly by the Ministry of Karma Force Registration, the Ministry of Soul Administration, and the Deva of Yin-Yang United Institute. When a Buddhist's material body dies, a judgment on his soul will follow.

Deva Realm is not divided into levels like a tall building; it is divided into domains. These domains are scattered across the entire solar system. The ninth Deva domain, however, is not too far from the Earth. Therefore, it is able to receive messages faster. The messages of the living beings chanting Buddha's name are propagated at the speed of light, which is 300,000 kilometers per second. Travelling from the Sun to the Earth at the speed of light requires eight minutes and thirty seconds. The distance between stars is measured in light years. The distance of one light year is 300,000 kilometers times the number of seconds of a year. In the galaxy that we know, the distance between Altair and Vega is approximately twelve light years. In other words, it will take twelve years travelling at the speed of light. The diameter of the galaxy is more than 100,000 light years, whereas the World of Utmost Joy of Amitabha Buddha is 44,580,000,000 light years away from our planet Earth. That is the reason the Deva of Buddha Institute is established in the material realm. Otherwise, it would seriously delay the processing of a soul from the time that the message was received.

Some people are very zealous in their Pure Land Sect practice, and they are qualified. They believe that they will be successful in reaching their destination after their death. Indeed, they can make it. They chant Amitabha before their death, and they are escorted to the Pure Land of Medicine Buddha or other Buddhas. This is the collaborative result of the Deva of Buddha Institute.

When teaching Buddhism in Yin-Yang Space, one cannot reveal every Pure Land and can only describe one or two as a representation. The backgrounds of the living beings, however, are very complex. These souls have connections with not just one or two Buddhas; some of them even do not have connection with Amitabha Buddha. These souls have been through many instances of transmigration and many worlds, over infinite Kalpas, and have established connections with many Buddhas. These souls are from different Pure Lands.

When a soul begins the Pure Land Sect practice, they are in a school of religious practice, and their deaths are their graduations. When they graduate, these students will be sent everywhere. They chant Amitabha, and they go to different Pure Lands because all Pure Lands are Worlds of Utmost Joy. This is also called "stream dispersion" (分流).

"Stream dispersion" means not all living beings who practice the Pure Land Sect go to the same Pure Land. They must be sent to different Pure Lands. This is a method of decentralized management used in managing living beings.

When the material realm is about to decay and disappear, the headquarters of the Deva of Buddha Institute will look for and contact the other newly born material realm. It will then transfer the souls who have not yet achieved Nano Bodies in the current material realm to the new material realm. The souls in the "Original Soul Palace" under the Ministry of Soul Administration will also be transferred; so will Heaven and Hell. Only the material bodies living in Coarse Space will have to wait until their bodies have died before their souls can be transferred. After the transfer is completed, the management system for the souls in the new material realm will be similar to the old material realm.

The living beings will not sense the relocations of Heaven, Hell, etc. How can we know if the galaxy or the solar system has moved in a certain direction for one million light years? For this reason, the relocation of Heaven or Hell cannot be sensed by the living beings.

10. The Deva of Low Fairies (下仙天)

From the point of view of level, fairies are classified into Deva fairies and earth fairies. Earth fairies live on earth, and Deva fairies, of course, live in the Deva Realm. This difference is totally determined by the levels achieved through cultivation.

Deva domains from this Deva domain, or the tenth Deva domain, to the twelfth Deva domain belong to "the Devas of Deva Fairies" of the Realm of Disassociation. These Deva domains are established in the "Dharma Body Pure Residence Deva Domains" in the Refined Space.

The Deva fairies living in this Deva domain are basically of the same level; their ideology and manifestations of supernatural power are pretty much the same. They are all at the entry stage among the Deva fairies.

The Heaven People living and enjoying blessed retribution in "The Deva of Thirty-Three Domains" are all people of great goodness. These people of great goodness are not required to enhance greatly their level of ideology or achieve progress in the matters of lust, alcohol, or "temperament" (心性). As long as they have hearts of goodness and are able to continue their acts of charity, it will be enough. The living beings living in the Devas of Deva Fairies, however, are different. It is far insufficient if they only have hearts of goodness and perform acts of charity; they need to make significant improvement in the matters of lust, alcohol, and "temperament."

Prior to achieving the stage of attainment of Deva fairy, they must succeed in studies of human physiology, life, and the material realm. They must believe: in souls, which exist and transmigrate after material bodies' deaths; in the Deva government and the under government; in cause-and-effect retribution and multiple spaces; in Qingticle (炁) (Spiritual Qi; 靈氣) as a kind of energy; that the integration of such eternal energy of universe and souls can produce Yang Spirit (陽神); that Yang Spirit is not broken down by fire, is not drowned in water, does not die when buried, is able to escape if incarcerated, and is able to enter and exit Yin and Yang Spaces at will; and that Yang Spirit can be achieved by cultivation, thereby achieving fairy stage. Then, they decrease their desire, concentrate their minds, realize the Way, and cultivate Yang Spirit. They even leave cities, abstain from sexual desire, hide in deep mountains and virgin forests, and engage in supramundane cultivation. They will eventually succeed in the cultivation of Yang Spirit and achieve the stage of Deva fairy.

Even though what they are cultivating themselves for is also the stage of Deva fairy, they hide deep in the mountains or forests for their cultivation; their success is not obtained within the bustling cities. Therefore, their mental training is not enough. Perhaps, if they are left among the people and surrounded by troubles, they will not succeed. Therefore, the stage of attainment granted to them is low fairy among the Deva fairies.

Cultivation to become a low fairy is a conservative way of cultivation. There will be plenty of physical pain associated with it before the cultivation may succeed, but it is easier to succeed. If one is too ambitious for a higher stage of attainment and cultivates oneself among people, due to unstable "temperament" (心性), such a person drifts among mundane people and perhaps may not even achieve the low fairy, the lowest level of Deva fairies.

Anyway, anyone who follows the trend of people is an ordinary person, and the one who goes against such a trend is a fairy. The ordinary one follows, whereas the fairy does not.

The Chinese character for fairy (仙) is a combination of "person" (人) and "mountain" (山). A person who cultivates in a mountain will become a fairy.

Alcohol, lust, wealth, and pride are four walls;
these walls trap all living beings.
Breaking through the walls
makes one Deva fairy, or at least benefits one's health.

The Deva Lord of the Deva of Low Fairies lives in the biggest and the most luxurious palace there. Most of the palaces are built and can be changed according to the taste of their respective owners. There are limitations, however, in the areas used and the heights of palaces.

Modern Buddhism argues that the lifespan of every Deva domain is fixed, which is also a serious fallacy. For example, all fairies in the Deva of low fairies are at the level of low fairy, but the lengths of lives of all fairies are different. It is also difficult to convert the average lifespan to the time of Yin-Yang Space. They have their own way of calculation, using the graphs and charts based on meritorious virtue and time. Only a few will go through transmigration after their lives have ended; they constantly seek the opportunity to reincarnate to progress to the next higher level. They have also accumulated meritorious virtue in the mundane world, and, therefore, their life spans change constantly as well.

There are living beings coming in and exiting the Deva Realm at any given moment. Some have very long remaining lives, and some have very short remaining lives. The remaining lives also change constantly; some are extended, and some are cut shorter. Therefore, there is no way to arrive at an average. Their stages of attainment, and even spheres and blessed retributions, are the same, but their life spans are not necessarily the same.

11.   The Deva of Middle Fairies (中仙天)

The eleventh Deva domain is the Deva of Middle Fairies. The people living in this domain have a level of ideology and "temperament" (心性) much higher than those in the Deva of Low Fairies. When they were cultivating themselves in the mundane world, they accumulated virtues through acts of goodness and realized the truths of life, the material realm, and the transmigration of souls. They also attempted taking severe tests of the dusty world. In addition to understanding Spiritual Qi, Yang Spirit, and the way of supramundane cultivation, they understand the way of mundane cultivation. When they engage in supramundane cultivation, they also spend time on mundane cultivation. They devote about 50 percent of their time to supramundane cultivation and another 50 percent to mundane cultivation. In addition to understanding the reason for cultivation, they adopt cultivation using half supramundane and half mundane methods. They have succeeded.

In fact, many middle fairies have attained this stage of attainment directly from the animal category. Because this book is basically written for human beings to read, it will primarily be based on the cultivation standards of human beings in the mundane world.

These middle fairies are much better than the low fairies in matters from social etiquette to the handling of "alcohol, lust, wealth, and pride," from mundane cultivation to supramundane cultivation, and from the analysis of issues to "temperament" stability, when cultivating in the human world. They are, therefore, appraised as middle fairies and are designated to live in the eleventh Deva domain.

The living beings living in the eleventh Deva domain have stronger supernatural power and a higher level of energy than the living beings living in the Deva of Low Fairies. Because they have accumulated much more meritorious virtue in the human world than the low fairies, they enjoy much more blessed retributions than low fairies.

12. The Deva of High Fairies (上仙天)

The high fairy is the highest level among the stages of Deva fairies. Further cultivation from this point on will lead to the stage of divine fairy, the highest level of cultivation for Yang Spirit (陽神) for Taoists.

There are many folk stories in China. Many of the most popular stories are about Deva fairies, such as the Voyage of the Eight Fairies and the Matching of Deva Fairies. The Matching of Deva Fairies is about seven fairy ladies descending to the human world, and the Voyage of the Eight Fairies is about the typical process of cultivation.

The stages of the Eight Fairies are all "high fairies." Therefore, they are also called the high Eight Fairies. They live in the twelfth Deva domain: the Deva of High Fairies.

There are all kinds of luxurious, comfortable palaces in the Deva of High Fairies. The central town of this Deva domain has a top grade castle-type palace, which is the palace of the Deva Lord of the twelfth Deva domain. All administrative tasks and operations concerning this Deva domain are controlled by the Deva Lord and his subjects.

When these high fairies cultivate in the human world, they already have hearts of goodness and are willing to give alms. At the same time, they have experienced the teachings of their mentor and have profound knowledge of Taoist theories (Taoist methods), Taoist techniques, physiology, and life. In addition, they have deep enlightenment in soul reincarnation, Spiritual Qi, and Yang Spirit (陽神). They completely understand multiple spaces in the material realm. On this basis, they are further characterized as having loyalty, justice, benevolence, and integrity. Their cultivation is done entirely in the mundane world. In the filthy stream of mud, they sail upstream without being contaminated. They may be poor, but they never steal; they may be rich, but never commit adultery. Their integrity drives them to prefer punishing badness and praising goodness.

They are dedicated to religious cultivation in the mundane world. They do when they should do, and they do not do when they should not do. To achieve the stage of fairy, they fear no tribulation; they greet tribulation with smiles and regard it as a "contributory condition."[48] They consider filial piety a priority; they are filially obedient to their parents, teachers, and ancient saints and sages. Because of their relentless progress, they always move forward, conquer all tribulations, and cut away all the worries that are commonly associated with cultivation among ordinary people. They have finally achieved the stage of high fairy and are placed in the twelfth Deva domain to enjoy long-lasting blessed retribution.

13. The Deva of Little Divine Fairies (小神仙天)

Starting from the thirteenth Deva domain is the Deva of Divine Fairies. Divine fairies have the thirteenth, fourteenth, and fifteenth Deva domains in Deva Realm; the residents of these domains are little divine fairies, middle divine fairies, and great divine fairies.

The stage of attainment below divine fairy is Deva fairy, and the stage of attainment above divine fairy is Deity. Divine fairy is the highest level of Yang Spirit (陽神) cultivation in Taoism; any further up will not be under the jurisdiction of the Fairy Category Administration.

The general manager of the Deva of Little Divine Fairies is the Deva Lord of this Deva domain.

When the little divine fairies are cultivating in the human world, they already possess all levels of Deva fairy. They cannot, however, engage in supramundane cultivation; they must cultivate in the mundane world. In addition, they must learn how to convert people, be ready to cultivate people at any time, and help people to achieve the stage of fairy and become enlisted in "the team of fairies."

When they learn how to convert people, they must first

learn how to observe, judge, and understand humanity, how to teach according to the nature of people, and all the useful methods for converting people. In the meantime, they must learn more mundane knowledge and skills. In addition to sustaining their own material bodies, they must help their subjects and become intimate friends of them, both of which are directed towards the ultimate end of converting their subjects.

They can use all kinds of methods to convert the chosen people, including creating religious sects and recruiting disciples.

Despite little divine fairies having only a few successes in converting people, they do have a heart for that, they are ready to do so, and they take it seriously. Their lack of experience, however, causes their low success rate.

For this reason, their stage of attainment is little divine fairy.

14.   The Deva of Middle Divine Fairies (中神仙天)

For a Chinese, the term divine fairy is never strange. There are many legends about divine fairies throughout history. Many of the stories have been produced as movies, published as books, or passed around as folklore (e.g., *the World of Divine Fairies*, *the Chronicle of Divine Fairies*, *the Biography of Divine Fairies*, and *the Encyclopedia of Chinese Divine Fairies*).

They become middle divine fairies because they are already qualified to be little divine fairies when they are in the human world, and they have made significant progress at the levels of ideology, personal character, and social etiquette. In particular, their methods and skills in converting people are becoming mature. They apply different methods according to the "natural capacities" (根器) and levels of their subjects, and that is why they can increase their rate of success. Therefore, they can convert some of their subjects and have them enlisted in "the team of fairies."

These middle divine fairies have been pursuing academic achievements throughout many lives. In fact, because of their accumulated learning throughout their previous lives, they excel in many aspects and specialties. This provides a great opportunity for them to become acquainted with people and make a good impression on the subjects to be converted, thereby making the subjects willing to accept their ideas.

Because they still have doubts about their abilities when they convert people, they do not have enough confidence to convert a great number of people. They only try their skills within their circles among their friends and relatives. Therefore, most of the subjects who have been successfully converted are their friends and relatives.

Because of their limited success in converting people, and because the subjects enlisted in "the team of fairies" are mostly their friends and relatives, they are given the stage of middle divine fairy.

15.   The Deva of Great Divine Fairies (大神仙天)

The Deva of Great Divine Fairies is the highest level of the stage of divine fairy. They have great supernatural power, high "blessed retributions," and long lives.

Great divine fairy is the highest state of Yang Spirit cultivation in Taoism. A further rise in the thought level, abstaining from affection for the material body and material realm, and changing the "cognition" deep in the ideology shall lead to liberation from the material realm and birth and death and the receipt of an eternal life.

The divine fairies at this level are all professional philosophers; they have practical theories for the country, society, life, and the world. They are the mentors of all of the other fairies.

When they are in the human world, they are already at the levels of Deva fairy and divine fairy. For example, they already know about all methods of cultivation for fairies, including the practice of dhyana, gathering Qingticle (炁), deep respiration, enhancement of both physiology and psychology, nurturing Yang Spirit, integration of material body and Yang Spirit, and "rainbow material body."[49] In addition, they also know methods of understanding people, including fortune telling by facial reading, palm reading, body reading, ear reading, foot reading, and bone reading. Concurrently, they also know the methods of health enhancement and natural healing, including the understanding and application of herbal medicine, the understanding and application of Yin and Yang, the understanding and application of meridians and collaterals, the understanding and application of Inner Spiritual Qi and Outer Spiritual Qi, and the understanding and control of alcohol, lust, wealth, and pride. In addition, they can master the skills of language and writing. They are good at using all kinds of literary skills in writing and speech and can be understood easily together with the context.

Eventually, their own ideas can be fully expressed and be acceptable to their audience.

They are professional converters. Some are professional thinkers, philosophers, religionists, and educationists. Some are lecturers and professors. They can master the methods of converting people and apply these methods to convert different kinds of people with great results. Not only can they give brilliant speeches, but they also write books. Therefore, they are at a level to "widely convert" other fairies. They are the teachers of all other fairies.

Their level is already high enough, what, then, differentiates them from Buddhists? Overall, the main difference is their "cognition" of the ideological level. Due to limited space here, the issue will be addressed in the next book. Only the most important difference will be introduced here, which is their persistence in the material realm and material body.

Simply put, the Fairy Category pursues "achievement through the present body," becoming a "true person," and achieving "rainbow material body" (虹化色身). In other words, they still have affection for the material body and material realm. When they have gained success, they continue to pursue immortality for their material bodies for eight hundred more years, eight thousand more years, tens of thousands more years, or even hundreds of millions more years of life. On the contrary, Buddhists pursue discontinued affection for material body and material realm. Once accomplished, the material body is to be abandoned, and the material realm is to be rejected, and there will not be transmigration to this world again.

Eventually, they want to be liberated from birth and death and receive eternal and true peaceful happiness.

16.   The Deva of Department One (一部天)

The nine Deva domains from the sixteenth Deva domain to the twenty-fourth Deva domain belong to the Devas of Deva Deities in the Realm of Disassociation.

Deity is one great stage of attainment that comes with a wide variety of supernatural powers, high "dharma powers" (法力), great blessed retribution, and a long life. Deity is a stage below Arhan and above Divine Deity. One level further up is the stage of Arhan in which there is no birth or death. The stage of deity, however, cannot be deliberately pursued. When they are in the human world, they do not know that they can become a deity until they have died. When they are alive, they have proven their loyalty (忠), justice (義), benevolence (仁), and integrity (正). When they die, and if there are vacancies open for deity positions, they will be given the stage of Deva deity or Earth deity and work for the material realm according to their respective karma force. If they are willing, they may become qualified public servants in the material realm.

The public servants in the material realm do not hold lifetime positions. Good performance is recognized, and poor performance leads to replacement. Once one has been replaced, the stage of deity remains, but the job title is downgraded. In some cases, there is no more job title.

The Deva of Department One is a deity administrative agency responsible for managing and registering data of all Earth deities and Deva deities in Yin Space and Yang Space.

Deities are distributed throughout all departments. Those who work in Deva domains are Deva deities (天神); those who work outside the twenty-eight Deva domains are Earth deities (地神). There are also deities in the human world worshiped by people and having no specific tasks to do except saving and converting people with "appearance dharma." They are "leisure deities" (散神).

Deities are everywhere in the material realm, and the Material Realm Deity Headquarters (色界神總部) is located at the Deva of Department One. In other words, Department One is the Material Realm Deity Headquarters.

The Material Realm Deity Headquarters is a giant agency with a huge workload and many departments. Whenever a deity is recognized by the Deva of Stage Appraisal Institute, a field worker will deliver the copies of the files to the Material Realm Deity Headquarters where further arrangements will be made.

The number of Deva Lords of all Deva domains in Yang Space plus the number of ministers of all ministries in Yin Space (the Deva of Thirty-Three Domains has thirty-three Deva domains, and the Deva of Dharma Guardians has four Deva domains) minus the five Deva Lords or ministers of the Deva of Buddha Institute, the Deva of Qingyang Institute, the Deva of Stage Appraisal Institute, the Ministry of Yin Space Central Authority, and the Ministry of Qingyang Enlightenment, gives sixty-eight Deva Lords or ministers, all of which are of deity stage.

Because the minister of the Ministry of Yin Space Central Authority and the Deva Lord of the Deva of Yin-Yang United

Institute are the same deity, these two agencies only take up one personnel quota.

When appraising stages of attainment and determining the stage of a deity, there is no difference between great and little deity. There are only high and low job positions. Their ranking positions are determined by their job positions.

17. The Deva of Department Two (二部天)

The seventeenth Deva domain is the Deity Position Department Two and is the administrative headquarters in charge of all "deity positions" (神職). The deity group is really huge. Many deities originate from the direct promotion of animals. Therefore, among the deities, there are many animals (e.g., the Deva Dragon Eight Commands and the Twelve Chinese Zodiac Animals). From Deva Kingdom to Yin Kingdom, from high mountains to the ocean, there are deities everywhere.

Most of the jobs from Yin Space to Yang Space must be completed by deities or "earth fairies" (地仙). When working, they must be organized and disciplined; anarchy is not allowed. Otherwise, the material realm would be complete chaos. It should be said that to a sentient being, any space has a manager and administrative agency with laws to be followed. Anyway, in our material realm, all sentient beings are rotated in an orderly fashion.

The "deity positions," such as "Thunder God and Lightning Goddess," Mountain Deities, Land Deities, Water Deities, and River Deities referred to in folklore, must be assigned by the Deity Position Administrative Headquarters

(神職行政總部) in the seventeenth Deva domain. If a position in a certain agency becomes vacant, and a replacement is needed, then the agency will report the situation to the Deity Position Administrative Headquarters. Upon receiving such an application, the Deity Position Administrative Headquarters forwards it to the Material Realm Deity Headquarters (色界神總部) for review. If there is a competent candidate, then the deity is assigned directly. If there is no adequate candidate, then the personnel requirement is forwarded to the Deva of Stage Appraisal Institute specifying the level of deity required with a detailed job description. The Deva of Stage Appraisal Institute will search for the adequate candidate throughout the world according to the request of the Material Realm Deity Headquarters. If there is such a candidate who is agreeable, then the candidate will be commissioned as a deity. Next, the file of this deity will be forwarded to the Material Realm Deity Headquarters to follow up.

The Thunder God and Lightning Goddess to which folklore often refers are not responsible for producing thunder and lightning as is thought by people. Rather, their jobs are monitoring thunder and lightning and preventing any "accidental" calamity in the material realm caused by thunder and lightning.

The Deity Position Administrative Headquarters is very large with many workers. In addition to managing the deity positions in Deva Kingdom, it manages the deity positions in Yin Kingdom, including the "leisure deities."

To be more precise, the Deva of Department One is responsible for file archives, while the Deva of Department

Two is responsible for the arrangement and management of deity positions.

18.   The Deva of Department Three (三部天)

Department Three is located in the eighteenth Deva domain and is also a department leading "deity positions." The Deva deities living in the Deva of Department Three are primarily responsible for internal security; it is the Internal Security Department.

Every deity working in Department Three is a highly trained fighter in martial arts. They fight faster than the speed of light. They specialize in close-quarters bare-hand combat techniques and are skilled in the eighteen weapons.

Department Three is different from Departments One and Two. Departments One and Two are responsible for the administration of the material realm, and Department Three is responsible for the internal security of "the Refined Space Deva Domains." The Deva domains directly under their protection are the four Deva domains in the Realm of Liberation and the eighteen Deva domains in the Realm of Disassociation.

There are six more Deva domains in the Realm of Desire, which also need internal security. Both the Realm of Desire and the Realm of Disassociation belong to the Deva Realm, but they are two different states of living. Therefore, deities with ideology of the Realm of Disassociation cannot be sent to the Realm of Desire to work. A group of deities that holds the ideology of the Realm of Desire and has not entered the ideology of the Realm of Disassociation must be organized and sent to the Realm of Desire to perform internal security tasks. Therefore, the Music Deity Division and Fragrance Deity Division are separately established. Together with the other six divisions of the Deva of Dharma Guardians, they are collectively called the Deva Dragon Eight Commands.

The Music Deity Division and Fragrance Deity Division are the Internal Security Department for the Deva domains in the Realm of Desire in Chinese Deva Kingdom. This department is a unique agency with dual leadership. During peacetime, it is ruled by Department Three. During wartime, both Music Deity Division and Fragrance Deity Division are ruled by the Deva of Dharma Guardians, and war is the priority. At such a time, all Deva Kingdoms in the material realm are united to fight against the external enemy.

Department Three focuses its effort mostly on the Deva of Deva Kingdom Central Authority, followed by the Deva of Deva Kingdom Justice, the Deva of Wisdom Life Management Committee, the Deva of Deva City Management Committee, and the Deva of United Enlightenment (Chinese Division).

These five Deva domains are the highest authorities for the Chinese Deva Kingdom. They are responsible for the normal operation of Deva Kingdom.

In Saha Land, the external security of all Deva Kingdoms is the responsibility of the "Deva Dragon Eight Commands," but the internal security is the responsibility of the Internal Security Department of each respective Kingdom. The Chinese Deva Kingdom is no exception. It has established its own Internal Security Department – Department Three.

19. The Deva of Department Four (四部天)

The nineteenth Deva domain is the Deity Position Department Four and is responsible for the general affairs of the Devas of Deva Kingdom Institutes (天國機構天). It is also called the Deva of General Affairs (雜務天).

Department Four is different from Departments One, Two, and Three. Departments One and Two are responsible for the administration of the material realm, and Department Three is responsible for the internal security of the Refined Space Devas. Department Four's scope of work, compared with the other three departments', is relatively small. It only administers the deities responsible for the general affairs of the Devas of Deva Kingdom Institutes.

The deities working for Department Four only work in five Deva domains. They focus primarily on the Deva of Deva Kingdom Central Authority, followed by the Deva of Deva Kingdom Justice, the Deva of Wisdom Life Management Committee, the Deva of Deva City Management Committee, and the Deva of United Enlightenment (Chinese Division).

Some may argue that Deva deity should be a significant role. Why is a Deva deity doing petty tasks like general affairs?

In the Devas of Deva Kingdom Institutes, it is normal for Deva deities to perform general affairs tasks, but such deities are mostly officials. When they are at work, they command their staff to do the work. Most of the staff members are Deva fairies, such as fairy ladies.

Hoodlum in Deva, a motion picture based on the novel *Journey to the West*, mentions Sun Wu-kung, who wishes to be commissioned as a deity. His wish is granted, and he is commissioned as Bimawun (literally the Protector of Horses). But, he despises this title and declares himself the Deva-High Great Saint.

In reality, such self-commissioning is mischievous regardless of who does it. It is similar in the human world where many people call themselves "Living Buddhas." There is no regulatory authority when they exist in their material bodies, but when their material bodies die, their souls are regulated. Then, they would not dare to call themselves "Living Buddhas." Sun Wu-kung's capability is much higher than a "Living Buddha," but he could not escape from the palm of Buddha. A folk saying goes "You can indulge your ruthless monkey business now, but later on, a list will be unfolded for you."

Life is short. Behave!

It is not rare for a deity to perform general affairs. Pick anyone who sweeps the floor for Buddha. He might just be a Pratyeka-buddha.

Although the Deva Lord of Department Four manages only a few "deity positions" and is not so busy, these deity positions' jobs are critical because they are performed around the "Deva Emperors." Everything must be considered and arranged carefully. Otherwise, the Deva Emperors may request a replacement. Therefore, all deities working for Department Four are carefully screened and selected by the Deity Position Administrative Head-quarters.

Most of the Deva deities working for Department Four have comprehensive knowledge with a high level of education. They have a good "temperament" (心性), calm-personality, great work ethic, and are thoroughly considerate. They must exercise good leadership and be capable of performing ideological tasks.

Of course, they must have the qualities of a deity, such as loyalty, justice, benevolence, and integrity. Without these criteria, there is no need for further discussion.

20.   The Deva of United Enlightenment (聯合教化天)

The Deva of United Enlightenment is an international organization in Deva Realm and is a direct subsidiary of the Deva of Material Realm United Authority (色界聯合集權天).

The twentieth Deva domain is the Chinese Division of the Deva of United Enlightenment.

The Deva of United Enlightenment's mission is specific: passing different "cognition and views" according to ethnic groups among different areas of the ordinary people, allowing the theories of such "cognition and views" to be supported and widely accepted, and achieving the same result of saving and converting with different methods regardless of how varied they are.

People frequently say, "Pervasively convert living beings" (普渡眾生). It is nothing more than a slogan. There are about six or seven billion people (as of 2009) in this world; there is no way an ordinary person may literally convert living beings "pervasively." In a person's lifetime, he must first go through infant stage. After his school years, he must also learn and understand the society, life, and humanity.

A person on average reaches maturity of mind at about fifty years of age. By such time, one should have achieved a certain level of comprehension in reasoning and be able to combine theory and practice. From this point forward, a person may have no more than a few decades of time to write books and convert people. There are really not many people that can be saved and converted over this period of time. In fact, only those who are connected with them can be saved and converted. The same also applies to the teaching of Buddhism by our great mentor, Sakyamuni Buddha.

In the circle of philosophy, there are not many young philosophers (under the age of fifty). Therefore, the mature period of philosophers, thinkers, and religious leaders begins as late as their fifties. Before the age of fifty, they are mainly studying and practicing.

There is a slogan at the Deva of United Enlightenment: "pervasively convert living beings." It indeed has done it. From Sakyamuni, Lao-zi, Jesus, to whoever may come in the future, the mission of religious teaching is all arranged by the Deva of United Enlightenment. It is also the Deva of United Enlightenment that decides and makes detailed plans about who shall be the next to carry on the legacy and promotion.

When the world needs to propagate a certain religion, and there is no expert to propagate such a religion in the-material realm, they will file a report to the "authority center" of this nebula. According to the report, a dele-gate will be sent to this material realm, and the Deva of United Enlightenment will contact other agencies for the arrangement of the matters regarding the reincarnation and "dharma" propagation.

The Deva of United Enlightenment is in charge of all religions, including folklore, Shamanism, Buddhism, Taoism, Shinto, Christianity, Islam, and others. As long as there are lives, the tasks of saving and converting will be arranged. From basic-level education to high-level education, none are ignored. It truly fulfills the dictum "pervasively convert living beings."

The Deva of United Enlightenment and the Devas of Devil Realm work closely together. They arrange Deva devils for the weaknesses in the mind of everyone, making such person constantly dream about what he or she fears most until the person no longer has such a fear. Once this challenge has been passed, a new challenge follows. Therefore, there will always be "devil tribulations" (魔難) in life. That is why there is the saying, "The devil always outsmarts attainments by one inch." Before a person achieves Buddhahood, there will be "devil tribulations" regardless of how high a person's level of cultivation may be. The strategy of the Deva of United Enlightenment is that it will never give up on any living being and will not let any opportunity pass by. It plans very delicately to make sure that every living being may progress further from wherever they are.

21. The Deva of Deva City Management Committee (天庭管委天)

The twenty-first Deva domain has established the Deva City Management Committee, which is a standing committee that comprises the delegates of all Deva domains.

Urban planning, urban development, the establishment and management of facilities such as banks, and the maintenance and management of the public environment and public hygiene of each Deva domain are all the responsibility of the Deva of Deva City Management Committee.

Every Deva domain was already planned a long time ago. The amount of space it may take has already been registered. If a Deva domain needs more space and plans for expansion, it is not a decision that the Deva Lord of the concerned Deva domain may make. Instead, such need must be reported to the Deva of Deva City Management Committee. Upon receiving the report, the Deva of Deva City Management Committee sends a specialist to make an on-site inspection. After the inspection, the result is reported to the standing committee. The standing committee analyzes it and makes a decision, and the applicant will be informed whether the expansion plan has been sanctioned. Expansion that goes unapproved shall be deemed as a violation of *the Law of Deva*. The violating Deva Lord will be punished. For a minor offense, the Deva Lord is impeached and replaced, whereas for an aggravated offense, the Deva Lord is expelled from the Deva City and sent to the human world through transmigration to suffer painful retribution.

When the development of a Deva domain is complete, supervision of the urban public facilities becomes the primary job of the Deva of Deva City Management Committee. In addition to supervising, it constantly improves the existing plans and facilities according to the information provided by all concerned parties.

The Deva Lord of the Deva of Deva City Management Committee is also a deity, who specializes in the management and development of the Deva City. Through his meticulous training, everyone in his staff is an expert in the management of the Deva Kingdom.

22.   The Deva of Wisdom Life Management Committee (慧命管委天)

When a living being receives a long and unlimited wisdom life, the living being also receives eternal liberation. If a living being receives a long but limited wisdom life, however, the living being will be very concerned about the length of his or her own life.

In the human world, everyone wishes for the enjoyment of happiness and naturally wishes for a longer life. After all, only a few commit suicide, and the majority still crave a long life. Some even say they would "rather live like a coward than die like a hero."

As souls transmigrate in material realm, they may be in different spaces and situations, but they share the same desire for long life.

The level of stage of attainment of a wisdom life in the material realm is determined according to appraisal, while the length of wisdom life is determined according to calculation and conversion.

The level of stage of attainment of a wisdom life is determined by the Deva of Stage Appraisal Institute, and the length of wisdom life is determined by the Deva of Wisdom Life Management Committee.

After the Deva of Stage Appraisal Institute has completed the stage appraisal of those wisdom lives who must continue to live in material realm, the appraisal results are forwarded to the Deva of Wisdom Life Management Committee. The calculation and conversion department will calculate the length of life and keep it on file. The data will then be transferred to "the secret code department" where the encrypted data (the secret code) will be entered into the original soul of the wisdom life. The secret code will be released automatically and slowly during the process of life, making life proceed according to the predetermined track.

A living being who wishes to change his or her own fate must fight against fate in order to change his or her future.

The purpose of coding the process of fate is to prevent a living being from knowing certain future situations in his or her life to ensure that he or she will work hard for a better tomorrow without knowledge of what will be happening tomorrow. Hope keeps life going, and self-confidence leads to success. Because people cannot decode their own secret code, they always live in hope.

Many wisdom lives still have affection for the material realm and tangible bodies; they are concerned about the lengths of lives of their bodies and file appeals frequently in the matter of life length. *The Law of Deva*, however, stipulates that only two appeals of such nature are allowed. One is an appeal at the court of the Deva of Wisdom Life Management Committee, and the other one is an appeal at "the Court of Appeals of Wisdom Life

Limit" of the Deva of Deva Kingdom Justice.

A long but limited wisdom life will be notified of the lifespan appraisal result by an agency under the Deva of Wisdom Life Management Committee. If such a plaintiff believes the appraised lifespan is too short, then an appeal can be filed with the Court of Appeals of the Deva of Wisdom Life Management Committee. If the court upholds the original decision, this wisdom life may yet file another appeal with "the Court of Appeals of Wisdom Life Limit" of the Deva of Deva Kingdom Justice.

"The Court of Appeals of Wisdom Life Limit" of the Deva of Deva Kingdom Justice is the highest authority in charge of appeal cases of such a nature. If the Court of Appeals of Wisdom Life Limit upholds the original decision, then the wisdom life will not be permitted to file an appeal to any agency.

The Deva of Wisdom Life Management Committee is an agency that appraises and determines the life span of wisdom life and manages the wisdom-life-limit files. Because of the large number of wisdom lives, there are tremendous numbers of files stored at the Deva of Wisdom Life Management Committee. Therefore, the Deva of Wisdom Life Management Committee hires a large number of workers to manage such files.

The Deva of Wisdom Life Management Committee has consequently formed a number of major palace areas: Deva Lord Palace area, Administrative Personnel Residence area, Court of Appeals area, Lifespan Appraisal area, File Management area, and Reception and

Receiving/Dispatching area.

23.   The Deva of Deva Kingdom Justice (天國司法天)

The twenty-third Deva domain is the Deva of Deva Kingdom Justice, which is the justice center for the entire Chinese Deva Kingdom. It is the justice agency established in this Deva domain that keeps the Deva Kingdom functioning in an orderly fashion in accordance with law.

The Deva Lord of the Deva of Deva Kingdom Justice lives in the castle at the center of the Deva walled city. He leads several Deva deities in running several departments.

The Legislative Department is one of the major justice agencies in the Deva of Deva Kingdom Justice. Since there were living beings in our material realm, the Legislative Department has been operating. Its primary task is the legislation of *the Law of Deva*. Because there are different periods in the material realm, the legislation of *the Law of Deva* must be adapted accordingly by adding or supplementing new clauses or replacing the clauses that no longer fit the new period.

The deities working in the Deva of Deva Kingdom Justice must receive special training before they are allowed to work in this Deva domain. Some of them have been studying laws in their previous lives and carry the quality of a deity, which is why they are selected to receive such training and become experts.

The courts are the busiest places in the Deva of Deva Kingdom Justice. These courts are classified according to the nature of the legal cases. Each court is only allowed to process the cases with which it is concerned. These courts are clearly defined and tightly controlled.

The phrase "not allowed under the justice of the Deva" means not permissible by *the Law of Deva*, which is the law of the Deva Kingdom. Any country that wants to maintain stability needs comprehensive laws. With aid from living beings' moral education, a country may remain stable, and its people may live happily in peace. Moral education originates from religion. Cause-and-effect retribution, education in soul transmigration, and education about Heaven and Hell are all indispensable, and such education must begin with children. The law can only punish those who have committed a crime, but religious ideas of "cause-and-effect retribution" and "soul transmigration" may stop and prevent crime. That is an indispensable foundation for a civilized country. Without such spiritual and cultural development, the people of a country become obsessed with pursuing satisfaction in wealth and desire. Such a country shall get onto the wrong track and suffer severe consequences in social security.

People, who do not believe in cause-and-effect relationships and souls, believe that they can do any bad thing during their lifetime as long as they can avoid the punishment of law.

People who believe in "cause-and-effect retribution" and "soul transmigration," however, are different. They believe they should not do anything offensive to Deva or reason; they believe "there is a deity watching just three feet above their heads;" they believe they must at least take thought for the next life even if not for the present life.

Therefore, they give up the idea of doing any bad thing that comes across their minds. If everyone follows the same pattern, then this country will be a wonderful world itself.

A country without spiritual civilization is not a civilized country. A real civilized country contains both material and spiritual civilization.

Deva Kingdom is a civilized country of such kind. Because religious education is popular in Deva Kingdom, and everyone knows very well about "cause-and-effect retribution" and "soul transmigration," the inhabitants behave accordingly as much as they can without violating *the Law of Deva* and will not interfere with the normal life of the ordinary human.

If they do not violate *the Law of Deva*, then why are the courts so busy? There are many clauses in *the Law of Deva* that only experts can fully understand. Accidental violation of *the Law of Deva* is not unusual. There is a common saying: "There is a Deva net; it may have seams, but it misses nothing." Every legal case must go to trial at court. Furthermore, spontaneous loss of self-control that ends up violating *the Law of Deva* happens all the time.

Besides, living beings of the Deva Kingdom do not always accept the conclusion of everything (such as residence arrangement, lifespan, reincarnation, and disputes among Deva People). Such disputes can be settled by resorting to the court of appeals, which is the right of the Deva People. People living in Deva Kingdom know how to exercise their rights for their interests. *The Law of Deva* is fair to everyone.

24. The Deva of Deva Kingdom Central Authority (天國中央集權天)

The Deva of Deva Kingdom Central Authority, the twenty-fourth Deva domain, is the highest authority of the Chinese Deva Kingdom.

The General Deva Lord of the Chinese Deva Kingdom, YuHuangDaDi (Jade Emperor, literally; 玉皇大帝), is the highest commander of the Chinese Deva Kingdom.

The palace of YuHuangDaDi sits at the center of the Deva city in the twenty-fourth Deva domain. The palace is colossal and magnificent; it is built with the Seven Treasures. The space it occupies is so huge that it ranks at the top among all palaces in the Deva Kingdom and takes up half of the space of the entire Deva city.

YuHuangDaDi is a deity. That means the stage of attainment of his Dharma Body is deity stage. He is a great deity.

The Deva of Deva Kingdom Central Authority is located at the Realm of Disassociation where the desires of sexuality and diet are disassociated. Therefore, YuHuangDaDi has no spouse or offspring.

In folklore, YuHuangDaDi has a wife, whose name is WangMuNiangNiang (Queen Mother, literally), and they have seven girls who are collectively called the Seven Fairy Ladies. This is all fallacy.

WangMuNiangNiang is also called YaoChiJinMu (Jade Pond Golden Mother, literally) and is also a great deity.

Her deity stage comes from her own cultivation, not the alleged marital status with YuHuangDaDi. Therefore, she is an independent deity.

In the entire Deva Kingdom, no one can produce offspring. In the Realm of Disassociation, there is no desire for sexuality at all. YuHuangDaDi may be the king of the Deva Kingdom, but he has no queen and imperial concubines at all. If he did, he could only be an emperor in the human world and would not qualify as the king of the Deva Kingdom. Ancient people deduced, according to the entitlements of ancient kings, that YuHuangDaDi should have more luxuries than the kings in the mundane world could ever have. This was only speculation. YuHuangDaDi does not have the same entitlement to pleasure as the ancient kings did, and that is why he can be the king of the Deva Kingdom.

YuHuangDaDi has the power to commission and de-commission the Deva Lords of all Deva domains. After commissioning, he delegates full authority to the Deva Lords, and the authorized Deva Lord must assume all responsibilities of the respective Deva domain. A Deva Lord must report to YuHuangDaDi periodically. Legal issues are the responsibility of the Deva of Deva Kingdom Justice, whereas stage of attainment issues are the responsibility of the Devas of High-Dharma Body Institutes. Deities are under the jurisdiction of the deity administration, whereas fairies are under the jurisdiction of the fairy administration. Therefore, YuHuangDaDi is a king who can sit back and relax.

YuHuangDaDi has the deity stage that is the highest stage of attainment among middle Dharma Bodies, but his life is still limited. Under the conversion of Buddha and Bodhisattva, he is currently continuing his cultivation and pursuing the Four Great Correct Stages (四大正果). He will eventually yield his throne to the next king; his intention is to obtain the supreme correct stage (無上正果) and to enter Nirvana without Remainder.

With this idea in mind, YuHuangDaDi often reincarnates, when the potentialities and conditions are appropriate, to the human world where he continues cultivation in pursuit of higher stages of attainment.

Stories of YuHuangDaDi and WangMuNiangNiang are popular among folks. Despite many being untrue and variations not agreeing all the time, these stories do serve the purpose of influencing folks.

25.   The Deva of Enterers-to-Be (預流天)

In the material realm, the Realm of Liberation has four Deva domains. The Deva of Enterers-to-Be in the twenty-fifth Deva domain is the first Deva domain in the Realm of Liberation.

The births and deaths throughout many lives and trans-migrations are one gigantic torrent. Some living beings, which have been in and out of this turbulent torrent that never ceases, have become tired and bored, and they have felt the pain. They want to stop, give it a rest, take a break, think about it, and focus on studying and learning about what will become of them if they commit themselves to making further progress.

They realize through their learning that their commit-ments may lead them to the Four Great Correct Stages.

Then, they can be liberated from the painful stream of repeated reincarnations, and they can enter the happy stream where there will be no birth or death. Then, they can jump out of the Three Realms, disassociate from their material bodies of the Five Elements, and receive Nano Bodies that are comprised of Spiritual Light. Then, they will obtain eternal and true happiness.

Therefore, these souls have become aware that they have to be ready to commit themselves. Many of them have formed an upstream torrent. Despite it being smaller when compared with the downstream torrent of the mundane people, it is still a torrent nevertheless.

Despite having studied the theories, having the belief in their minds, and being mentally prepared, they have not yet put it into action.

Those who have made up their minds to join the upstream torrent, but are not yet in the upstream torrent, will be assigned after their deaths to stay in the Deva of Enterers-to-Be where they can enjoy their "blessed retribution."

In the Deva of Enterers-to-Be, they will take the training programs that the Deva Lord of the Deva of Enterers-to-Be has prepared for them for further cultivation that enables them to fulfill their goal when they are reincarnated to the human world again.

The invited instructors of the programs offered at the Deva of Enterers-to-Be are all Great Bodhisattvas from the Deva of Qingyang Institute. The contents include theory and practice. These programs may greatly help the students when they are reincarnated to the human world. These programs are deeply imprinted in their souls, making them study and practice hard. They finally shall be able to enter the upstream torrent and pursue Nirvana.

The palace of the Deva Lord is established at the center of the twenty-fifth Deva domain. A "dharma lecture auditorium" sits in the palace. The auditorium is the place where Great Bodhisattvas give lectures on Buddhism dharmas to living beings of the Deva of Enterers-to-Be. All living beings living in the Deva of Enterers-to-Be have their own palaces surrounding the palace of the Deva Lord. Each palace is gorgeous and splendid.

26. The Deva of Stream Enterers (入流天)
The Deva of Stream Enterers in the twenty-sixth Deva domain is a residence of blessed retribution that is especially established for the living beings that have entered the torrent leading away from transmigration and are cultivating towards the joy of Nirvana.

A living being that wishes to be liberated from constant transmigration may begin his journey of religious cultivation after the mind preparation period. At this moment, such a living being has entered the upstream torrent and is flowing toward the ocean of Nirvana like all living beings that are leaving the transmigrations of births and deaths. These are called stream enterers, which means entering the upstream torrent and travelling in a direction opposite to the downstream.

Because the downstream has much greater force than upstream, one either makes progress or fails entirely. The living beings that have just been stream enterers rarely succeed. When their material bodies die, they fail to land on the shore of Nirvana. Those practitioners, who have lost their material bodies, will be assigned after their deaths to the Deva of Stream Enterers where they can enjoy their blessed retribution and, at the same time, receive training for the next challenge against the downstream.

From the beginning as a stream enterer to landing on the shore of Nirvana, a practitioner must first go through several births and deaths. The practitioner, at this time, is like a phoenix, which is a legendary immortal bird that is reborn again and again from the bath of fire until it enters Nirvana. Every rebirth after death makes this immortal bird of the Sun even prettier, more powerful, and more energetic, as well as places it at a higher level.

For a phoenix to set itself on fire and burn itself into ash requires a tremendous amount of courage and tolerance of extreme pain. A practitioner who wishes to attain Nirvana must have the following qualities of a hero: not proud in success, not discouraged in failure; staying alert when there is nothing happening; struggling more when the environment becomes tougher; and forfeiting nothing when being defeated.

Failure in one's life is nothing. Train, try again, and fear no failure. Have no fear of birth and death. If other people can do it, then you can do it. If others can succeed, then you can succeed. Paddle the boat against the current. Go bravely into the riptide. Having failed, just try again. Fight on and never surrender despite living life after life. One day you will succeed!

27. The Deva of Returners (再來天)

A living being that has vowed to reach Nirvana and achieved stream enterer stage in the human world will receive a stream-enterer body after death. Then, this living being will be assigned to stay in the Deva of Stream Enterers for further training. When the potentialities and conditions are right, this living being will reincarnate to the human world to continue his cultivation of the Way of Nirvana.

This time in the human world, they must, based on the existing achievement, challenge a higher level of cultivation. They "seek their own liberation" (獨善其身) by either supramundane practice (出世修行) or mundane practice (入世修行). Either way, they must raise their level of "cognition" about life and the world. On this basis, they must further break away from "derivative ignorance." Then, this practitioner will surpass the entry level of "stream enterer." He or she will join the great cultivation and become an aggressive member of the upstream torrent and take a key role in the Way of Nirvana.

Because these practitioners are highly self-disciplined and are good role models, they have established a good image among the general living beings. They have also brought great influence onto the progress of ethical civilization in the society.

These people may have not written any book, preached "dharmas," or widely converted living beings, but their positive image does influence people around them and provide good preparatory work for the Bodhisattvas who are coming to convert living beings.

The practitioners at this level will go through many tribulations and sustain many karmic retributions. By doing so, they are readying themselves to enter Nirvana with Remainder in the near future.

After their material bodies have died, they will not return to the Deva of Stream Enterers. Instead, they will go to the Deva of Returners for training and enjoyment of blessed retribution. They are here to accumulate more resources that will allow them to conduct the cultivation of the upstream torrent when once again in the human world.

Practitioners at this stage will come and leave the Deva of Returners for n times depending on the situation of their level of cultivation and status of karma settlement.

If a practitioner has many karmas in the human world, and there are other people demanding karma settlement, then he or she must not leave until these karmas have been settled even though this practitioner is qualified to enter Nirvana. It is like someone who owes a debt and wants to escape, and there is someone stopping the person from escaping. If the creditor demands that the debtor not leave without repaying the debt, then the debtor must not enter Nirvana. This debtor will not be coming back if he has already entered Nirvana, and the creditor will lose the debt forever.

"Returner" means the living beings at this level have made serious vows to realize Nirvana and will never stop until they have reached their goal. Therefore, they reincarnate to the human world for cultivation in the upstream torrent (while settling up their karmas). If one life is not enough, then they will try a second life, and so on until they finally succeed. That is the meaning of "returner."

Modern Buddhists believe that it shall take seven births and seven deaths of cultivation from "stream enterer" to Arhan. This is actually a fallacy. There is no specific rule that stipulates the number of times of returning; it is determined according to individual cases. It may be longer or shorter than seven births and seven deaths; it is not a fixed term.

28. The Deva of Non-Returners (不還天)

The Deva of Non-Returners is established in the twenty-eighth Deva domain. It is the last Deva domain in the Realm of Liberation and the last Deva domain in the Deva Kingdom.

The living beings receiving training and blessed retribution in this Deva domain may enter "Nirvana with Remainder" after one more birth and one more death in the mundane world. Then, they will be forever away from the material realm and material body and free from the suffering of transmigration and the pain that comes with it. This is the meaning of the Realm of Liberation. "Non-returner" means that after this departure from the Deva Realm, a living being will never again return to the Deva city if nothing goes wrong during the living being's stay in the mundane world. After that, this living being enters the Nano Realm where there is no birth or death and receives eternal and true ease and happiness.

Prior to entering the Deva of Non-Returners, the living

being preparing for Nirvana must continue transmigration back and forth between the Deva of Returners and the human world to clear the debt owed in the previous lives. While repaying the old debts, there must be no new debt, or the cycle will continue. This is exactly the reason why one must take precepts before coming to the Deva of Non-Returners. Taking precepts is critical in this period.

Taking precepts is removing "derivative ignorance" to prevent acquiring new debts while repaying the old debts.

When settling karmas, one still has to raise one's "ideological level" (mental realm; 思想境界), for example, raising the level of behavior in the mundane world, thoroughly realizing the true meaning of the universe and life, strictly maintaining precepts, cultivating a high level of "endurance of difficulty and temptation" (忍辱), and completely abstaining from affection for the material realm and material body. To pursue eternal great happiness of Nano Realm and Nano Body, one must give up temporary minor happiness. To achieve Nirvana, one is able to abandon all impermanent things and objects in the human world.

When a living being that comes from the Deva of Returners has settled up everything in the human world, deep in the mind of such a living being is no more affection for any person, issue, or object. He (or she) knows very well that everything is uncertain. He has reached a certain level in terms of enlightenment, taking precepts, and conducting oneself. After this practitioner has died in the human world, he is assigned a residence in the Deva of Non-Returners where he enjoys blessed retribution and receives new training.

The new training is primarily about how to enter Nirvana, what the realms after Nirvana are, how to live life after Nirvana, and where to stay. In addition to theoretical training, they will visit other worlds for inspection, particularly Buddhas' Pure Lands. Then, they may choose the living realms they prefer. After Nirvana, the living being will live in the realm that he or she has chosen.

After the training, proper potentialities and conditions will be arranged for the living being to reincarnate to the mundane world for the final effort – to achieve "Nirvana with Remainder."

If this living being fails in the final effort, such a living being must return to the Deva of Returners and start over again!

ESSENTIALS OF VOLUME THREE

42. Deva Eye (天眼)

Deva eye is a simple physiologic function, one of the entry-level supernatural powers, and is an "organ" that comes with the material body.

In modern days, many Buddhist monks have cheated their way to prestigious positions. They do not have any supernatural power because they have failed to cultivate and practice well in the first place, or they do not know the great way of practice and cultivation; all they know is chanting the scriptures. To keep their followers and maintain their dignity as masters, they audaciously claim that there is no such a thing as supernatural power in Buddhism.

It is not that there is no supernatural power in Buddhism, but it is not appropriate to demonstrate supernatural power as a show in an arrogant manner. There is supernatural power in Buddhism, but it is regarded as merely a small trick. A supernatural power is a byproduct in the process of pursuing Nirvana by common people. Having supernatural power is not particularly unusual, and one must not become arrogant because of that. All supernatural powers are pathetic tricks, and only Nirvana is great. Having a supernatural power does not guarantee the attainment of Nirvana, but the attainment of Nirvana will bring supernatural power.

Even a supernatural power cannot alter the karma force. The karma force is extremely strong. That is one of the reasons why Buddhism encourages practice and cultivation instead of supernatural powers.

The fact that Buddhism does not encourage supernatural power does not mean there is no supernatural power. All of the disciples who followed Sakyamuni Buddha had high-level supernatural powers. For example, Aniruddha, also known as the Number One Deva Eye, and Maudgalyayana, also known as the Number One Supernatural Power, had supernatural powers that outran those of anyone else.

A supernatural power is a physiologic potentiality and a function that everyone has; it is a born capability for survival that deteriorates if not unlocked once we are born. If, however, we follow a certain procedure, it can be unlocked or restored.

Assuming that Nirvana is a primary product, then the phenomenon of supernatural powers emerging in the process of pursuing Nirvana is a byproduct of the Way of Nirvana. It is also like growing rice where there are rice husks and rice stalks as byproducts of the rice grain. In this case, practice and cultivation, if done correctly, will lead to the possession of supernatural power. In other words, the enhancement of our knowledge about supernatural powers will greatly help with upgrading our insight when pursuing the Way of Nirvana.

Only a few supernatural powers, which are already familiar to the readers, will be introduced in this book: the five eyes and six supernatural powers.

Five eyes: Physical eye, Deva eye, Wisdom eye, Dharma eye, and Buddha eye.

Six supernatural powers: supernatural power of Deva eye, supernatural power of Deva ear, supernatural power of knowing past lifetimes, supernatural power of reading minds, supernatural power of divine foot, and supernatural power of exhaustion of leakage.

"Five eyes" are the functions that everyone has. They are potential functions before cultivation or being manifested. When manifested, these potential functions become manifest functions. Then, they are "unlocked" (become supernatural powers). Actually, "five eyes" contain "six supernatural powers." We will introduce them separately for details.

[1]   Physical Eye (肉眼)
Everyone has physical eyes; does that count as a supernatural power? Literally speaking, it is not a supernatural power if it is locked. But, when it is unlocked, it is a supernatural power. The only thing is that it is a physiological supernatural power, and it is a supernatural power of the lowest level.

From the aspect of human "cognition and view," there are many forms of bodies that also possess supernatural powers in addition to human beings, such as the Heaven People, ghosts, and Dharma Bodies. Only two forms of bodies are discussed in this book: human beings on the planet Earth and Dharma Bodies.

"Physical eye" as mentioned here is actually the supernatural power of physical eye, which is a function of the human body. Those who have this function may see the Spiritual Qi and Spiritual Light. The high-level supernatural power of physical eye also sees bodies in multiple spaces. This function is of a low level because it allows only the vision of bodies in multiple spaces without two-way communication, which requires additional supernatural powers.

Those who possess the supernatural power of physical eye may acquire the functions described below without having to study or read professional books. Such functions are also collectively referred to as physiognomy (相學) or the "physiognomic techniques" (相術), or in Chinese medicine, diagnostics.

(a) Sense of Hand
- Using one's hand to sense another person's physical condition as well as the past, present, and future. Bone-sensing technique is an example of sense of hand. By sensing another person's bones, one may understand everything about such a person. It is also called bone-reading.

- Observing another person's palm provides understanding of the other person's physical condition, temperament, character, luck, and even past, present, and future. Fortune telling using this technique is called palm reading.

(b) Sense of Body

Sense another person's physical condition and other aspects with one's own body.

(c) Ear Observation

By observing another person's ears, one may tell that person's physical condition and other aspects of life. It is also called ear reading.

(d) Foot Observation

By observing another person's feet, one may tell that person's physical condition and other aspects of life. It is also called foot reading.

(e) Face Observation

By observing another person's face, one may tell that person's physical condition, temperament, character, and fate, including the past, present, and future of the person. Face observation can be applied in medical diagnosis as it is in Chinese medicine. Face observation also tells the history of a person as is done in "numerology" (命理學), which refers to face observation as face reading.

There is a saying: "One's appearance tells one's mind." A person's mind, physiology, and life are all written on one's appearance. If you know these "techniques," you then know the "physiognomic techniques" (相術).

In ancient times, people acquired the physiognomic techniques through cultivation. Gradually, they found the patterns. As written language emerged, such knowledge was written down and passed onto disciples and the generations to come. Today, there are many books about the physiognomic techniques; anyone fascinated may learn the physiognomic techniques through study (by first memorizing, followed by practicing).

A Chinese medicine physician must also study face observation in the physiognomic techniques. It is therefore said that study is also one type of cultivation.

[2]   Deva Eye (天眼)

Once the Deva eye is unlocked, it becomes the supernatural power of Deva eye (天眼通), which will be introduced in this section. Once the Deva eye is unlocked, the Physical-eye will be unlocked automatically.

Deva eye has several modern terms: Eye of the Deva, Opened Eye of Deva, and "Deva-Eye-Acupoint" (天目穴). The last one consists of one meridian and three positions of the brain. There is a "mirror" in the upper rear part of the brain, sitting at an angle facing slightly down. This mirror is called "Deva." A high-level supernatural power of Deva eye can produce images on "Deva" directly like a screen, resulting in a screen effect. The "Deva" reflects the "divine light" (神光) (which is a special kind of Spiritual Light that allows one to see through materials of multiple spaces). The "divine light" lights up the "eye" existing at the pineal (or Mud-pellet Palace as referred by Taoists). Alternatively, the screen may directly display images for the "eye" to see. An "acupoint" at the slightly upper side of the center between two eyebrows receives and emits the "divine light." The meridian runs through the three positions of "Deva," "eye," and "acupoint" in a straight or curved manner, and the trinity of this combination is "Deva eye."

Deva eye is an imaging system that receives and processes information from the multiple spaces. The frequency used by every person is independent. The sources of information are the "bodies" in the multiple spaces, and the level of information source is dependent on the practitioner's condition. This is related to the level of cultivation in the previous lives, the stage of attainment prior to reincarnation, the virtue in the present life, and the level of cultivation and enlightenment achieved.

The often-heard "soul departure from acupoint" (靈魂 出竅) is of the supernatural power of Deva eye level.

In addition to receiving and processing the information from the multiple spaces, the supernatural power of Deva eye also has the following three functions:

(a) Inner Vision (內視)

Li Shi-zheng, a highly self-disciplined Chinese medicine researcher and practitioner in ancient times, indicated, as early as four hundred years ago, that "the inner vision tunnel is only visible and accessible to those who self-examine and self-review." Not only can the meridians and collaterals be observed with inner vision, one may inspect one's own internal organs through self-observation (自觀). *Sheng Ji Zong Lu* (聖濟總錄), a classic of Chinese text written during the Song Dynasty, states, "With inner vision, one may clearly observe one's own internal organs even with the physical eyes closed."

Inner vision comes after the attainment of supernatural power of Deva eye and allows one to self-observe one's own physiological status, which is difficult to examine under normal conditions. For example, inner vision may observe one's own skeleton, muscles, internal organs, meridians and collaterals, acupoints, "inner Spiritual Qi," inner "Spiritual Light," circulatory system, and other physiological functions.

(b) Transparent Vision (透視)

Transparent vision is one of the functions allowed with supernatural power of Deva eye. It comes in several types as described below:

- **See through wall vision (**隔牆透視**)**

This is a supernatural power of Deva eye of a higher level. Watching the "screen" with unlocked Deva eye allows one to see people and objects in another room.

- **See through ground vision (**透視地下**)**

This is also a Deva eye of a higher level. Watching the "screen" with unlocked Deva eye allows one to see objects buried underground, even mineral vein, underground water, and so on.

- **See through human body vision (**透視人體**)**

This is a standard function of supernatural power of Deva eye. Watching the "screen" with unlocked Deva eye allows one to see another person's internal organs, meridians and collaterals, blood, muscles, tumor, calculi, "inner Spiritual Qi," "inner Spiritual Light," existence of "Holy Infant" (聖嬰) and its age, and so on.

- **Microscopic transparent vision (**顯微透視**)**

"Microscopic transparent vision" is also a higher-level function of supernatural power of Deva eye. During a human body scan with unlocked Deva eye, "microscopic transparent vision" allows one to see the other person's internal bacterial activity. For example, it can see the calcification of recovered tuberculosis and bacterial activity, if any.

(c) Remote Vision (遙視)

Remote vision is a higher-level function of supernatural power of Deva eye. A practitioner sitting at home may see people, things, and objects thousands, or even tens of thousands, of miles away. This phenomenon corresponds to the ancient saying, "To know everything in the world without leaving home."

Remote vision can be applied in conjunction with other functions, such as the functions of transparent vision.

There are four types of remote vision functions.

- **Information reception (接受信息)**

Information transmitted by a specific information source from multiple spaces is decoded and presented (in the form of text or image) onto the "screen" inside the brain to realize the purpose of remote vision. This is information reception that depends on "other-power" (他力).

- **Soul departure from acupoint (靈魂出竅)**

This task depends on one's own soul. After the soul has departed, it follows its owner's command and flies at the speed of light to the designated location. The soul sees as if the material body was present, and the person may correctly describe a remote scene. This is information reception that depends on "self-power" (自力).

- **External Body (身外身)**

An External Body is the True Self, as well as an "energy body," that is attained through practice and cultivation in the present life. Using the External Body to benefit one's own "material body" is not against *the Law of Deva* (天條). (A Dharma Body cultivated by a material body is called an External Body if the material body still has "Yin-Yang life" and still exists in "Yin-Yang Space.") A Dharma Body of the previous life, or the Dharma Body cultivated by the material body of one's previous life, is restricted; *the Law of Deva* prohibits assistance to the material body of the present life from the Dharma Body of the previous life.

Using the External Body to help the material body with remote vision is naturally a good practice.

- **Body possession (附體)**

"Body possession" allows functions at many levels, including remote vision. "Body possession," however, is not a way of practice and cultivation that we pursue. All functions as mentioned here are attained through cultivating our own material body and will follow us to the future lives. Body possession is a different story; its functions are attached to the possessor and are irrelevant to our material bodies. After the body possessor recedes, our normal status resumes; there is no attainment of supernatural power after all. The supernatural power is attached to the body possessor; when the possession ends, the supernatural power is gone.

As body possession is a third-party function as opposed to one's own, the "five eyes" and "six supernatural powers" mentioned here (all of which are one's own functions) are irrelevant to body possession, and all functions mentioned here do not include body possession.

[3]   Wisdom Eye (慧眼)

The supernatural power of wisdom eye is built upon and of a level higher than the supernatural power of Deva eye. There are cases that some practitioners attain wisdom eye directly without going through the level of Deva eye. When the wisdom eye is unlocked, the Deva eye and physical eye are automatically unlocked.

The supernatural power of wisdom eye is primarily about the upgrade of the level of the information source, which must be the body at the level of Buddha or Bodhisattva. The Dharma Bodies at such high levels remotely control a material body, so this material body may convert living beings through supernatural powers, allowing the living beings to realize, believe, and study mysterious cultures until they start their enlightenment and gradually "enter the stream." That is how they practice and cultivate the way of Nirvana and finally achieve correct stages of attainment.

Compared with the supernatural power of Deva eye, supernatural power of wisdom eye receives information from wider sources. Also, it requires the practitioners of wisdom eye to upgrade their cultivation to focus on their minds to keep their minds at peace when facing the wider information sources, thereby better servicing living beings. That is why the practitioners of supernatural power of wisdom eye are also the subjects that Buddha is converting.

All levels of multiple spaces will be presented in front of those who possess the supernatural power of wisdom eye.

"Up to the devas and down to the underworld, from the space of Yin to the space of Yang," it supersedes the supernatural power of Deva eye because whoever has the supernatural power of wisdom eye has been given a critical "order card" (令牌). The "order card" grants them access to any department in the material realm to make inquiries about the karmic retribution, "the Life and Death Book" (生死簿), the stage of attainment, and the past, present, and future of a living being as a reference for the arrangement of "karma conversion" (化業) for this living being.

Alternatively, "thought telepathy" (思維傳感) can be applied to understand the other person's status of mind to precisely and accurately save and convert such person.

In addition to the functions mentioned above, it also gives two major functions:

(a) Tracking (追測功能)

With the tracking function, a person with the supernatural power of wisdom eye may track down the how, why, and whole process of an event, despite such event having taken place and only the result being known without the details of what happened.

(b) Prediction (預測功能)

Prediction function is not deduction or speculation. It is about a high Dharma Body informing a person with the supernatural power of wisdom eye, according to the cause and effect relationship of an event, and the person with the supernatural power of wisdom eye then telling the conveyed information to the other person.

The cause of an event determines its effect, which is inevitable with occasional variation in a certain pattern. As an event develops, certain changes might appear. This is because "karma conversion" emerges and alters the effect. Take predicting something that will happen after ten years as an example, the prediction made in the present year may or may not be the same as the one made after five years even if the prediction is made by the same person. If the predictions are inconsistent, it is not unusual, and there must be a cause for that inconsistency.

In terms of prediction accuracy, the further time is projected, the greater the possibility of inconsistency and the lower the accuracy. On the other hand, the closer the time is projected, the lower the possibility of inconsistency and the greater the accuracy. For example, predicting the decay and disappearance of the Earth is projecting a time extremely far out; only an approximate period can be told, not a precise date. On the contrary, the weather station can do a pretty good job of predicting tomorrow's weather. A prediction of the weather for some day one hundred days from now by the weather station, however, may not be accurate, but a person with the supernatural power of wisdom eye can give a highly accurate prediction.

[4]　Dharma Eye (法眼)

Dharma-eye is a high-level function and is a form of supernatural power commonly referred to as a "paranormal function" (特異功能) at the present time. There are two situations for "dharma eye": the Dharma Body's dharma eye (法眼) and the material body's supernatural power of dharma eye (法眼通).

(a) Dharma Body's Dharma Eye (法眼)

Dharma Body comes in a hierarchy of levels and energy classes. Every Dharma Body is born with dharma eye, and dharma eyes are different only in their levels, not in being locked or unlocked.

If a Dharma Body (External Body) that owns a material body is willing to integrate or collaborate with its material body, then this material body will possess the following supernatural powers: body duplication; breaking through spatial obstacles (e.g., moving through walls); invisible body; immobile body (定身); great relocation; transformation; bringing the dead back; rejuvenation; object duplication; moving mountains/changing landscape; body hovering; Samadhi True-Flame; "one-hundred uncaged beasts;" nidus transfer (nidus: the central point of bacterial growth); weather control; grasping objects through air; stealth; and so on. (All functions are mentioned as a convenience; some of the supernatural powers originate from the same function.)

(b) Material Body's Supernatural Power of Dharma Eye (法眼通)

The material body's supernatural power of dharma eye also comes in different levels according to its respective information sources. In other words, the information source is the determinant of the level of the material body's supernatural power of dharma eye.

High-level supernatural power of dharma eye receives information directly from Buddha; a question is asked directly of Buddha, and an answer or correct dharma is directly returned. A person who has attained supernatural power of dharma eye at this level must have been a

Great Bodhisattva reincarnated with the mission of converting living beings. That is why such a person is allowed access to the dharma directly taught by Buddha (in order to widely convert living beings). It is the level that propagates the correct dharma for "widely converting living beings" (廣渡眾生).

The material body's supernatural powers of dharma eye at lower levels receive information transmitted from Dharma Bodies of other levels. Such information varies when converting different living beings with whom the material body has connections. This is the level of converting the connected individuals using supernatural powers and is different from the level of "widely converting living beings" as mentioned above.

[5]　Buddha Eye (佛眼)

Supernatural power of Buddha eye is a high-level function. Similar to the supernatural power of dharma eye, the supernatural power of Buddha eye comes in two types: Dharma Body's Buddha eye (佛眼); and material body's supernatural power of Buddha eye (佛眼通).

(a) Dharma Body's Buddha Eye (佛眼)

In addition to all the supernatural powers of Dharma Body's dharma eye, the Dharma Body's Buddha eye has even more superb supernatural powers that are applied in "martial arts" and "polite literature."

- **"Martial Arts" (武)**

It is the "manifestations of supernatural power" (神通變化) of the "dharma power" (a common term for supernatural function or its strength). Some examples include the creation of Nature, the operations of the Deva, the Earth, and the souls, and the creation of Buddha's Pure Lands. The well-known World of Utmost Joy in the West was created by Amitabha Buddha using the "dharma power" of Buddha eye. The functions and the uniqueness of that world are beyond the power of language.

Only a Dharma Body that has attained "supreme correct enlightenment" (無上正等正覺) has Buddha eye. That is, only Buddha has Buddha eye. The "dharma power" and "supernatural power" of Buddha eye may dominate all Dharma Bodies at the level of dharma eye, making them willingly obedient and behave without disturbing the mundane world. The strength and technique of Buddha's martial arts have reached their peaks. For example, when both perform boxing with the superluminal speeds, Buddha is much greater than the ones at dharma eye level in terms of fist striking speed and strength.

- ### "Polite Literature" (文)
This is the supernatural power in "ideological level" (思想境界). (Supernatural power itself is only the "cognition" of the material body. As a Dharma Body has cultivated to a certain level, these supernatural powers come with progress. It is like comparing low-level animals with high-level animals; functions that are natural to high-level animals are supernatural power to animals at a low level.) Buddha has impeccably completed his studying and practicing; he knows every dharma, he perfectly explains every dharma, he makes great use of every dharma, and he perfectly preaches every dharma. The cultural attainment of Buddha has reached the highest level, and he can use any language, spoken or written, without any difficulty as he does when exercising all dharmas.

In addition to the difference between "martial arts" and "polite literature," the Dharma Body's Buddha eye also has ten functions:

- **Full comprehension of the good places and bad places**

Buddha eye knows every karmic cause committed by the living beings and knows to what realms (karmic effect) the living beings will be led. In other words, Buddha eye has the full comprehension of whether these karmas will lead the living beings to good places for happiness and liberation or bad places for suffering and troubles.

The ability to predict correctly the good or bad effected retribution in the future according to the present karmic cause is the function of full comprehension of the good places and bad places.

- **Full comprehension of the "maturity of karmic-retribution"**

Buddha eye knows the karmic retribution stories of every living being, and, at the same time, knows the maturity time and situation of every karmic cause and its karmic effect. Buddha knows completely the entangled relationship among all karmas.

Buddha eye is fully aware of any karma made by any living being and what has caused a living being to be led to the present condition. Regardless of whether the karma made by a living being is minor or major, recent or historical, in which life, matured or immature, Buddha eye can tell the full details. This function of a Dharma Body is the full comprehension of the maturity of karma.

- **Full comprehension of the states of meditation (禪定)**

The cultivation for Nirvana must go through meditation, which is also a type of Kung Fu (Gong Fu). It is why meditation is also called the Dhyana Kung (Dhyana Practice; 禪功).

The "mind power" (心力) and the physiology of living beings differ for all sorts of reasons. In terms of "mind power," some are strong and focused, while some others are weak and loose. Therefore, a standardized Dhyana Kung practice does not necessarily work for everyone.

Buddha eye can make thorough observation of the level, potential advantage, and potential achievement of the "mind power" of a living being. It allows for customized and personalized teaching; living beings with different "natural capacities" (根器) may get different dharmas (methods; 法門). That is why there are eighty-four thousand dharmas that eventually lead to the same goal: Nirvana.

Having experienced all states of meditation, being able to know other people's states of meditation, being able to master and utilize the dharmas of meditation, being adaptive to other people's states, being able to instruct living beings with the practice of Dhyana Kung, and enabling living beings to succeed at the end is the full comprehension of the states of meditation.

- **Full comprehension of "natural capacities" (根器)**

Since beginninglessness, living beings have experienced different events, environments, and people. Such experiences constantly evolve as time moves on. Different

characters and "habituated tendencies" (習氣) are, therefore, formed and dominate everyone's life. These different
lifestyles have caused the moral quality and personality of
a living being to be shaped in a basic and fixed pattern.
That is the "natural capacity" of a person.

A good "habituated tendency" produces a "good
nature" (善根), whereas a bad "habituated tendency"
produces a "bad nature" (惡根). Good natures will lead a
living being to a good place for happiness and liberation,
whereas bad natures will lead a living being to a bad
place for suffering and troubles.

The transmigrations between births and deaths of living
beings since beginninglessness have accumulated all
kinds of karmic causes and countless good and bad
natures. These natures are very complex; some of them
benefit one another, while some of them suppress one
another. These reactions are boiled down to a unique "natural capacity." Upon contact with external conditions, a
unique natural capacity develops a unique reaction.

Buddha eye can see clearly the "natural capacity" of
every living being; it knows what they can do and what
they cannot do, what they want to do and what they do
not want to do, how to save and convert accordingly, and
what to do with them.

The ability to have insight into (and perform adaptive
applications of) the good and bad "natural capacity," as
well as the behavior and characters, of living beings is the
full comprehension of "natural capacity."

- **Full comprehension of desire**

This is a function of knowing the desires or intentions of living beings.

Buddha eye can observe the desire and quest of every living being. It does not matter whether it is a good or bad desire, a mundane or supramundane desire, or an insatiable or humble desire. Once the desire begins to arise in mind, Buddha eye can detect it. This insight of living beings' desire is the "full comprehension of desire."

- **Full comprehension of the inside and outside of the nebula**

Buddha eye can clearly see the Nature and the "conditioned genesis" (緣起) of every world that is inside or outside the nebula in the past, present, or future. Therefore, the "formation, existence, decay, and disappearance," the "birth, extinction, change and variation," or the state of being "neither born nor ended" of every world inside or outside the nebula are all within the sight of Buddha eye. This ability to know all truths of every world is the full comprehension of the inside and outside of the nebula.

- **Full comprehension of "the dharma of pain and joy"**

"The dharma of pain and joy" is the method by which the living beings escape from pain and attain joy.

Buddha eye can observe all the methods to escape from pain and attain joy. "The dharma of pain and joy" at different levels works for living beings of different levels. Buddha eye can tell the following precisely: which way works best for which living being; what level can be attained by a living being if a certain way is adopted; what the result will be; what the chance of success is; and so on.

Applying such a dharma to save and convert living beings may help keep living beings on the right track and, therefore, increase the chance of success greatly. This observation, understanding, and application of the dharma of liberation are the full comprehension of the dharmas of pain and joy.

- **Full comprehension of "past lifetimes"**

Not only can Buddha eye see how he himself transmigrated in previous lives and how he attained Nirvana without Remainder (無餘涅槃), but he can also see the past lives of any living being as if looking at his own. For example, how one was born, how karma was made, how one died, how one transmigrated, and the complex relationship of the karma forces among living beings (how the karmic retributions interacted with one another, how their births and deaths were related, how they gave one another hard times, how they remained intimate, and so on).

With such details of a living being, it is easy to know the fate of such a living being. With deliberate arrangements made according to fate, the living being may be saved and converted in a shorter time with better result. This ability to know the past lifetimes of all living beings is the "full comprehension of past lifetimes."

- **Full comprehension of "multiple spaces"**

The mundane living beings are limited by their physical eyes and can only see the world in the Coarse Space (粗維空間). Consequently, they assume that the world in the Coarse Space is the real world. They have, therefore, lost their direction, become trapped in an upside down and illusory fantasy, and cannot escape from the painful transmigration in material realm (色界).

Buddha eye can thoroughly see and understand multiple spaces. It can tell which space is real and which is not. Buddha eye can thoroughly see every space; no spatial obstacle or object in space can block its vision. Nothing can escape from its observation. The manifestations of supernatural power (神通變化) of any dharma eye will be recognized by Buddha eye. For example, when a Dharma body disguises as a tree, to a physical eye, it is a tree, but to the observation of Buddha eye, it is not a tree but some Dharma Body.

When observing multiple spaces, Buddha eye sees the Coarse Space as a realm of fantasy; the Thin Space (細維空間) and Refined Space (精維空間) are both regarded as transitional spaces, and the Nano Space (納維空間) is the real world with neither birth nor end. This ability to observe and recognize the illusion and reality of Multiple Spaces is the full comprehension of Multiple Spaces.

- **Full comprehension of "exhaustion of leakage" (漏盡)**
Leakage symbolizes contamination, defect, shortfall, error, weakness, insufficiency, damage, flaw, divulgence, loss, seam, evasion, and being imperfect or inconsiderate.

There is an analogy for leakage. This coast is suffering, and the coast on the other side is joy. In between the two coasts lies the ocean of pain. To cross the ocean, a boat is needed. Steering the boat is like the practice of religion. If the boat leaks, then the practitioner sinks into the ocean of pain. If there is no leakage, then the boat can reach the other side.

Buddha eye can tell if there is leakage on the boat of living beings and knows how to fix existing leakage, if any, and prevent future leakage. It thus instructs living beings how to eliminate all leakage to enable them to sail to the other side for permanent enjoyment. This ability to know the leakage of living beings and instruct them to eliminate the leakage is the full comprehension of exhaustion of leakage.

(b) Material Body's Supernatural Power of Buddha Eye (佛眼通)

The Dharma Body's Buddha eye can be very complicated and has many functions that can only be introduced briefly.

The material body's supernatural power of Buddha eye is much simpler when compared with the Dharma Body's Buddha eye. The material body's supernatural power of Buddha eye does not have the functions of the Dharma Body's Buddha eye; it only has one function - communicating with Buddhas.

Once the material body's Buddha eye is unlocked, one may instantly see the world of Buddha and Buddha himself. In other words, one may seek answers from Buddha, talk to Buddha, and receive instruction from Buddha until one's own Dharma Body has also attained Buddha eye in the future lives. This ability to see Buddha and receive instruction from Buddha at any time is the material body's supernatural power of Buddha eye.

[6] Supernatural Power of Deva Eye (天眼通)

The supernatural power of Deva eye of "the six supernatural powers" and the Deva eye of "the five eyes" has been introduced under the section of Deva eye. Everyone has the "equipment" of Deva eye, but most people have not unlocked it. Supernatural power of Deva eye, on the other hand, is the unlocked equipment that is not owned by everyone. It is like a cellphone in that everyone may buy one, and all they have to do is subscribe to a service from the carriers. Deva eye is like a cell phone with locked network access, and the supernatural power of Deva eye is an unlocked cell phone ready for use.

[7]   Supernatural Power of Deva Ear (天耳通)

Similar to Deva eye, Deva ear is the "equipment" that everyone has, and the supernatural power of Deva ear is the unlocked "equipment."

Supernatural power of Deva ear receives information through the audio nerves in the brain as opposed to physical ears. Therefore, a person with supernatural power of Deva ear can still hear clearly the "voice" that comes from Multiple Spaces even with their physical ears sealed.

Some people's supernatural power of Deva ear is stand-alone and not attached to other kinds of supernatural powers. Some other people, however, are given other supernatural powers when they have attained the supernatural power of Deva ear.

Supernatural power of Deva ear comes in active or passive types. Active supernatural power of Deva ear may pose questions and receive responses from an information source. On the other hand, passive supernatural power of Deva ear can only wait for the information source to transmit; the information actively sent by a person seldom receives a response from the information source.

When supernatural power of Deva ear first appears, it is difficult to tell if it is one's own hallucination or incoming information. Even if one knows there is information coming from outside, there will still be doubt. After a period of training, one may distinguish the difference naturally.

[8] Supernatural Power of Knowing Past Lifetimes (宿命通)

Supernatural power of knowing past lifetimes is similar to the "full comprehension of past lifetimes" of the Dharma Body's Buddha eye. It is singled out here because it is of a different level. At the Buddha-eye level, the functions of Dharma Body are focused, while the supernatural power of knowing past lifetimes focuses on the functions of the material body.

Supernatural power of knowing past lifetimes attained by a material body has limited functions unlike the widely applicable full comprehension of past lifetimes of Dharma Body.

The material body's supernatural power of knowing past lifetimes allows one to know "the causes and effects in the past, present, and future lives" (三世因果) and examine the person's situations of past lives. High-level supernatural power of knowing past lifetimes allows one to know the highest stage of attainment that a Dharma Body has cultivated in the previous life, the reason for reincarnation, what kind of dharmas should be practiced in this life, what stage of attainment may be achieved at the end of life or in the future, etc.

The material body's supernatural power of knowing past lifetimes is an effective tool for saving and converting living beings using supernatural powers. The path of cultivation for attainment can be customized for any person, and it works very well. This customized path allows living beings to understand what kind of dharmas to be practiced and how to practice in the most efficient way without wasting time and effort. For example, a Little Bodhisattva has come through reincarnation to learn the techniques of saving and converting people from a Great Bodhisattva. After the Little Bodhisattva has come to the human world, however, he does not know what he should do. Instead of learning the techniques of saving and converting people, he has turned to pursue the way of Arhan. That is against the sequence of cultivation.

A practitioner in this case may still accomplish the original mission if a person who has the supernatural power of knowing past lifetimes comes along to give a reminder that leads the practitioner to enlightenment.

[9] Supernatural Power of Reading Minds (他心通)
Supernatural power of reading minds is also called thought telepathy or information transmission. There are two ways to attain supernatural power of reading minds.

(a) Training
The emotions and activity of humans follow a certain rhythm. By analyzing such rhythms, one may observe another person's mind through the outer appearance. It is a part of psychology.

After enough study and training in psychology, one may attain the supernatural power of reading minds. That is, one may understand the world inside another person by observing the external appearance of such a person.

(b) Practicing Dhyana Kung (禪功)

Some people have never studied or been trained in psychology at all but suddenly possess some kind of function when practicing Dhyana Kung. Just think about another person and one may know what is on that person's mind, what the person's opinion about a certain issue is, or what the person is planning to do. This function is the supernatural power of reading minds attained by practicing Dhyana Kung.

The supernatural power of reading minds attained by practicing Dhyana Kung can be upgraded to the "full comprehension of desire" of the Dharma Body's Buddha eye. The supernatural power at this time can better help save and convert people (the function is now attained with the aid of the information received).

When converting living beings, the supernatural power of reading minds can help with the understanding about the status of the method being applied, and the method of converting can be constantly adjusted for each living being. Supernatural power of reading minds is still a lower-level supernatural power.

[10] Supernatural Power of Divine Foot (神足通)

Supernatural power of divine foot is a function exclusive to the Dharma Body. It is the Dharma Body that brings the supernatural power of divine foot to a material body; the material body cannot develop this power on its own. When a material body integrates with its Dharma Body, then there is really no difference.

Supernatural power of divine foot is differentiated by weight, distance, speed, and the number of obstacles in Multiple Spaces through which it break. These differences are determined by the level and energy class of Dharma Body. For example, the distance from Point A to Point B is 5,000 kilometers. Dharma Body A is moving its own material body from Point A to Point B, and it has taken him sixty minutes to do so. Dharma Body B is moving the material body of Dharma Body A from Point B to Point A, and it has taken only twenty minutes. Thus, sixty minutes minus twenty minutes is forty minutes, and forty minutes is the difference in strength of supernatural power of divine foot, or dharma power difference, between Dharma Body A and Dharma Body B.

[11]   Supernatural Power of "Exhaustion of Leakage" (漏盡通)

Supernatural power of exhaustion of leakage is 100 percent a function of the Dharma Body; it is unavailable to the material body.

Many modern Buddhists believe that only Buddha has the supernatural power of exhaustion of leakage. This is wrong; it is a basic supernatural power of all Dharma Bodies and, therefore, is not exclusive to Buddha. It is a lower level of supernatural power of Dharma Bodies.

Supernatural power of exhaustion of leakage is an information reception function and is a term that appears as a result of the comparison between the Dharma Body and the material body. Actually, it is simply a normal function of the Dharma Body similar to the aural ability of a material body who can hear people nearby calling his name without mistake.

Here is a good example. The material body and the Dharma Body of the author are in the same room. At the same time, there are ten thousand people around the world asking the author to enhance their Spiritual Qi. These people are chanting: *"Bai Tong Qing Yang Shen Wai Shen"* (literally "worship the Qingyang External Body"; 拜通青陽身外身). The information of these requests is transmitted at the speed of light all over the world. The material body of the author can hear nothing, but the Dharma Body of the author hears all the information without missing a single chant. The Dharma Body then duplicates ten thousand "Response Bodies" (應身) that travel all over the world at a superluminal speed.

Ten thousand pieces of information have passed through the brain of the material body of the author, all of which have been lost. The Dharma Body, however, has received every one of them; not a single one has been lost. That is called "without leakage." "Without leakage" means "with leakage" has come to the end. It also means "exhaustion of leakage" and no more "leaking." The ability to receive calling information in the world without any mistake is the supernatural power of "exhaustion of leakage."

43. Convert Karma (化業)

Karma conversion is not settling karma, cancelling karma, and, in particular, not eliminating karma. No living being's karma can be eliminated, not even by Buddha or Bodhisattva. Karma conversion is about physically changing or converting karma under the condition that there is no elimination. Eliminating karma is prohibited, impossible, and unviable. Approved karma conversion, however, is allowed, possible, and viable. One must settle one's own karma; it cannot be done by any other person. If it could, then Amitabha Buddha would not have needed to spend so many years cultivating Buddhahood. In fact, a great portion of time in the process of Buddhahood attainment is spent on settling karma.

The conversion of "blessed virtue" to "meritorious virtue" is karma conversion, and vice versa. Borrowing the karmic retribution from future lives to be used in the present life is karma conversion. Transferring the karma due to be settled in the present life to future lives is also karma conversion. Dividing the retribution of 100 kilograms of karma into one hundred retributions (1 kg per retribution) is karma conversion. Consolidating one hundred retributions of 1 kg of karma into one retribution of 100 kilograms of karma is also karma conversion.

Karma conversion is a highly complex knowledge. A Great Bodhisattva on a great mission must first complete a training program at the Qingyang Zang (青陽藏) of the "Kingdom of United Nebulae" (星雲內外聯合王國) and receive the "pardon order cards" (特赦令牌) before he may go to the human world to save and convert living beings and convert karmas for living beings.

Prior to a person's reincarnation, the "karmic retribution code" (業報密碼) is edited according to karmas committed in the previous lives and stored in the original soul (原魂). After birth, these retributions will be fulfilled one by one.

A person with the supernatural power of wisdom eye can decipher the secret code but cannot disclose all of it.

If everyone knows the folded cards (i.e., if everyone knows the result of the game already), then this game is not fun at all. It is as though someone has bought a set of TV series DVDs and begins viewing from the very last episode before viewing the first episode. That makes the storyline boring.

If the karmic retribution code is decoded, then one will know what will happen. There is another arrangement of the code. There are intersections in life, each of which has several routes available. Each route leads to a dramatically different consequence. When life comes to such intersection, a hint can be very useful. Karma conversion can block all routes except one. Then, one does not have to worry about what to choose.

Say the karmic retribution code for this life is 123456. 123 has passed, and 456 is something really bad. Everyone wants to eliminate something really bad, but that will not be the case. Here is a way to perform karma conversion. First, check the files of the future lives to see if there is any good karmic retribution. If there is not any, then one must plant good seeds in the "field of blessedness" (福田) in the present life. The newly planted "field of blessedness" has no grain yet. Calculate in which life the grain will be produced at how much output. If the grain will be produced in the next life and that grain is 789, then 789 is borrowed to replace 456, and 456 is placed in the future lives and evenly distributed in three times or for three lives.

The above is only an example; those who are wise enough can come up with more examples. In fact, karma conversion is very complex; it cannot be performed by ordinary Dharma Bodies. There are many ways to convert karmas. For example, meritorious virtue can be traded by issuing notes. Or, if one complains that the blessed retribution in the present life is not enough, then some of the meritorious virtue in previous lives can be converted into blessed virtue to be used in the present life.

44.   Sarira (舍利子)

Sarira inside a human body is cosmic energy (Spiritual Qi) gathering at high density. Taoists call it Dan (丹), and Confucians call it Ren-Yi (Benevolence-Justice; 仁義). Sarira can go through a physical transformation from a gaseous state to a liquid state or from a liquid state to a gaseous state. The cremation of a dead material body in a unique process will produce the material of Coarse Space in solid state. It is a crystallized material that comes in different sizes; it can be white or other colors.

The so-called bone Sarira or hair Sarira are not Sarira; they are bone ashes. Calling bone ashes Sarira is wrong. The polymer produced by cremating condensed Spiritual Qi at high temperature is the real Sarira.

Sariputra (奢利弗多羅, 舍利弗) is the name of a person, who was a disciple of Sakyamuni Buddha. Some people call Sarira "Sariputra" by mistake, which is all wrong and should be corrected as the two terms are very different.

Sarira exists at Dan Fields in the human body. There are the small Dan Fields and the large Dan Fields. The large ones are Lower Dan Field, Middle Dan Field, and Upper Dan Field. The cremation of the material body of a practitioner, if properly processed, will produce Sarira. The

author has seen the cremation of a person that has produced three Sariras. These Sarira came from Upper Dan
Field, Middle Dan Field, and Lower Dan Field, respectively.
The one from Lower Dan Field is the largest; its diameter is
about four to five centimeters. The one from Middle Dan
Field is smaller, and the one from Upper Dan Field is the
smallest.

After the cultivation of the three major Dan Fields has
been successfully completed, several smaller Dan Fields
will then be established gradually. The saying, "Every part
of a body has a Dan Field," means that the entire body is
fully charged with Spiritual Qi. The small Dan Fields grown
later on will give fragmented crystals after cremation.
These crystals are called Sarira flowers (舍利花).

Actually, these Sariras produced through cremation
have no use for living practitioners at all. They cannot help
with our attainment, and they cannot give us energy. All
they do is to serve as proof that the deceased is truly a
practitioner (but that does not guarantee the deceased
has attained Nirvana). Therefore, as enlightened people,
we should not be obsessed with Sarira produced after the
death of material body. Instead, we should focus on
cultivating ourselves while we are still alive and how to
grow physically changed Sarira. That is the Sarira that is
useful to us. Further cultivation, based on this foundation,
for the attainment of Nirvana is what the correct way
should be.

45. The Five Qi (五氣)
Simplified Table of the Five Elements (五行)

The Nature					Five Elements	Human Body				
Five Seasons	Five Directions	Five Colors	Five Transformations	Five Moments		Five Zang-Viscera	Five Fu-Viscera	Appearance	Five Facial Organs	Moods
Spring	East	Green	Birth	Sunrise	**Wood**	Liver	Gall	Tendon	Eyes	Anger
Summer	South	Red	Growth	Noon	**Fire**	Heart	Small intestine	Blood vessel	Tongue	Happiness
Long summer	Center	Yellow	Transformation	Afternoon	**Earth**	Spleen	Stomach	Muscle	Mouth	Deliberation
Autumn	West	White	Harvest	Sunset	**Metal**	Lung	Large intestine	Skin and hair	Nose	Worry
Winter	North	Black	Storage	Midnight	**Water**	Kidney	Bladder	Bone	Ears	Fear

The "Five Qi" are the Spiritual Qi of the Five Elements.

To understand the Five Qi, the Five Elements must be explained first. The Five Elements are metal, wood, water, fire, and earth. Practitioners are not independent of Yin and Yang and the Five Elements. Both the world and the human body are comprised of the Five Elements. Please refer to the table above for their respective relationship with the human body.

The Five Qi are the Spiritual Qi of metal, wood, water, fire, and earth. Spiritual Qi is classified into Yin and Yang; the Five Qi, too, are classified into Yin and Yang.

According to the table above, the Spiritual Qi of the Five Elements correspond to the entire human body. Therefore, by gathering the Spiritual Qi of the Five Elements at a specific position (a specific position where the fetus of the Dharma Body may form), a "holy fetus" (聖胎) may be formed. It is the long lost secret dharma: Five Qi Concentration (五氣朝元).

46. Samadhi True Flame (三昧真火)

Literally, "Samadhi" has no meaning; it is transliterated from Sanskrit and Pali.

The meaning of Samadhi in its original language is a state of cultivation that is achieved through the training of "temperament" (心性). When "temperament" has been cultivated to a certain level, the spirit can be comforted to such a great extent that the soul can depart from the body to travel around the Multiple Spaces. Such travel allows the soul to learn more about the true meaning of life, and the level of enlightenment will be enhanced to enable one to attain a Dharma Body pretty soon.

Samadhi True Flame is at the level of Dharma Body and is a function of Dharma Body's dharma eye. Before material body has integrated with Dharma Body, there is no way to blast out Samadhi True Flame.

The flame is no ordinary flame of the Coarse Space; it is the flame of the Thin Space, the Refined Space, and the Nano Space. It is a flame that originates from True Qi and is the flame used by "true body." That is why it is called True Flame. Any material in the Coarse Space, such as water, wind, sand, or earth, cannot stop or help the combustion of the True Flame. Even though the material in the Coarse Space cannot intervene in the combustion of the True Flame, the True Flame can burn the material in the Coarse Space.

Samadhi True Flame means a mundane person has reached the state of Samadhi through practice and cultivation and has attained the Dharma Body. Because the True Flame is at the disposal of a Dharma Body, it is therefore called Samadhi True Flame.

47.   Eight-Meritorious-Virtue Water (八功德水)

The correct name of the Eight-Meritorious-Virtue Water is Eight-Virtue Water. Some people call it Eight-Meritorious-Virtue Water to emphasize the achievements and merits. In addition to the name of Eight-Meritorious-Virtue Water, there are other names like Eight-Meditation Water, Eight-Flavor Water, Eight-Attribute Water, and Water of Eight Types of Virtues.

Eight-Virtue Water is pure water only available in Refined Space, Nano Space, and the "Yang Space" portion of Thin Space. Such water can be used for drinking, bathing, and swimming.

In each of Buddha's Pure Lands, such as the World of Utmost Joy in the West or the World of Pure Lazurite in the East, the Eight-Virtue Pool exists. In the Deva Kingdom of this material realm, many Deva domains (天域) have Eight-Virtue Pools as well. For example, the Eight-Virtue Pool has been built in every palace of the Deva of Buddha Institute (佛陀機構天) and the Deva of Qingyang Institute (青陽機構天).

The Eight-Virtue Water is produced by practitioners, who have attained the Eight Virtues, using the "dharma power" acquired through the cultivation of the Eight Virtues. Therefore, such water is only available to those who own at least one of the Eight Virtues.

[1]   Eight Virtues
The Eight Virtues are filial obedience, kindness and pity, benefaction, people helping, lenient criticism, cleaning and influencing, good guiding, and life releasing.

(a) Filial Obedience (孝順)
Filial piety has been explained in No. 2 of the Essentials of Volume One, including the great filial piety, minor filial piety, remote filial piety, near filial piety, mundane filial piety, and supramundane filial piety.

Although "filial piety is at the top of all good deeds," "obedience" is more difficult than "filial piety."

The master once told the author that "obedience" is "compliance" (隨順) but not "blind compliance." It is about interpersonal skill and the technique that practitioners of Bodhisattva use to save and convert people.

Compliance is easier said than done. The "four methods of winning people over" (四攝) used by Bodhisattva practitioners are the high-level "compliance with living beings" (隨順眾生) that is used to serve the purpose of saving and converting living beings.

"Filial piety" is about taking the initiative, while "obedience" is about being yielding and agreeable to the orders given, which takes "endurance." Correct obedience leads to correct results. Therefore, one must have the correct "cognition and view" (知見) and thought.

A person with integrity, a good heart, and bright hope can gradually self-develop a personality toward perfection through the technique of "compliance."

(b) Kindness and Pity (慈悲)

The meaning of kindness and pity has been discussed in detail in No. 31 of the Essentials of Volume Two.

"Kindness" means bestowing joy or happiness, and "pity" means saving others from pain. A heart of kindness and pity is a heart that gives joy and removes the pain of other people. Kindness and pity is a great virtue and is altruistic. Sometimes, these altruistic acts can even hurt one's own interest. Obviously, such altruistic acts are not based on egoism.

Kindness and pity must find its ground in "goodness." It is meaningless to talk about kindness and pity without "the heart of goodness."

(c) Benefaction (施捨)

Benefaction is not an easy thing to do; it is an altruistic act that benefits other people and hurts oneself. Some give away fortune; some give away "dharmas;" some give away time; some give away physical effort.

In Chinese, "benefaction" is comprised of two characters, "giving" (施) and "forsaking" (捨). "Forsaking" means giving up one's own interest to benefit other people. This is the virtue of forsaking.

Some even forsake their own material bodies to benefit other people. It is an act of dignity and a high-level benefaction.

In an environment where self-interest dominates, having the wish deep in one's heart to forsake is a reflection of the profound "good nature."

Throughout history, many saints have forsaken transient leisure of their material bodies in exchange for the attainment of Nirvana. When our great mentor, Sakyamuni Buddha, was cultivating at the "causal stage" (因地) in his previous lives, he had forsaken his body to the hungry tiger and cut off the flesh to feed the hawk. It was a highly dignified benefaction.

(d) People Helping (助人)

"Help people do good deeds and take pleasure in helping others." That is what good people will do. Human beings are high-class social animals; sooner or later in life, one will need help with some kind of trouble. A person living in a society often needs help from other people when there is a difficulty. Therefore, while living in this world, we must help one another.

Helping other people is a voluntary act of goodness. It may sound complex, but it is easy to do. Lending a hand, for example, is an act of goodness.

Doing good deeds and helping others can be done anywhere and anytime in daily life; it does not have to be done deliberately.

A person takes pleasure in helping others because a seed of goodness has already been planted deep in this person's heart.

(e) Lenient Criticism (寬諍)

"Lenient" means being tolerant and forgiving. "Criticism" means straightforward admonition.

Treating others with a lenient heart is not easy. "Understanding" can be liberation of mind. Ancient people said: "Greatness comes from tolerance." This is also the mental state of "the person with a tolerant heart." Driven by such mental state, the person will treat others nicely and bring reconciliation to hatred. This mental state will make such person commit less bad karma or not commit bad karma at all. It will also make his speech/action incline to the good direction constantly, not only positively influencing other people, but also bringing both mental and physical health into his present life and blessed retributions into his future lives.

Criticism is pointing out the mistake or defect of another

person in a straightforward manner. Such correction is not expressing one's discontent. Instead, it helps the person avoid making the same mistake again. It helps the other person to correct the wrong without fear of offending such person.

A friend who will give straightforward admonition is often unpopular among friends; those who use flattering words and tell pleasant lies can become "confidants." An old saying goes, "The truth bites on the ears." A friend who gives the straightforward admonition is a friend hard to find in the lifetime.

If a person already has a heart of tolerance and is able to point out another person's mistake or weakness calmly without offending him, thereby making him willing to accept the criticism, this person has already attained the virtue of "lenient criticism" among the Eight Virtues.

(f) Cleaning and Influencing (淨染)

Cleaning and influencing means using one's moral cultivation and clean acts to inspire and educate surrounding people. Such a clean act can influence others silently.

A clean act can be anything, but it is done primarily in conduct and speech.

In the aspect of speech: clean speech reflects good quality of cultural etiquette, respect for other people, politeness, a gentle tone, sincerity, credibility, earnestness, and frequent use of quality and straightforward language. It not only avoids hurting others, but it also cleans and positively influences the surrounding people through daily conversation. This is oral virtue in interpersonal relationship.

In the aspect of conduct: a person is judged according to his or her conduct. Good or bad conduct in a person is what makes us categorize such a person as a good person or bad person. Clean conduct is critical if a person wants to be regarded as a good person. Examples of clean conduct include compliance with the laws and moral standards of society, practicing adequate etiquette in social settings, not offending other people's rights, maintaining equality and harmony with people, treating people gently, keeping a respectable demeanor, living an industrious and thrifty lifestyle, being humble and giving precedence, etc.

A person with such acts at a certain moral level can greatly influence surrounding people. This influential power generated by practicing clean acts is "cleaning and influencing."

(g) Good Guiding (善導)

Disseminating all sorts of practical culture and knowledge to people in a good way, thereby allowing people to move from a lower level to a higher level, enriching their culture and knowledge, enhancing their life skills, work skills, and livelihood, and sublimating their level as human beings, is called good guiding.

Cultivating the virtue of good guiding is an easy task. Anyone with correct thought, concept, culture, and knowledge can share some of them in a slow, but positive, way with those who are connected anytime and anywhere.

The modern world has highly developed telecommunication; practical culture and knowledge is being broadcast to the general public through media. Passing practical culture and knowledge to people through the media is also good guiding.

Good guiding does not have to be done in a formal setting; social chatting and leisure activity are all great occasions for disseminating subtly.

(h) Life Releasing (放生)

In real life, some people have committed significant wrongdoing and made a large illicit fortune. To redeem bad karmas and accumulate virtue, they periodically purchase live fish or livestock and release them.

Modern Buddhism has misunderstood the real purpose of "life releasing." "Life releasing" primarily focuses on human beings; it means reconciling accumulated conflict, solving hatred, giving people a break, and letting go of the motive to kill and the chance to kill. Hatred begets nothing but hatred. Just let go of the desire to get revenge, and leave it to cause and effect. Justice works in a mysterious way, and it never forgets. Everything will be brought to justice somehow, and the Deva will deliver the final judgment.

Even letting go of the idea of revenge without tangible action is an active fulfillment of "good deed," and that is something special about the virtue of "life releasing." Everyone believes that a "good deed" must be an act, and the same should be applied to "life releasing." People really do hold an animal in hand and release it into Nature. It is totally wrong. The difference that sets the virtue of "life releasing" apart from other "good deeds" is that as long as one can reconcile injustice, enmity, resentment, or hatred in one's mind, then it is a "good deed" already.

The Eight Virtues have been introduced above. Eight-Virtue Water is for the use of the souls and the bodies of other spaces as opposed to the material body. Eight-Virtue Water is only available to the living beings who possess at least one of the Eight Virtues. It seems Eight-Virtue Water is difficult to come by; what does it do anyway?

[2]   Eight Effects of Eight-Virtue Water

Eight-Virtue Water has eight effects: purification, mind control, sweetening, gentleness, moisturizing, peace of mind, satisfaction, and nurture.

(a) Purification (澄淨)

Eight-Virtue Water is crystal clear; one can always see the bottom of the water regardless of the depth. It is absolutely clean, and it is not contaminated at all.

Water of any kind in this world will be contaminated eventually, particularly water used for bathing and swimming; the material body is not clean, and the water in contact with it will be quickly contaminated.

Eight-Virtue Water is different. Because of the "dharma power" of the Eight Virtues, any contamination in Eight-Virtue Water will be purified automatically and instantly. Therefore, one may drink Eight-Virtue Water while bathing with or swimming in it; it is guaranteed to be pure.

(b) Mind Control (意控)

When taking leisure in a pool filled with Eight-Virtue Water, one may control the temperature and depth at will. For example, if one wishes the temperature to be set at 25° Celsius, the water temperature will change instantly to 25° Celsius; if one wishes the temperature to be set at 30° Celsius, the water temperature will change instantly to 30° Celsius. If one feels the water temperature is somewhat too hot, the water temperature will cool down a little bit automatically, and vice versa. If one wishes the water surface to be shallower and be set at waist depth, the surface will lower to the waist instantly; if one wishes for chest depth, the surface will rise to the chest instantly. If one wishes to move forward, the body will be propelled forward automatically; if one wishes to move backward, the body will be propelled backward automatically. It is the same for shifting right and left. Whether it is the water or the body, it can be controlled by one's mind.

(c) Sweetening (甘美)

Eight-Virtue Water can be used for drinking and bathing. Either way, it gives a sweet taste. Such sweetness goes right into one's heart and lungs. It is so refreshing and comforting that one can pleasantly feel the sweetness from the depth of the heart.

(d) Gentleness (輕柔)

The water in the Coarse Space is subject to the force of gravity and, therefore, has weight, which can cause damage to the material body in certain circumstances. For example, a person falls from a height onto the surface of water, a considerable amount of water is poured onto a person, or a person takes a direct hit from a highly pressurized water column. These can all inflict injuries of different severity or even death.

Eight-Virtue Water has no weight and is soft like cotton; it cannot cause damage to the human body. It does not cause painful feeling to a person who collides with it. It gently and softly dampens any collision.

(e) Moisturizing (潤澤)

Eight-Virtue Water moisturizes and gives a shine.

Anyone who uses Eight-Virtue Water will receive such benefit equally. Regardless of the amount of virtue or level of cultivation, any living being who uses Eight-Virtue Water will receive the same treatment without any discrimination.

Eight-Virtue Water moisturizes skin and gives it a shiny look.

(f) Peace of Mind (安和)

A living being, who has used Eight-Virtue Water, will feel peaceful about the "good deeds" that he or she has done and secure about his or her situation. A disturbed mind will be stabilized, and a wary mind will be comforted.

A living being who has used Eight-Virtue Water will be given a feeling of security and peace. The body and mind will then be in a harmonic state, and personality will be more friendly and pleasant. Such a living being will enjoy harmonious relationships with others and learn more about resolution of hatred. The facial expression will become increasingly peaceful. Because such a living being is rewarded for the practice of virtue, further practice of virtue will be encouraged. The future will then be smoother, the mood happier, the tone of voice more pleasant, and life more appropriate.

(g) Satisfaction (滿足)

Eight-Virtue Water is saturated with more than enough Spiritual Qi. This Spiritual Qi is energy. Upon entering the

Eight-Virtue Pool and drinking some Eight-Virtue Water, one will instantly feel satisfied regardless of how thirsty or hungry. Lying peacefully in the pool, both body and mind are relaxed in comfort and are totally satisfied. Everything becomes meaningless except the practice of "good deeds." There will be no more need for struggling because struggling is so tiresome. In the Eight-Virtue Pool, any struggling that does not concern virtue is meaningless. Anything that one may wish for will be satisfied instantly.

(h) Nourishing (養根)

Any body with a soul has six sensing organs: eyes, ears, nose, tongue, body, and mind.

The eighth effect of Eight-Virtue Water is nourishing the sensing organs.

When any body with six sensing organs, except the material body, uses Eight-Virtue Water, the six sensing organs will be nourished. With this nourishing effect, the physiology of the six sensing organs will be tuned, functions enhanced, and mind increased with "good natures."

48. Contributory Condition (增上緣)

Modern Buddhism is getting more sophisticated and hard to learn. Taking "contributory condition" as an example, some people have invented in their imagination positive contributory condition and negative contributory condition. Contributory condition is contributory condition; there is no such difference as "positive" or "negative."

Everything concerning a human being in this world is subject to cause (因) and condition (緣) and the cause and effect relationship (因果關係). "Cause and condition" roughly means prerequisite and relationship. Provided that everything is about condition, then why is there an additional contributory condition? Ancient people said, "Challenge sometimes works better than persuasion." There are cases where positive lecturing produces no result, but negative lecturing serves the original purpose.

Some living beings progress faster in response to the condition in an unfavorable (adverse) circumstance than in a favorable circumstance. The factor that drives the living beings to make progress in an unfavorable circumstance is called contributory condition.

Both favorable and unfavorable circumstances are conditions. In an unfavorable circumstance, there is resistance, which is also called pressure, tribulation, or difficulty. Such resistance is a contributory condition. When we flip a ball of crumpled-up paper away with our index finger, the index finger must exert and build up pressure against the thumb. Without the thumb, the ball cannot be flipped away very far. The thumb is the resistance for the index finger, and it, therefore, is the contributory condition of the index finger.

Conversely, a favorable circumstance is not a contributory condition. We call an unfavorable circumstance a contributory condition because it has resistances and tribulations. A favorable circumstance is merely a condition. Only the resistance (or tribulation) encountered in an unfavorable circumstance is a contributory condition.

When there is a resistance, only breaking through it

may constitute a contributory condition. If there is no breakthrough of resistance, then there will be no such term as contributory condition.

In conclusion, contributory condition is contributory condition; there is no such difference as positive or negative.

49.   Rainbow Material Body (虹化色身)

Rainbow material body is the highest state of practice and cultivation regarded by the Rainbow Faction Taoism. Rainbow material body means a material body that may change like a rainbow. A life, rich and colorful as a rainbow, disappears along with the death of the material body. The material body, however, will appear once again like the rainbow does after rain. Life is like a rainbow; it is beautiful but brief. A practitioner who has attained the Yang Spirit (陽神) may transform his (or her) material body into a rainbow.

Rainbow material body is a level of cultivation and is a dharma eye function of the Yang Spirit; it is of the "great relocation" level. The Yang Spirit can relocate its own material body from a sealed space.

In ancient times, practitioners who were enthusiastic about cultivation followed their master and gathered somewhere deep in the mountains. Rainbow material body is a practitioner's verification of the attainment of the Yang Spirit.

After a practitioner has finished his cultivation and is ready to leave the mundane world, he notifies the fellow practitioners. He will choose a site for his own grave, have his coffin made, and pick the time for becoming a rainbow. When the date has come, the practitioner enters the coffin to "die." The fellow practitioners seal the coffin with long nails, bury it under the ground, and finish the tomb by making a pile of earth on top of it.

Three days later the fellow practitioners excavate the tomb and open the coffin. If the buried practitioner is still lying there, then that practitioner has failed the attainment of the Yang Spirit and has died. Alternatively, as opposed to finding the buried practitioner lying in the coffin, the fellow practitioners may find a long machete with a bundle of red strings tied to the ring at the end of the handle.

The red strings symbolize a "joyous occasion;" the ring symbolizes "perfection;" the "machete" symbolizes the decisive force of chopping off all attached troubles. All of the three collectively represent the pleasant mental state for full separation from all troubles.

APPENDICES:

DHARMAS FOR THOSE WITH DUE CONDITIONS

Epilogue
Membership Benefits
Membership Registration Form

EPILOGUE

The writing of this book progressed slowly because it has to answer to living beings; every issue has to be considered carefully and repeatedly to prevent misleading the living beings. If not for that, with the help of modern technology, even completing several books in one year would not be a problem.

Before this book was printed, the publisher asked for an introduction to the author. I must ask for your forgiveness for not providing such an introduction or details about the author. The author has no wish for fame or wealth from this book or from Buddha-to-Be Religion; the author only wishes to pass the correct dharmas of Buddha-to-Be Religion to living beings in the remaining years of life.

In fact, a person who really saves and converts people does not need to brag repeatedly about how great his (or her) supernatural powers, functions, or dharma powers (法力; another name for "supernatural powers") are or how much higher he is above others. Such a person should try every way to explain dharma principles clearly and help the living beings be saved and converted.

Folklore says, "Other people have planted trees before, so the people now may have tree shade." The author has enjoyed many rewards in his lifetime and does not need to worry about money or a livelihood. If the author can finish all his books before Nirvana with Remainder comes, then the author's mission is accomplished.

The founding father of Taoism, Lao-zi, spent most of his time living as a hermit. He did not write the classic *Daodejing* until he was about to leave the human world. People still benefit from his book even today, which indicates the profound meaning, circulating scope, and pervasive teaching of his book.

Buddha-to-Be Religion is a newly emerging religion and brings many new thoughts to the people of the world. These new thoughts (correct dharmas of Buddha-to-Be Religion) need people to pass them around. Propagating new thoughts is inherently difficult. In order to encourage the spread of the new thoughts, the author has especially filed application with the Devas of High Dharma Body Institutes to grant some special privileges to anyone who adopts and promotes the "new dharmas." The application has been approved.

Anyone who thoroughly studies and circulates this book and promotes the thoughts of this book shall be recorded by the Ministry of Karma Force Registration as good karma for promoting Buddha-to-Be Religion and shall receive four virtues of kindness and pity, benefaction, people helping, and good guiding among the Eight Virtues. At the same time, such a person shall be entitled to ten types of benefits (ten types of good retributions) as follows:

1. Spiritual Qi supplement
2. Increase in "attainments"

3. Blessing and protection from Religion Guardians
4. Soul-level promotion
5. Dignified appearances in future lives
6. Extra points for stage of attainment appraisal
7. Increased blessed virtue
8. Extended limit of wisdom life
9. Enhanced wisdom
10. Accelerated Buddhahood attainment

The above ten types of benefits are not comparable to the benefits "bestowed" by modern Buddhism.

Modern Buddhism often claims that the benefits received will allow one to achieve Buddhahood through the Present Body (即身成佛) or eliminate bad karmas as many as the number of sands in the Ganges (罪滅河沙). In fact, these are all lies. In the correct dharmas of Buddhism, there is absolutely no such thing.

There is no Buddhahood through the Present Body or generous pardon. There is no way that tremendous numbers of crimes can be pardoned; not even a minor crime can be pardoned. A bad karma is a bad karma; a good karma is a good karma. They cannot offset each other. They will be recorded individually and have their respective retributions. Any living being shall sustain the karmic retributions with his or her respective "retributive body."

It is regretful that this book cannot completely explain Dharma Bodies in detail. The next book (the second scripture of Buddha-to-Be Religion) shall explain Dharma Bodies in detail and at every ideological level.

The name of the second scripture of Buddha-to-Be Religion is temporarily determined to be "The Mysteries of Dharma Bodies." Those who are interested are humbly asked to look forward to its publication.

MEMBERSHIP BENEFITS
(Notice from the World Buddha-to-Be Religion Society)

The World Buddha-to-Be Religion Society was registered in Canada on April 30, 2008 and is currently recruiting permanent members.

The External Body of Sakyaqingyang (釋迦青陽), after working closely with his material body, has been appraised by the stage appraisal done by the Devas of High Dharma Body Institutes to be at the stage of "Dharma-Cloud Ground" (法雲地). Now, the External Body is able to concurrently produce an unlimited number of "Response Bodies" (應身) to benefit the members with Spiritual Qi enhancement.

The Dharma-Cloud Ground is not a stage of attainment of the material body; it is a stage of attainment of the Dharma Body. The Dharma-Cloud Ground is the fiftieth stage among Bodhisattva's fifty-two stages of cultivation and is the final "ground" for the Ten-Ground Bodhisattvas. A Dharma Body that has achieved the stage of Dharma-Cloud Ground can produce unlimited numbers of Duplicated Bodies (分身), including Response Bodies (應身) and Transformation Bodies (化身). These bodies can appear anywhere in the world and can assemble as one at any time just as there can be cloud and rain anywhere in the world. A Dharma Body at this "ground" can administer "dharma" to living beings like cloud and rain. Such a cloud may cast shade onto living beings to shield them from oppressive misery and troubles, and such rain may nourish the wisdom lives of living beings. The living beings' need of correct dharma from the Dharma-Cloud Ground is like the parched land's desperate need of cloud and rain.

ACCESS TO MEMBER BENEFITS
I. Practicing Qingyang Dhyana Method
Part One of Qingyang Dhyana Method is Dhyana of Spiritual Qi; Part Two is Dhyana of Spiritual Light, and Part Three is Dhyana of Non-Rebirth.

Part One has three steps of dhyana methods; members start with the practice of the first step.

Step One Dhyana is Natural Dhyana and is also called Qingyang Natural Dhyana, or simply Natural Dhyana.

◆   Method for practicing Natural Dhyana

There is no strict requirement for environment, time, or location. A practitioner may choose a preferred position of sitting, lying, standing, or lying on one side. Just choose any position that makes you feel comfortable.

After the position has been chosen, maintain this position. Then gently close your eyes and lips. Moisten your lips with your saliva. Keep your mind calm with a smile on your face. Loosen up your body. Once you are completely relaxed, chant in your mind: *"Bai Tong Qing Yang Shen Wai Shen"* (worship the Qingyang External Body) from the beginning to the end. At this time, the External Bodies of Sakyaqingyang and his disciples will come to you at superluminal speeds to enhance your Spiritual Qi.

Once you have opened up your "channel," the Qing-yang External Body will be there for you whenever you call it in your life. There is no limit on the length of time or frequency of your daily practice.

Those who have not yet opened up their "channels" may practice Natural Dhyana, too. When practicing, the same effect of "dhyana" can be obtained as well.

When the practice is about to end, the practitioner chants, "I am exiting dhyana," three times. Then, slowly open your eyes, walk around, and talk.

II.   How to Open the "Channel"

(A)   Obtain Membership Registration Form
   1.   Visit the website of World Buddha-to-Be Religion Society and download (http://www.buddha-to-be.org/).
   2.   Use the application form supplied at the rear of this book. Photocopies are acceptable.

(B)   Fill out the Membership Registration Form
   1.   Download the file and fill out the form directly on your computer.
   2.   Fill each blank required on the Membership Registration Form supplied with this book. Please write neatly. Avoid pens with ink that may fade.

(C)   Make a donation of any amount
The World Buddha-to-Be Religion Society is a non-profit-seeking organization established and registered by the adherents. Donations made by the adherents will be used to promote the religion.

Believers in Buddha-to-Be Religion may show their sincerity by donating any amount as membership fees. They will be granted permanent membership with lifetime membership benefits.

ତ୨

Methods of Donation

1.   Internet
Visit http://www.buddha-to-be.org/ (World Buddha-to-Be Religion Society website) and click on "Donation." Make your donation through PayPal; it is fast, convenient, safe, and reliable.

2.   Fund Remittance
Remit your donation directly to the bank account of "World Buddha-to-Be Religion Society."

(1) Canadian Dollar Account:
Bank name: Bank of Montreal (Richmond Main Office)
Address: 6088 No. 3 Road
          Richmond, BC
          Canada V6Y 2B3
Account No.: 07820-001-1084231
Account Name: World Buddha-to-Be Religion Society

SWIFT Code: BOFMCAM2

(2) U.S. Dollar Account:
Bank name: Bank of Montreal (Richmond Main Office)
Address: 6088 No. 3 Road
　　　　　Richmond, BC
　　　　　Canada V6Y 2B3
Account No.: 07820-001-4608247
Account Name: World Buddha-to-Be Religion Society
SWIFT Code: BOFMCAM2 PNBPUS3NNYC

3.　　Mail
Please send your check by mail to:
Address: 130-8191 Westminster Hwy
　　　　　Richmond, BC
　　　　　Canada V6X 1A7
Receiver: World Buddha-to-Be Religion Society

༜

(D)　Submit Membership Registration Form
There are three ways to submit the Membership Registration Form:

1.　Email
　　Please send the completed Application Form to World Buddha-to-Be Religion Society at btb@buddha-to-be.org.
2.　Fax
　　Please fax the completed form to 1-778-297-6336.
3.　Mail
　　Please mail the completed form to

Address: 130-8191 Westminster Hwy
Richmond, BC
Canada V6X 1A7
Receiver: World Buddha-to-Be Religion
Society

Upon receipt of the Membership Registration Form, the form will be registered by dedicated personnel, and the applicant will then be a permanent member. The member's channel for enhancement of Spiritual Qi by the Qingyang External Body will be opened.

World Buddha-to-Be Religion Society

MEMBERSHIP
REGISTRATION FORM

Last Name:	First Name & Middle Ini.:
Gender:	Date of Birth:
Telephone:	Nationality:
Date of Registration:	Education:

Email:
Mailing Address:
Other Contact Methods:
Notes:
Registration No.

**Form prepared by the World Buddha-to-Be
Religion Society**

TRANSLATION NOTES

The translation of any Buddhist literature or scripture is never easy. In this case, many Buddhism terms used in the Chinese version of this book are either transliterations or verbatim translations of the original Sanskrit terms. Now, these Chinese terms have to be translated into English so that they are comprehensible to native English readers. It is inevitable that there will be certain ambiguities in this edition of the English version, and the translator humbly invites and welcomes any suggestions that may improve the later edition of this book in English.

Please kindly be advised of several translation principles that may be adopted in this book.

As a gesture of respect to the original author whose birthplace is China, translation of the Chinese terms in this book adopts the spelling method commonly accepted in China although there are other methods currently used in other Chinese-speaking regions.

With all due respect for the consideration and diligence taken in an attempt to perfect the English translation, if there is any conflict, ambiguity, error, or mistake, the original Chinese version shall take precedence.

Your opinions and comments are important to this book and to the mission of the global teaching of Buddha-to-Be Religion. Should you have any translation suggestions for this book, please do not hesitate to inform us at cosmosculture @gmail.com.

Made in the USA
San Bernardino, CA
03 December 2014